# Suicide
# in Children
# and
# Adolescents

# Child Behavior and Development

*Series Editor* Dennis P. Cantwell, MD

ISSN 0193-7421

**Suicide in Children and Adolescents.** Syed Arshad Husain and Trish Vandiver.

**Affective Disorders in Childhood and Adolescence—An Update.** Dennis P. Cantwell and Gabrielle A. Carlson, editors.

**Emotional Disorders in Children and Adolescents: Medical and Psychological Approaches to Treatment.** G. Pirooz Sholevar, Ronald M. Benson, and Barton J. Blinder, editors.

**Clinical Treatment and Research in Child Psychopathology.** A.J. Finch, Jr., and Philip C. Kendall, editors.

**Autism: Diagnosis, Current Research, and Management.** Edward R. Ritvo, Betty Jo Freeman, Edward M. Ornitz, and Peter Tanguay, editors.

**The Hyperactive Child: Diagnosis, Management, Current Research.** Dennis P. Cantwell, editor.

# Suicide in Children and Adolescents

by
**Syed Arshad Husain, M.D.**
and
**Trish Vandiver, M.S.**

Department of Psychiatry
University of Missouri-Columbia
Columbia, Missouri

**SP MEDICAL & SCIENTIFIC BOOKS**
a division of Spectrum Publications, Inc.
New York

SPECTRUM PUBLICATIONS, INC.
175-20 Wexford Terrace
Jamaica, NY 11432

**Library of Congress Cataloging in Publication Data**

Husain, Syed Arshad.
  Suicide in children and adolescents.

  (Child behavior and development)
  Includes index.
  1. Children—United States—Suicidal behavior.
2. Youth—United States—Suicidal behavior.
I. Vandiver, Trish. II. Title. III. Series. [DNLM: 1. Suicide—In
infancy and childhood. 2. Suicide—In adolescence.
WI CH/44M v.5 / HV 6546 H968s]
HV6546.H87      1984        362.2        83-13728
ISBN 0-89335-190-3

Printed in the United States of America

*Dedicated to*

*Jennifer, Keary, Darius*

*Harry, Beulah, Susan*

*our families*

# Foreword

The death of a friend, a colleague, a relative, or a patient can be a devastating experience, particularly when that death is self determined. It is devastating to us as human beings to lose someone we cared about; it is devastating to us as professionals to wonder what we might have done that could have helped; and it is devastating to us as psychiatrists, because it makes us realize that for all we do know, there is still a great deal more that we do not know. When the person exhibiting suicidal behaviors or completing the act of self-murder (as the Germans call it) is a child or adolescent, the tragedy seems even greater.

Completed suicide among the younger age groups (especially in the English-speaking and Scandinavian countries) has increased dramatically over the past three decades and is continuing to do so. Suicide is now, in fact, the second cause of death among adolescents and young adults in the United States, according to the latest statistical reports. It is exceeded as a cause of death in these ages only by accidents (some of which are undoubtedly hidden suicides, probably more so among such younger persons), with suicide death rates even rising above those from homicide during the past few years.

While actual completed suicide among children below the age of puberty remains relatively rare, it too is increasing. As far as attempted suicide is concerned, no one knows the true rates—but there is strong evidence that such behavior is much more common than previously thought, and increasing among persons under the age of 25 or so. Despite these facts, suicide remains a sociopsychiatric phenomenon about which much confusion exists. Inextricably involved with the attitudes, folkways, mores, taboos, and laws of culture and subculture, with emotions and values, with clinical psychiatric disorder, with genetic diatheses and environmental and family influences, suicide as a subject for scientific study engenders complex and difficult problems, whether that study is actuarial, clinical, or oriented to depth psychology on the one hand or biochemical investigation on the other. There is a plethora of literature on the subject, but much of it is speculative, superficial, or anecdotal. Nowhere, until now, has there been a truly comprehensive and critical review of what has been discovered about suicidal behaviors in children and adolescents, and nowhere, until now, has there been developed a set of profile patterns that delineate the several kinds of young people most likely to be at high risk, the sequence of their actions, and the possible courses for treatment.

The work of Dr. Husain and Ms. Vandiver is all the more important, then, for providing mental health professionals and other concerned parties with a collected, organized way of viewing these overdetermined and difficult-to-understand self-destructive behaviors. The authors describe how the human being's concept of death changes from early childhood through adolescence, discuss the family, social, environmental, and psychodynamic factors related to the etiology of suicidal behaviors in children and adolescents, as well as the specific predisposing and precipitating factors, note in detail the characteristics and presenting symptoms of those younger people involved in such actions, traverse the changing outline of the methods utilized, and review the varieties of treatment available. The final section of the book provides a unique analysis of case studies which mark out the behavioral profiles of those children and adolescents who actually have demonstrated suicidal behaviors, categorized not only by sex but by age groups from 4½ to 20 years old.

The authors who planned, organized, reviewed, and carried out this vital task, which they have completed with noticeable sophistication, deserve congratulations. Several recent studies have indicated that the physician's emotional response to death and dying is likely to be sympathetic identification with feelings of inadequacy, impotence, lowered self-esteem, and frustration. Coping strategies to deal with such difficult feelings involve not only attempting to understand and master one's emotions, but also obtaining an adequate knowledge base on which to plan one's program of evaluation and therapy. This book, therefore, contains incisive messages not only for the medical and mental health professions, but also for teachers and parents everywhere. It points the way to present care and future research. It should arouse responsible citizens sufficiently so that they will be willing to spend more money, effort, and time, for investigation, for evaluation, for treatment, and especially for prevention of what has been a minor epidemic but what is rapidly becoming a major problem for our society.

James M. A. Weiss, MD, M.P.H., F.A.C.P., F.R.C.Psych.
Professor and Chairman, Department of Psychiatry
and Professor of Community Medicine
University of Missouri Health Sciences Center
Columbia, Missouri

# Contents

# Part I
# Suicide in Children

# 1

# Introduction

Children who are 15 years of age or younger and who have attempted or committed suicide are the focus of the first part of this book, although both children and adolescents are grouped together in many other studies of suicide and suicide attempts. Grouping persons under age 20 in one group, however, ignores the developmental phases and changing social roles experienced during the first two decades of life. "Suicide and Suicidal Attempts in Children and Adolescents," published in *The Lancet* in 1964, suggests that the child and adolescent population should be divided into age groups spanning five or even three years per category.

## WHY SUICIDE MAY NOT BE DETECTED IN CHILDREN

Suicide and attempted suicide often remain unknown to the public. Lukianowicz (1968) lists the following reasons why this is true in the case of children:

1. In most cases of threatened or attempted suicide in children, the parents may not take this gesture seriously and may

3

not seek medical advice; 2. In many other cases, the parents, however strongly they might have been disturbed and upset, do not report the event, being afraid of publicity, social embarrassment and disgrace; 3. Some parents may hush up the incident for fear of an investigation and a possible prosecution for neglect or cruelty.

Shaw and Schelkun (1965) discovered several reasons, which vary inversely with age and which conspire to lower the recorded number of suicides among children:

Methods—Methods of suicide utilized by children often result in deaths classified as accidents. Since children have limited access to lethal weapons or drugs and rarely know how to use these devices effectively, they are more prone to resort to such familiar dangerous behavior as jumping from heights or running into traffic.

Lack of communication—Suicide notes, often the chief evidence relied on by coroners, are less likely to be left by children, who either may be too young to write or may not be conditioned to written communication.

Tradition—Western culture, in general, tends to underestimate the strength of children's emotions and motivations; therefore, suicidal motives in children are usually unthinkable—and therefore uninvestigated—in the majority of cases.

## DEVELOPMENTAL LEVEL AS AN INDICATOR FOR DIVIDING CHILDREN FROM ADOLESCENTS

As previously mentioned, the developmental level of the child indicates that latency-age suicides should be separated from adolescent suicides. The precise age at which a traumatic experience occurs, for example, is probably important in the reaction to that experience (Suicide and Suicidal Attempts in Children and Adolescents, *The Lancet*, 1964). Such factors as identification, suggestion, and impulsiveness probably play a larger role in suicides among children. Particularly in terms of aggression, Lourie (1966) notes that the child acquires experience from earlier psychological experiences. A child may learn for example, that when she or he turns away from a returning parent and the parent appears to be hurt, she or he can hurt the parent by removing herself or himself from a situation (or symbolically committing suicide).

Children appear to kill themselves more impulsively and with fewer rational motivations than do adults, possibly because of fear or spite or both (Zilboorg, 1937). Impulsive suicides seem unmotivated. In Shaw and Schelkun's (1965) words, "These children seem —from the evidence at hand—to kill themselves as casually as if they were merely pouring themselves a drink of water."

Ackerly (1967) says that the latency-age child who threatens suicide "is giving expression to a complex interplay of psychic forces resulting from the vicissitudes of his aggressive drives and his narcissistic orientation to life." This self-destructive behavior is an expression of rage and aggression directed at the parent (usually the mother) and is a result of early-life frustrations and disappointments. Attempted or threatened suicide is a symptom of acute emotional distress (Morrison and Collier, 1969). Children who have made such attempts or threats require immediate intervention to identify and alleviate the distress of both the child and the child's family (Pfeffer, 1977).

## INCIDENCE

A number of authors believe that suicide committed by a child is a rare event (Aleksandrowicz, 1975; Glaser, 1971; Gould, 1965; Jacobziner, 1960; Shaffer, 1974; Suicide and Suicidal Attempts in Children and Adolescents, *The Lancet*, 1964). Gould, however, states that "the actual number is much higher than statistics indicate" (Gould, 1965). Toolan (1975) reports that suicide ranks as the fourth leading cause of death in young people aged 15 to 19. He suggests that suicides by children and adolescents are underestimated and that as many as 50% of all suicides by children have been disguised as accidents.

The National Office of Vital Statistics has documented an increase in suicides in the 10- to 14-year-old age group from 0.4 per 100,000 in 1955 to 1.2 per 100,000 in 1975 (Pfeffer, 1981). Bakwin (1957) noted that the death rate from suicide in the 10- to 14-year-old age group was "not inconsiderable" and added: "It is important to keep in mind that the number of deaths from suicide is probably considerably greater than is given in the mortality data."

Schrut (1964) reported that, at the Suicide Prevention Center of Los Angeles, there was an "increasing awareness of the fact that a large percentage of suicides (perhaps as many as 50% or more) are disguised or not reported for various reasons. It also is evident that there are others who commit suicide by 'accidental means.' "

McIntire and Angle (1970) reported that "accidental poisoning" is a socially acceptable diagnosis. They further reported that there are "absolutely no data on the incidence of suicidal gestures and attempts at self-poisoning by children 5 to 15 years of age." Apparently the question of incidence of child suicides still requires a great deal of study.

# 2
# The Child's Concept of Death

Authors who have discussed the child's concept of death in their research on suicide threats and attempts by children and adolescents include: Ackerly (1967), Glaser (1971); Gould (1965); McIntire and Angle (1970, 1971); Pfeffer (1981); and Pfeffer, Conte, Plutchik, and Jerrett (1980, 1979). McIntire and Angle (1971) state that possible suicide cannot be diagnosed if the subject does not comprehend the finality of death; others would probably disagree.

The consensus of opinion of many authors who have discussed the child's concept of death is that beliefs about death and consciousness proceed through states as the child develops cognitively and emotionally. Piaget (1960) concluded that the child's attributing consciousness to things proceeded through four stages. In the first stage, everything that is active in any way is believed to be conscious, even if it does not move. In the second stage, consciousness is attributed only to things that can move. In the third stage, consciousness is attributed to things that move by themselves (often including clouds and water), but not to things that move because of outside agents (such as a bicycle). During the fourth stage, consciousness is restricted to the animal world.

Likewise, in the early stages, the child may endow all things with consciousness but not with consciousness of everything, so

7

that activity or resistance may be required (a wall, for example, may not feel a prick, but it would feel being knocked down) (Piaget, 1960). Piaget adds that "it is when some phenomenon appears doubtful, strange, and, above all, frightening that the child credits it with a purpose" and "the child believes in the all-powerful nature of man's command over things and animism serves to explain the obedience of things."

It is not until the fourth stage that systematization becomes reflective rather than implicit, and then the child may discard animism and the attribution of consciousness to things other than those in the animal world. The first stage lasts usually until the ages of 6 or 7; the second stage lasts from ages 6 and 7 to 8 and 9; and the third stage from 8 and 9 to 11 and 12. However, Piaget (1960) says that some of the 5- and 6-year-olds were in later stages. The fourth stage begins at 11 or 12.

Nagy, in two articles (1948, 1959), discusses children's views of death based on a sample of 378 children in Budapest, from whom she acquired compositions, drawings, and discussions. Her children appeared to develop concepts of death in three stages. A summary of her findings include: (1) The child who is younger than 5 years of age does not see death as an irreversible fact; (2) From about 5 years of age to about 9 years of age, death is personified; (3) At about age 9 or later, the child begins to view death as a process which happens to people according to certain laws.

Nagy (1948) says that the child in the first stage attributes life and consciousness to the dead and sees death either as a sleep (a complete denial of death) or as gradual or temporary. The child in the second stage personifies death or identifies death with the dead (no separation in meaning of the two words). In the third stage, the child realizes that death is the cessation of corporeal life. At this stage, the child understands that death is a process operating within the person, and realizes its universal nature.

Piaget's first three stages correspond in age-divisions with Nagy's three stages of death concept. Safier (1964) compared Piaget's "animism" stages to Nagy's death stages in children and discovered that the stages are parallel in their development. Also, there is a positive relationship between life- and death-concept formation in children.

Hug-Hellmuth (1965) offers an account from a diary record-ing a young boy's first thoughts about death. It is an entry that clearly illustrates Nagy's (1948, 1959) first-stage children who see death as gradual or occurring in degrees. To quote the diary re-ported by Hug-Hellmuth:

> A dung-beetle was crawling with difficulty on the floor. Ernie was delighted and wanted to give the "dear beetle" to his cousin, Lottie. But he didn't get far before he put the beetle on the path and stepped on it lightly. Then he picked the squashed beetle up again. "But Ernie, the poor beetle!" "Well, he was crawling on my hand too much, and he made it wet. So I crushed him a little bit dead, so he would lie quietly. When Lottie comes he'll wake up again." Ernie stumbled over stones and roots of trees, but carefully, with love, he carried the dung-beetle along. It surprised him that Lottie didn't share his pleasure in the beetle. For him it was still the "dear dung-beetle", even if he was a "little dead", that is, only a form of being asleep. Ernie was firmly convinced that the beetle would soon crawl vigorously.[1]*

Both Nagy (1948) and Hug-Hellmuth (1965) mentioned that the worst aspect of death to the young child is separation, and death and separation appear to be indistinguishable to the child.

Two studies conducted in the 1970s were focused on children's concepts of death and showed that children were not anxious about the questions asked. McIntire, Angle, and Struempler (1972), in an interview with 598 Midwestern children of ages 5 to 18, found that the 7-year-old child was the most willing to consider death as total cessation. Responses to the questions (which included asking what happened to the body of a pet and of a person at death) were coded as: (1) fantasy (including reincarnation); (2) organic decom-position; and (3) "religious" decomposition to dust or ashes.

It was discovered that, particularly in regard to reincarnation, fantasies involving a person and a pet were retained by about 20%

---

*See Appendix C for permission annotations on material cited in the text. Annotations in tables appear as table footnotes.

of the 15- and 16-year olds. The children who had lost a parent through death were more likely to respond that the body decomposed, with "rotted" as the most frequent response. Only about 20% of the 5- and 6-year-olds saw death as reversible. Children who said they had wished they were dead "frequently" (about 3% of the sample) and who were considered to have a possible suicidal ideation had a concept of death that was less naturalistic and with more fantasy and imagery of reincarnation (McIntire, Angle, and Struempler, 1972).

Koocher (1974) interviewed 75 children from ages 6 to 15. He found that 8 children between the ages of 6.0 and 7.1 believed that dead things could be made to come back to life. When asked about what happens at death, 52% said, "You were buried." Other responses included some hints of an afterlife by 21%, references to a funeral by 19%, specific predictions of how death occurred by 10%, references to some aspect of sleep by 7%, references to being remembered by others by 5%, references to reincarnation by 4%, and references to cremation by 3%.

In a study of the concept of death in suicidal, aggressive, and normal children ages 10 to 12, Orbach and Glaubman (1979a) discovered that suicidal children distorted the death concept and produced more wishful thinking about death than the other two groups, although the suicidal children did not differ from the other two groups on other measures. The authors concluded that the distortion of death concept in suicidal children is a defensive process, and that this may serve as a new motivation for suicide. Orbach and Glaubman (1979b) found the same results in a report of three case studies of suicidal children.

A number of authors have included a section on children's concepts of death in their reports on suicidal children. McIntire and Angle (1971) discovered that 16% of 17- and 18-year-olds in their study admitted to the fantasy of reversibility or cognizance after death and McIntire and Angle (1971) feel that this "suggests that not only the child but the older adolescent and even the adult may 'measure their own life value with a defective yardstick.' "

Ackerly (1967) says that the young child describes death as reversible and temporary as a defense. Also, conceptions of heaven or life after death appear to arise spontaneously in the child, even without religious instruction. These "nice places to go" are constructed by the child to avoid confronting the reality of death by burial in the ground.

Both Gould (1965) and Glaser (1971) report that the child sees death as a reversible process. Gould reports that this reversibility concept is a result of intellectual development, cultural attitudes, and the influence of television and movies. Glaser feels that, because of this reversibility concept, seriously disturbed children may act upon their threats more readily.

McIntire and Angle (1970) report that suicidal intent is rarely lethal. The child who attempts suicide does not seek a cessation of life, but only an escape from certain aspects of life. Children and adolescents may totally deny the possibility of death.

Pfeffer, Conte, Plutchik and Jerrett (1979) found that suicidal children were significantly more preoccupied with thoughts about death than nonsuicidal children. Other data that correlated significantly for suicidal children included preoccupation with death and the dangerousness of suicidal behavior. Also, the belief that death is a pleasant state and the degree of dangerousness of suicidal behavior was found to correlate significantly for suicidal children. Suicidal children were more worried about members of their family dying. Even more, they were extremely upset by the death of someone they considered important to them personally. They differed significantly from nonsuicidal children in their concept that death is temporary.

Children may envision suicide as an opportunity to join a lost loved person, to make an important person love them, or as a symbolic rebirth after death and "wiping the slate clean" (Gould, 1965).

Children who attempt suicide to punish their parents seem to believe that they will somehow survive and be able to observe the effects of their actions on the parents (Garfinkel and Golombek, 1974).

Shaw and Schelkun (1965) and Gould (1965) note that the child sees the reversibility of death as a sign of her or his own invulnerability. This magic thought of the child's grandiose and omnipotent feelings about death compensates for the child's feelings of helplessness and inadequacy.

## SUMMARY: THE CHILD'S CONCEPT OF DEATH

Authors who have discussed the child's death concept, including Nagy (1948, 1959) and Safier (1964) believe that a child passes through stages of cognitive and emotional development in the formation of death concept similar to Piaget's (1960) cognitive development stages. Suicidal children may distort death concept and engage in "magical thinking" about death, so that death is seen as a temporary state. McIntire and Angle (1971) found that even 17- and 18-year-old suicidal adolescents admitted to fantasies of reversibility or cognizance after death.

Different authors report different findings regarding death concepts in young children. These differences may be partly due to cultural and sophistication differences in the children questioned, the way the question was worded, and the categories various authors created for children's responses.

# 3

# Family Factors

## THE EFFECT OF LOSS

### Death of a Family Member

The most significant environmental factor present in suicidal children and adolescents seems to be the loss through death, desertion, or separation of a close family member or associate, according to Shaw and Schelkun (1965). These authors note that such a loss probably has the following consequences:

(1) Conditioning of the suggestible child, who identifies with the lost love object (particularly if of the same sex). (2) Precipitation of anxiety and depression through a sense of threat, guilt, or loss. (3) Decrease in the child's sense of his own worth: The child views death as an abandonment and often feels a loss of status when a parent is lost. (4) Disruption of the interpersonal relationships which the child has previously established: The death of a near relative often brings with it overwhelming environmental change.

Zilboorg (1937) says that the person most likely to be suicidal is one who has identified with a dead person; the one who loses a

13

father, brother, mother, or sister at the height of the Oedipus complex or transition to puberty is in true danger of suicide. Often, a suicide or suicide attempt occurs on the anniversary of such a loss.

Of 34 suicidal children in Morrison and Collier's study (1969), 76% had experienced a significant loss, a separation, or the anniversary of such a loss within days or weeks before their suicide attempts. These separations included death, illness, hospitalization, marital separation and household moves of a parent or parent surrogate.

Bender and Schilder (1937) feel that the death of the parents, particularly when occurring suddenly and mysteriously, makes the psychological situation so unbearable for a young child that even a small deprivation can lead to a suicidal wish. One child in their study had lost her mother when she was 3 years of age and her father when she was 12. Another girl felt the loss of love because of her mother's mental disease and her father's indifference.

In Greer's (1966) study of suicidal adults, it was discovered that their parental loss in childhood, particularly when that loss occurs during their first 4 years of life and involves the loss of both parents, may produce suicidal behavior in neurotic, disordered patients.

In Connell's 1972 study of 15 children under 15 years of age who were admitted to a hospital after a suicide attempt, 2 girls had lost their mothers through death. One of the children was 6 years old and had been left with an alcoholic father. The mother of the other was killed in a car accident 19 months before her daughter attempted suicide. One girl had lost her grandmother 18 months before her suicide attempt. The grandmother had been her chief emotional support in a disorganized family.

In a study of 70 suicidal children living in New York City by Winn and Halla (1966), 50% had never known their real fathers and 75% were not living with their real fathers at the time of admission to the hospital after their suicide attempt. In Winn and Halla's study, 15% suffered the permanent loss of one or both parents by death; 85% of the children had experienced prolonged separation from a parent or parent surrogate, and many of these children had experienced multiple separations.

Of 75 suicidal children studied by Mattsson, Seese and Hawkins (1969), 6 had lost one parent and 8 had lost both parents through death.

### Effect of Family Disorganization

Crook and Raskin (1975) indicate that the separation of parent and child in itself does not predispose the child to attempt suicide, but that the loss resulting from factors associated with marital discord and pathological patterns of family interaction is often associated with suicide attempts. To quote Pfeffer, Conte, Plutchik and Jerrett (1979):

> Chronic environmental traumas of deprivation, family disorganization, separations, displays of violence, and overt sexual encounters influence the course of ego development of the child. The resultant effects include multiple deficits in ego functioning and the evolution of a fragile defense system that is vulnerable to decompensation. The children experienced intense feelings of frustration and their states of extreme rage were marginally maintained under control. They viewed the world as hostile, ungiving.

Shaw and Schelkun (1965) report a high incidence of broken or disorganized homes in suicide attempters and say that loss by death, desertion, or divorce causes the child to fear for his existence, since he has lost the support of an adult upon whom he depended. The child may also feel a sense of guilt because she or he may feel responsible in some way for the death or desertion.

Haldane and Haider (1967) discovered in their study of suicidal children that homes broken by death, divorce or separation affected less than one-quarter of their sample, but the majority of homes were "broken" in the sense that relationships were unsatisfactory. The family situation most often seemed to include an aggressive, dominant father; an anxious, submissive mother; and a lack of positive, affectionate paternal support for the mother or children.

Lawler, Nakielny, and Wright (1963) reported that the majority of the suicidal children in their study were living in homes with grossly disturbed family relationships, with domineering parents who had little capacity to give to their children in a mature manner, or with the loss of a parent by death or desertion. Toolan (1975) said that fewer than one-third of the children in his study came from homes in which both parents were present, and most of these had fathers who were conspicuously absent from the homes.

Shaffer (1974), in a study of 31 children under age 15 who completed suicide, found that 2 sets of parents had been divorced between the time of the children's death and the study 1 to 4 years later. This may reflect that either the child's death created stress or the threat of separation or divorce was present at the time of the child's death.

In the majority of cases in their studies of suicidal children, both Haider (1968) and Tishler (1980) noted that the homes were disorganized in many ways, including unsatisfactory relationships between parents, frequent quarrels, divorce, suicidal attempts or completions, and substance abuse by the parents.

Connell (1972) states that a parent substitute was present in the homes of 4 of the 15 children he studied, and the parent substitutes all were hated by the children. Three of the substitute parents overtly rejected the children and the fourth was ambivalent. Quarrels were frequent in 14 of the 15 families.

Winn and Halla (1966) discovered that only 8% of their 70 suicidal children came from intact families: 25% of the children were illegitimate, 10% had never known their real mothers, and 25% were not living with their real mothers at the time of their admission to the hospital after their suicide attempt. Mattsson, Seese and Hawkins (1969) observed that about half of the children in their study came from intact families. Of the 75 suicidal children included in their study, 27 had experienced their parents' divorce or separation; 14 had experienced a loss through death.

Tuckman and Youngman (1964) studied suicidal adults and also discovered that family breakdown and disorganization characterizes the life experiences of persons attempting suicide. In 63% of families with service-agency contacts, two or more members of the family were involved in independent contacts. In 53% of the cases, two or three generations were involved. In a study of families with children who had repeated accidents, Husband and Hinton

(1972) noted that 29% of the parents were divorced, separated, or unmarried and not cohabiting.

In a study of self-destructive battered children, Green (1978) found that abuse is generally connected with family disorganization, parental dysfunction, neglect, interruption of maternal care, and early experiences with object loss. Abusive parents "fail to provide the child with average, expectable psychological and physical nurturance. When the basic needs of these children for love, nurturance, and physical contact are generally unmet, the stimulation afforded them during the abusive interaction might reinforce further pain-seeking behavior." Green found that severely deprived children seem to prefer beatings to abandonment.

The following case studies are examples of disorganized homes of families with a child who attempts suicide:

> G is a 5-year-old white boy referred for psychological evaluation (after medical treatment) by the emergency room after swallowing 47 aspirins. An emergency room staff doctor said G stated that "he knew that aspirin could kill him." According to the patient's mother, G climbed on a bathtub, then to the sink, and took the aspirin out of the medicine cabinet, leaving only one tablet in the bottle for "his mother." He told his mother at the time that he was angry that his siblings would not play with him.
>
> G is a cute blond and physically active. He interacted well during the interview. He told the interviewer that he had taken the aspirin because he had a "toothache and wanted to die and speak with Jesus." He referred to dying a number of times stating "If I drop a cigarette, the house would burn up and you would die" and "If I jump out of the window I die." He asked the interviewer if he would be killed if he jumped out of the office window. G spoke of wanting to die so he could see Jesus and his maternal grandmother who died six months before. G's maternal grandfather was planning to remarry in a few days, creating additional stress on G. He had a history of setting fires, running away from home, and torturing animals. His affect was inappropriate and he described "liking it when

people are sick or hurt." There were sleep onset difficulties. G awoke two or three times nightly and described "scary dreams" in which snakes and spiders harm people.

There was no report of physical abuse toward this child, but G had reportedly observed his mother being physically abused. At age 16, G's mother had overdosed, an admitted suicide attempt. She had psychiatric hospitalization twice and had been in outpatient psychotherapy for about a year. She took a variety of medications. G's mother had been married three times; the first husband died after reportedly abusing drugs. The mother married G's natural father, whom G's mother described as a drug abuser. G reportedly fought with his two siblings and neighborhood children. His mother said he was "spoiled rotten." When she tried to be stricter, G cried more often and showed wide swings in mood and behavior.

P is a nine-year-old white girl who arose from the dinner table and fell to the floor, eyes rolled back, and was incontinent of urine. At the emergency room, she was combative, responded to her name, and reacted appropriately to pain. She admitted having taken some pills. When a resident asked, "Why did you do such a silly thing like this," she replied, "because we were having bad family problems. Dad and Mom split up before Christmas and the rent came and Mom didn't even have the money for the rent. It's been awful." Toxicology confirmed that the patient had taken salicylates and imipramine. When interviewed by a psychologist, P avoided questions regarding suicidal intent by saying she did not remember. However, she did talk freely about the distressing events that precipitated the overdose, particularly the dispute between her mother and father that led to their divorce. The parents had attempted reconciliation but then came a second separation after an interval of 12 months. Her mother had chastised her the day before the overdose for lying to her father while attempting to defend the mother. Although of average intelligence, she had a year-long history of school difficulties. Her eight-year-old brother had been attending a mental health center for emotional/behavior problems. The patient was referred for outpatient psychotherapy and follow-up to the same mental health clinic. (Tischler, 1980)[2]

## Effect of Lack of Emotional Support

Lukianowicz (1968) noted that disturbed relations with their parents was the most important extrinsic factor in the emotional disturbance of the 10 suicidal children he interviewed. None of the parents had a well-integrated, mature, stable personality. Most of the fathers were passive or disinterested in their children: one was rigid and restrictive and one was an alcoholic and cruel. Of the mothers, 4 were hostile, aggressive, and rejecting; 3 were anxious and insecure; and 2 were permissive but dull and inefficient. The abnormal parental personality was considered to be the main cause for the suicidal attempts or preoccupations in 7 of the 10 children.

Hendin (1975) says that the bond of emotional death between suicidal children and parents with impaired relationships was as powerful as that experienced by an actual parent death, and that bond defined the relationship of parent and child and continued to control their lives, even if the parent later died. Hendin describes this emotional death as the result of experiencing death, depression, and misery which has been built into the parent-child relationship since childhood as a result of parental tension, rage, and emotional deadness. Hendin blames this on a society which he says is unable to happily adjust to children.

Emotionally detached parents cause children to feel unloved and unwanted, according to Glaser (1965). Such parents are not available as resources and do not satisfy the child's dependency needs. In about half of the cases he studied, the father played a passive and disinterested role in the family.

Pfeffer, Conte, Plutchik, and Jerrett (1980) found that parents sometimes seem incapable of appropriately responding to a child's developmental needs. This may be a result of the parent's being unaware and unknowledgeable of child development, and because the parent may experience problems with object relations. The parents may be dependent, unable to delay gratification, and experience intense mood shifts. They may lack internalization of appropriate parenting qualities and are unable to differentiate their needs from those of their children. One mother described her son in these terms: "John was the second child just like me. I had no friends, just like John. I always fought and was teased, just like John."

In McIntire and Angle's (1973) study of suicidal children and a control group, hostility, indifference, and overt rejection by the parents or substitute parents seemed to be the rule for the suicidal child, but was an exception for controls.

Schrut (1964) studied 19 suicidal children and adolescents from age 7 to 19. In more than half of these cases, the child was made to feel that he or she was a burden to the parents, either by the parents' coldness and hypercritical discipline or by the absence of mothering concern. Those parents who seemed to totally reject the parental role most likely had children who were depressed (in this group of suicidal children), while those mothers whose distaste for mothering was modified by guilt or remorse (and thus expressed ambivalence) tended to have children who misbehaved, were often delinquent, and were frequently chronically self-destructive.

The following case study of a 7½-year-old girl described by Aleksandrowicz (1975) is characterized as a situation of "biological strangers" in which there is a "mismatch" between the child's characteristics and the mother's personality. "Too much noise and movement" caused Daphna's mother to have "paralyzing headaches." Lack of privacy, gossip, noise, and Daphna's restlessness and crying as an infant drove the mother out of the house and to a full-time job. Daphna was left in the charge of a neighbor and she had a number of infant illnesses that included respiratory disease, stomach aches, and diarrhea. She cried at the door of the preschool and refused to enter. Daphna was envious and jealous of a younger brother and sister. When the family moved to a new city when Daphna was in second grade, she did not adjust well to the new school and she began to have headaches and eye-blinking. Aleksandrowicz's account of this case continues:

> One night, seven-and-a-half-year-old Daphna opened the window in her room on the third floor of a Jerusalem apartment house and jumped out. Luckily a sheet was drying on the lines underneath the window sill. Daphna must have rolled into this sheet when she fell. She was even more fortunate in falling on

some bushes only a few yards away from a deep, slaked-lime pit.

Daphna must have lost consciousness but later laboriously and painfully climbed on all fours up the three flights of stairs. She knocked on the door, repeatedly crying, "Open the door; please don't be mad at me." It was 3:00 a.m. when Daphna's parents, at last realizing who was knocking on the door, opened it. They took Daphna to a hospital where she was found to have four fractures in her pelvis.

Daphna's desperate act was the ultimate attempt to reunite with her love object and to find the love which she could neither evoke nor give.

Daphna and her mother seemed to have been locked in a magic circle where each of them tried intensely, in her own way, to love and be loved by the other, yet they could not reach each other and had to bear the frustration and suppressed rage. (Aleksandrowicz, 1975)[3]

The following case study illustrates the situation of a father-absent home with a hostile, anxious mother who seems not to be able to meet the child's needs:

This 10-year-old girl took, over three days, an unknown amount of aspirin, pentobarbital, and other medicine belonging to her mother. She said she had taken the barbiturates once before but these had only made her sleepy so this time she took more. She said, however, she didn't really want to die and defined death as "after you're buried you are no longer here but are in a different life, it's like going to sleep but you never wake up." She had been found in a semi-conscious state by her mother who noted, only in retrospect, that she had appeared very sleepy for 2 days. The girl lived with her divorced mother and grandmother. Her parents were divorced five years before, after the alcoholic father was jailed for wifebeating, and the father was missed by the girl. The girl appeared frail, fearful, and inhibited. Weight loss and anorexia had been noted for the two months since Christmas. When asked for three wishes she said she had none at all. The girl said the thing she was most upset about was that just before Christmas her mother had sent her dog to be destroyed since it was going to have puppies. She said the thing she most wanted, besides her dog, was the chance to go to school so she could study hard and grow up to be a famous veterinarian. The school psychologist had previously seen the girl because of her extreme anxiety, poor performance despite a high IQ, and frequent absences. She was kept home from school, according to her mother, "because she takes school too seriously and because I need her help when I'm sick and her grandmother is working." The mother was anxious, hostile, and hypochondriacal and had a myriad of prescription drugs that she asked the girl to give her on schedule. The girl said she did not talk to anyone when things were wrong but she did communicate freely with the visiting nurse on subsequent visits, with the school psychologist and the case worker. (McIntire and Angle, 1973)[4]

## THE EFFECT OF VIOLENCE IN THE FAMILY

In Green's (1978) study of self-destructive behavior in battered children, parental behaviors included acute physical and psychological assault, a harsh and punitive child-rearing atmosphere, early maternal deprivation and object loss, and scapegoating. The child who is exposed to the threat of annihilation and/or abandonment becomes anxious and exhibits ego disorganization. This child may attempt to escape from the situation by making a suicide gesture or attempt. The parent may be rejecting, harsh, and punitive, and the child often learns to regard himself or herself with this same hostility and criticism. When the child is deprived of love, nurturance, and physical contact in a situation of neglect, interruption of maternal care, and early experiences with object loss, the child may prefer beatings to abandonment. The child is often blamed for the shortcomings and inadequacy of the parents. Consequently, the child assumes that she or he is to blame and deserves the punishment. The child's self-hatred and low self-esteem then increase and become the nucleus for subsequent self-destructive behavior.

Connell (1972) noted a strikingly high level of aggression in homes with a suicidal child. Physical abuse was common in 7 of 15 families studied, and one mother had been admitted to the hospital twice because her husband had assaulted her. One couple came close to blows during the interview with the researcher.

In Paulson, Stone, and Sposto's 1978 study of 34 families, violent fighting with knives, razors, and guns was common in several homes. The children retaliated with fire-setting and homicidal threats directed at their family members. Threats and attacks with knives or scissors, attempted strangulation of a sibling with a shoelace, attempted suffocation of an infant sibling with a pillow, drugging a sibling, and stabbing peers with a knife were reported in this group.

Rosenberg and Latimer (1966) reported in their study of 26 suicidal children that the mother encouraged the father to be abusive in one case, the parents were extremely punitive in one case, the parents were completely rejecting and beat the child-patient in one case, and the father rejected all the other children but was very possessive of the child-patient and was suspected of incest in one case.

## CORRELATION WITH FAMILY SUICIDES AND ILLNESSES

Previous physical or mental illness, suicide attempts, or completed suicides by a member of the immediate family were common in suicidal children's families. In Shaffer's (1974) study of 31 children who had completed suicide, 16 families (55%) had one or more members who had consulted a psychiatrist or received treatment for emotional symptoms before the child's suicide. Suicidal behavior by a parent or sibling was recorded in 4 cases before the child's suicide. There were 3 cases of attempted suicide by a first-degree relative. In 9 cases (8 fathers, 1 mother), the parents are described as heavy drinkers. Table 1 outlines these statistics.

Pfeffer, Conte, Plutchik, and Jerrett (1979) report that mothers of suicidal children were depressed more frequently than mothers

Table 1    Psychiatric Disorder in Families of Children
Who Committed Suicide

|  | Boy | | Girl | | Total | |
|---|---|---|---|---|---|---|
|  | N | Percent | N | Percent | N | Percent |
| Parent or sibling attempted suicide before child's death | 2 | 9.5 | 2 | 22 | 4 | 13 |
| Parent or sibling depressed before child's death | 5 | 24 | 1 | 11 | 6 | 29 |
| Parent or sibling psychotic before child's death | 2 | 9.5 | 1 | 11 | 3 | 10 |
| 'Nervous debility' or 'anxiety state' before child's death | 2 | 9.5 | 1 | 11 | 3 | 10 |
| Total | 11 | 55 | 5 | 55 | 16 | 55 |

From Shaffer (1974). Copyright 1974, *Journal of Child Psychology and Psychiatry and Allied Disciplines.*

of nonsuicidal children in their study. There was also a significant correlation between parents who were depressed and suicidal and the degree of dangerousness of suicidal behavior in children of these parents. In the population of 58 children studied, 13 mothers (22%) had suicidal ideas, 10 mothers (17%) attempted suicide, and 2 mothers (3%) completed suicide. Among the fathers, 2 (3%) had thought of suicide, 3 (5%) attempted suicide, and 1 (2%) completed suicide.

In Connell's (1972) study of 15 children who were suicidal, 4 of their parents admitted threatening suicide and 1 mother had made two attempts at suicide by taking an overdose in front of the child.

Of the 34 children in Paulson, Stone, and Sposto's 1978 study, 3 had close relatives (a grandmother, mother, and brother) who had completed suicide; 2 other families had immediate relatives who attempted suicide one or more times.

Rosenberg and Latimer (1966) noted that of the 26 parents of suicidal children, 2 (a mother and a father) had been in mental hospitals. Also, 2 family members (a stepfather and a sister) had committed suicide, and a brother had made an unsuccessful attempt.

In addition, 2 mothers had made suicide attempts, and frequently the children had siblings who were disturbed or delinquent.

Haldane and Haider (1967) reported that of 16 suicidal girls, 7 of the girls' fathers had some chronic or recurrent physical illness and 4 of their mothers had a chronic or recurrent physical illness. Only 1 of the 7 boys in the study had a mother who was physically ill. None of the boys had fathers who were physically ill; 1 father and 2 mothers of the boys had had psychiatric treatment.

## BIRTH ORDER AND FAMILY PRESSURES

Shaffer (1974) found that 13 children in his sample were the eldest children in their families and 11 children were the youngest. Only 6 children were in other positions. While only 3 of the children in the study were only children, 7 of the 17 children who were either youngest or intermediately placed were at least 5 years younger than the next-eldest sibling and might be considered as a special or only child.

Lawler, Nakielny, and Wright (1963) studied 22 children and found that 7 were the oldest, 5 were the youngest, and 3 were only children in their respective families. They concluded that the inability of these children to cope with problems arising from their position in the sibling order contributed to their suicide attempts.

A child with limited intellectual resources in comparison to parents and siblings may be placed under considerable pressure for better school performance, according to Glaser (1971). The parents express their frustrations with reproaches, accusations, punishment, and comparisons with other siblings. This produces guilt and hopelessness in the child, who feels inadequate, worthless, helpless in the situation, and convinced of never being able to gain the parents' acceptance and love.

## SUMMARY: FAMILY FACTORS AND CHILD SUICIDAL BEHAVIOR

Loss is the most significant environmental factor in the consideration of child suicide behavior. In studies of suicidal children, a number of authors have found significant numbers of these children have experienced the loss through death or separation of a parent or other family member important to the child. Family disorganization was another important family factor occurring in the backgrounds of suicidal children. At least one set of authors (Haldane and Haider, 1967) report that homes actually broken by death, divorce, or separations were unnecessary; homes that demonstrated a lack of emotional support for the children and aggressive, dominant fathers were predominant in suicidal children's backgrounds that they studied. Abusive behavior of parents toward children also figured in disorganized family situations of suicidal children.

Suicidal children often experience disturbed emotional relations with their parents. Hendin (1975) describes this in a group of children who he says are in a "bond of emotional death" with their parents. Homes with overt fighting, abusive behavior, and punitive parents also were important factors in the backgrounds of suicidal children. Many of the suicidal children's families had parents who had physical or mental illness or who had attempted or completed suicide. Most of the children appeared to hold a special place in the family as oldest, youngest, or only child.

# 4

# Social and Environmental Factors

## SOCIOECONOMIC LEVEL AND INCIDENCE OF SUICIDE

There appears to be little information about this factor in the literature on child and adolescent suicide. The article, "Suicide and Suicide Attempts in Children and Adolescents" (*The Lancet*, 1964), mentions a study in which members of lower income groups were overrepresented with regard to suicide attempts and admission to a hospital. The author speculates that attempted suicides in the higher income groups are less likely to lead the individuals to admission to public hospitals or any hospitals at all. Also, this overrepresentation of low income suicides reported may apply to children and adolescents more frequently than to adults, according to the author. Gould (1965) reported that in his sample, most children who attempted suicide came from the lower socioeconomic and cultural groups. Winn and Halla (1966) reported that their sample of children drawn from "poorer families" are in a situation in which: (1) mothers must warn their children of falling off the subway platform; (2) most of the children come from houses that empty directly onto the street, except for the sidewalk; and (3) roofs, fireescapes, and the streets serve as play areas for the children. The mothers must warn children of the dangers of these play areas. It has been reported that young children often use these environmental situations as methods of their suicide attempts (i.e., jumping from a high place, running into traffic, or jumping in front of a subway train). Paulson, Stone, and Sposto (1978) reported that the majority of parents in their study of suicidal children were of low income and were semiskilled, with a mean annual income of $7,900; 14% were on welfare.

## RACE AND CULTURE AND INCIDENCE OF SUICIDE

Jacobziner (1960) found that whereas Puerto Ricans compose about 11.8% of New York City's population, they are responsible for 28% of the suicide attempts in children. Black children also made a higher percentage of attempted suicides than would be anticipated from their population distribution, but this was not statistically significant in Jacobziner's study. Gould (1965) also found that a higher percentage of Puerto Rican children attempted suicide than white or black children. Black children made slightly more suicide attempts, but not significantly more. Gould reports that Puerto Rican youngsters have more "hysterical" traits, and that also was true for blacks who came to the city from rural areas some years ago. They made up a larger percentage of hospital admissions after suicide attempts when the influx from rural areas was large than they did at the time of Gould's study (1965) after assimilation and acculturation to urban New York City life.

To quote McIntire and Angle (1971) on this issue:

There is absolutely no national data on the racial incidence of self-poisoning, ages 0 to 4, to compare with the 40% incidence of Negroes in the 6- to 10-year-old group, although mortality statistics from 1960, the last year available, show death from accidental ingestions 0-4 to be four times as high for Negro as for Caucasian males. The decrease with age in this study of nonwhites could represent differences in patient population or referral for treatment, the development of expertise in drug use and abuse, or the availability of culturally acceptable outlets for impulsive acting-out. This contrasts with the increase with age of Jewish boys from the upper socioeconomic group possibly denied such outlets in a more restrictive environment.

Bakwin observed in 1957 that the strictness of a social system (which he describes as a "Prussian" way of life) may demand a rigid conformity that allows its members too few alternatives. Punishment is prompt, frequent, and severe. This attitude, which may be dominant in the home, school, and community may be a major factor leading to suicide.

Bakwin (1957) further notes that in Japan children of the nobility and military classes formerly were made aware of the concept of suicide in their earliest years. Life must be surrendered when duty or honor demanded it. Ohara (1963) reports that parent-child suicide (with the mother taking the life of her child and then committing suicide) accounts for 16% of multiple suicides in Japan. Ohara adds, "No political, religious or educational efforts have ever succeeded in discouraging parent-child suicide in Japan. As a matter of fact, no one has ever thought of discouraging it seriously."

Bakwin (1957) says that the social attitude toward suicide is important. In cultures that regard suicide as an honorable and noble way to die (Germany and Austria for example), suicide is more frequent than in countries where suicide is considered as cowardly behavior or a sign of mental aberration (England and the United States).

In Japan, according to Ohara (1963), no matter how sinful they may have been when they were alive, the dead are considered divine. Their sins are forgiven at their deaths, and they are worshipped as holy spirits. Many people in Japan who have financial difficulties, physical afflictions, or psychological problems prefer death to dependence upon others. Also, Japanese parents feel that their chilcren should think the way they do and share their intentions, happiness, and sorrows.

## SUMMARY: SOCIAL AND ENVIRONMENTAL FACTORS
## AND SUICIDAL CHILDREN

Suicidal behaviors appear more prevalent for children of low socioeconomic backgrounds, especially those in urban areas whose play areas often serve as the method of their suicidal behaviors (i.e., jumping from roofs, jumping from subway platforms, and running into traffic on their busy neighborhood streets).

Puerto Rican children who are unaccustomed to life in the urban areas of the United States make more suicide attempts than would be expected from their population. It was noted (Gould, 1965) that blacks also had higher suicide rates some years ago when they were moving into urban areas in large numbers, but that these figures have ceased to rise so dramatically since assimilation and acculturation have taken place.

Social and cultural attitude also appears to figure prominantly in a country's suicide rate, including the rate of child suicides.

# 5

# Characteristics and Presenting Symptoms in Suicidal Children

## WARNINGS

Children who attempt or complete suicide may show signs of instability or disturbance, or they may give some kind of warning to important people in their environment before they attempt suicide (Glaser, 1965). The type of warning or even the nature of the suicidal act should not be used as an indicator of the seriousness of the patient's condition, nor to judge the likelihood of recurrence.

Glaser (1965) classifies warnings of suicide as *just talk, gesture, threat,* or *attempt. Just talk,* casual expressions that generally are not meant to be taken in their literal sense, are so common that they are rarely brought to the attention of the physician. If such remarks are mentioned by the mother to the physician or repeated frequently by very young children, Glaser suggests that the child should be further evaluated. *Gesture* refers to a suicidal act, carefully planned so as to be noticed by an important person in the child's life. *Threat* is a more serious act than the gesture, but often is difficult to distinguish in its expression from *just talk.* An *attempt,* a strong, often last and desperate warning, involves a definite risk. Below are case studies illustrating each of the above categories.

*Just talk*:

An eleven-year-old boy had 'mentioned killing himself,' according to the mother. The parents were greatly concerned about the boy's lack of friends and relatively poor school performance in the presence of very high intelligence. However, this was a constant behavior pattern with no recent change in mood, and the threat was not repeated. (Glaser, 1965)[5]

*Gesture*:

A seventeen-year-old girl told the interviewer: 'I just scratched my wrist—many do.' She wanted to prevent or delay her return to the parents after visiting an aunt. But she was socially well adjusted, her school progress was satisfactory, and she had applied for and obtained college admission. (Glaser, 1965)[5]

*Threat*:

[The subject was] a twelve-year-old boy for whom the transfer from elementary to junior high school was an unduly stressful experience. He also felt threatened by other students whom he had reported while acting as 'safety patrol' the preceding year. He refused to attend school and developed physical symptoms.

In the interview, he indicated that he considered suicide as 'the only way out.' The stress appeared overwhelming: he felt cornered, helpless, and unable to solve his conflict. On further study it became evident that the conflict was deeper. He felt different and embarrassed because of his unusual breast development, and wanted to avoid exposure during showers. (Glaser, 1965)[5]

*Attempt*:

A thirteen-year-old girl took phenobarbital, which she had available for the control of her epileptic seizures. She left a note indicating the number of pills she was taking. By limiting the number of pills and practically leaving instructions for her rescue, she obviously did not seriously intend to take her life but circumstances, such as a delay in her parents' return, could have foiled the rescue. (Glaser, 1965)[5]

## CONSTITUTIONAL CORRELATIONS

Heredity as a determiner of the intensity of reaction to the environment has entered the discussions of suicide (Shaw and Schelkun, 1965). Constitutional correlations that can be included in a discussion of suicide are hypersensitivity, suggestibility, related psychological or physical pathology, and developmental disturbances. They will be included in this discussion.

Children lacking normally supportive adult relationships were shown by Connell (1972) to have inadequate personality structures for coping with environmental stress and their own aggressive drives. These children had a background of increasing decompensation that finally led to a seemingly trivial event that, in turn, led to an impulsive but very serious suicide attempt. The three factors needed were: (1) an unstable and aggressive family background and inadequate personality resources to deal with lack of family support; (2) an increased emotional decompensation; and (3) a trivial event that triggered the impulsive suicide attempt.

Specific constitutional conditions pointed out by Winn and Halla (1966) included two mothers who had attempted suicide by ingesting sleeping pills while pregnant. Another 15% of the 70 children included in this study had prenatal complications such as prematurity, 15% had postnatal trauma such as encephalitis or cerebral concussion, and 30% had been "head-bangers" during preschool age. In addition, 15% had been slow to develop, and many others had been hyperactive and had feeding problems or other difficulties at an early age.

Zilboorg (1937) interprets suicide as an elemental drive that performs some function in the biological scheme of things. This was suggested by its being present universally at various stages of civilization and at various levels of individual development.

Freud (1965) says that no clinical picture in childhood is determined by only one set of factors and that most pathological formations are dependent on both a child's particular constitution and the constitution's reaction to a particular set of external circumstances.

### Hypersensitivity

Shaw and Schelkun (1965) say that children who seem to be constitutionally susceptible to suicidal behavior are intense reactors and are characterized by a low tolerance for frustration.

### Suggestibility

Although adults vary in their susceptibility to suggestion, nearly all children are susceptible to suggestion to a greater degree than adults (Shaw and Schelkun, 1965). These authors suggest that strong death wishes directed toward the child and held by those close to her or him may cause the child to feel that she or he "has to die." "Suicide epidemics" among adolescents also indicate the power of suggestion.

Lourie (1966) reports that suggestion plays a major role in the method selected for suicide attempts. Television, movies, or constant talk or threats of suicide are often copied by children. When children repeat suicide attempts, however, they seldom repeat their first methods.

### Psychological or Physical Pathology

Zilboorg (1937) describes a psychosis in which the individual who is unable to master reality denies its existence and then restores it by projecting her or his own fantasies into real life. This projection itself is not pathological (as with a child who makes blocks into a train and the poet who believes in her or his own fantasies) because it serves the biological purpose of both mastering and recreating reality. However, when reality is totally abolished and instead is filled with the ego projection, the ego, in an attempt to save itself, may choose death.

Winnicott (1965) discusses schizophrenia or psychotic conditions that emerge as a "highly sophisticated defense organization." This defense is against anxiety produced by environmental failure at a stage when the child is almost completely dependent upon a caretaker. In this situation, the child experiences a loss of reality and the capacity to relate to objects, and the defense isolates that child and allows a position of invulnerability through introversion.

Lawler, Nakielny, and Wright (1963) and Winn and Halla (1966) discuss hallucinations occurring in suicidal patients in their studies. Lawler, Nakielny, and Wright discuss 4 schizophrenic patients who had marked ego weakness, impaired reality-testing, and disturbed body image and who employed projection and introjection and had hallucinations that were primarily auditory. They all had a fantasy life filled with hostile references, as well as flattened and inappropriate affect and difficulties with interpersonal relationships. Winn and Halla indicate that 59% of their 70 suicidal patients had hallucinations directing them to kill themselves, and 35% had hallucinations directing them to kill someone else. They further noted that 15% had hallucinations of persons or animals threatening to kill them, but most of these were younger children whose dreams of monsters persisted while they were awake. In Winn and Halla's study, 15% of the children had dreams in which they were dead or badly injured, and 20% saw caskets, funerals, or other dead people in their dreams. Only 2 children in this group dreamed of intentionally wanting to kill or harm themselves.

In Lourie's (1966) group of 40 suicidal children, 4 had a psychosis of the nature of childhood schizophrenia and 1 had a psychosis associated with postencephalitic process.

In his study of Swedish suicidal children who had undergone psychiatric exploration, Otto (1967) reported that 53% were neurotic, 16.5% were psychotic, 11.8% were schizophrenic, and 4.7% had manic-depressive psychosis.

In Shaffer's (1974) study of children who completed suicide, 9 (8 boys, 1 girl) or 30% of the sample, were either currently seeing a psychiatrist or on a waiting list of a psychiatric clinic at the time of their death. Only 2, however, had been referred for their attempted suicide.

In a comparison of suicidal inpatient and outpatient children, Pfeffer, Conte, Plutchik, and Jerrett (1980) report that inpatients had a higher incidence of multiple deficits in ego functioning; the outpatients had a higher incidence of neurosis; and the inpatients had a higher incidence of serious psychopathological behavior, learning disabilities, and organic brain syndromes. The inpatients showed more serious suicidal behavior, such as threats and attempts.

Shaw and Schelkun (1965) report that the psychological disorders that show a significant correlation with suicide are schizophrenia, psychoneurosis, and impulsive hyperactivity associated with brain damage.

The following case studies are of children with psychological disorders and suicidal behaviors.

Wendell is an eight-year-old boy who twice ran in front of cars to be killed. On the third try, he was actually hit and suffered a concussion. Earlier, he had been noted to go into ecstatic states in front of the television. He believed he had magical powers and had fantasies of being able to turn into a girl. He was markedly fearful of bulldogs and cats, and at an earlier age was afraid of thunder. He had always been hyperactive, was a problem at school, and had once set fire to a school desk. His symptoms had become pronounced after his father left the mother to enter a common law relationship. The father returned after one year. He was a policeman of paranoid personality who fought violently with his wife but he was gentle with his son. Wendell is of low normal intelligence and his EEG is normal.

Monroe is a 9½-year-old boy who threatened to kill himself by being hit by a car. He described an introjected white man who lived in his chest and was eating his insides. The introjected white man subsequently became externalized in the form of a Negro man living at a great distance who sent electricity into his head and talked to him through the light fixtures. The boy had a snake phobia and was preoccupied with dying violently. A typical nightmare was of a red face moving through the window to attack him with a knife. His spontaneous drawings were of a boy being killed by a car or burned to death. Monroe was born to an alcoholic prostitute who abandoned him at birth. He was in several foster homes at first but had been in the same stable home since he was five. He was of low normal intelligence and his EEG was mildly abnormal. (Winn and Halla, 1966)[6]

The two above case studies are of children who have been diagnosed as schizophrenic. Rosenberg and Latimer (1966) describe a set of 13-year-old twin girls, one of whom was depressed and approaching a psychotic break after the stepmother requested the twins be removed from the home when she discovered their homosexual behavior with each other. The second twin used denial and repression to handle her problems, and these seemed to work well for her.

## Developmental Disturbances

Garfinkel and Golombek (1974) say that the child who is entering early adolescence must relinquish emotional attachment to the parents and begin to shift attachments to his or her peers, cultural heroes, and adults of some prominence in the child's life, such as coaches, counselors, and teachers. The young person in this position has fewer resources to fall back on during times of stress, and a child of this age may feel increased anger, sadness, and helplessness. This developmental level causes the young person to have fewer problem-solving capabilities as she or he tends to resort to previously acquired methods of handling problems. This could give rise to thoughts of suicide as the only escape from stressful situations.

Shaw and Schelkun (1965) have the following to say about developmental disturbances:

> The sharp increase in reported suicides at the age of puberty suggests that this time of life, with its powerful sex drive and the attendant physical, psychological, and social changes, produces such difficult adjustment problems that the balance of determining factors is weighed toward self-destruction in some cases. Younger children, too, undergo upsetting and sometimes rather rapid changes during the course of development, and the resulting disturbance of homeostasis may combine with other factors to induce suicidal behavior.

## IQ

Winn and Halla (1966) found that the average full-scale IQ of all the children in their study was 87. Rosenberg and Latimer (1966) found no significant difference in distribution of IQs from

.he generally accepted norms, although 75% of these girls were 1 to 4 years behind their class in school. Boys in the study, when separated from the girls, did not approximate the generally accepted norms as closely as the girls with a lower median and mode than normal distribution. All but 2 of the boys were 1 to 4 years behind their class in school placement.

## STRESS TOLERANCE

Children who have a low tolerance for frustration or who have been subjected to continuing and overwhelming stressful situations may attempt suicide (Shaw and Schelkun, 1965).

Children who are in abusive situations may be threatened with annihilation and/or abandonment (Green, 1978). These children may feel overwhelmed by "noxious stimulation that often cannot be adequately processed by the young victim's defensive structures, resulting in severe anxiety, painful affect, and ego disorganization." Children who are abused may attempt to escape from their intolerable situation by a suicidal gesture or attempt.

This hopelessness, weariness, and desire for relief are apparent in the following suicide note left by a 17-year-old Chicago boy who shot himself to death. It is quoted by Shaw and Schelkun (1965) and was originally reported by Litman, Shneidman, and Farberow (1961)[7]:

> I'm sick and there is no obvious cure. God forgive me. I smoke and I cannot stop. I cannot control my diabetes. I steal. I lie. I'm failing in typing and trigonometry. I have been thrown out of physics class. My teachers are not to blame, they did their best. My parents, partly, they did not prepare me for life. I'm sorry for the troubles I'm causing. But my troubles will be over. Please have them sing the hymn "Amazing Grace" at my funeral.[8]

## AFFECTIVE FACTORS

Connell (1972) reports the following information about the affective state of 15 suicidal children in the following paragraph:

The children were impulsive and lacked adequate control of their strong aggressive drives; yet in their disturbed backgrounds they seemed unable to express their aggression openly. In 11 cases a quarrel with a family member, in a situation where the child could not show overt hostility, preceded the attempt at suicide. Generally, this involved a loss of self-esteem, the child being the object of derogatory remarks. It was this or a loss of material possessions (bicycle, money, new clothes) which appeared to be a major contributory factor. In all 15 cases the picture was one of increasing decompensation in the face of stress, culminating in some often trivial event which precipitated an impulsive suicidal act. Examples of the triviality were presented by a boy whose parents forcibly cut his hair, and a girl who lost 15 marks in an examination through a foolish mistake.[9]

Carlson and Cantwell (1979) report the percentages of symptoms in children with suicidal behavior who had been diagnosed as having affective disorders (see Table 2).

Pfeffer, Conte, Plutchik, and Jerrett (1979) have looked at multiple factors associated with the high risk for suicidal behavior in latency-age children. These behaviors have been broken down

### Table 2    Percentages of Suicidal Children with Affective Disorders

|                          | Percent |
| ------------------------ | ------- |
| Dysphoric mood           | 70.4    |
| Low self-esteem          | 74.1    |
| Poor school performance  | 48.1    |
| Anhedonia                | 66.7    |
| Changed appetite         | 40.7    |
| Tired                    | 66.7    |
| Insomnia                 | 70.4    |
| Somatic complaints       | 70.4    |
| Suicidal ideation        | 88.9    |
| Hopelessness             | 70.4    |

Modified from Carlson and Cantwell (1979).

into two groups by these authors: (1) factors associated with severe childhood psychopathology in general and (2) factors that may be used to distinguish between suicidal and nonsuicidal children. These factors in these two categories are listed below.

*Specific Factors Significantly Correlating with Suicidal Behavior*

Depression
Hopelessness
Worthlessness
Wish to die
Severe depression in mother
Depression and suicidal behavior in parents
Preoccupations with death
Concept that death is temporary
Concept that death is pleasant

*Factors Associated with Severe Psychopathology*

Severe anxiety
Severe aggression
Preoccupations about school failure
Learning disabilities
Fear of parental punishment
Parental separations
Abusive home atmosphere
Disturbed peer relationships
Multiple deficits in ego functioning

In addition to the variables found in suicidal children such as sadness, depression, hopelessness, worthlessness, and statements about wishing to die, the suicidal behavior and depression of the parents were specifically correlated with childhood suicidal behavior. Perception and identification with parental traits such as these may be internalized as self-images (Pfeffer, Conte, Plutchik, and Jerrett, 1979).

## Depression

Carlson and Cantwell (1982) used the Children's Depression Inventory (CDI) and semistructured interviews with 102 psychiatrically referred children and adolescents to test the correlation of suicidal ideation and depression. They found a direct correlation between feeling depressed and feeling suicidal in these children. For subjects with depressed scores on the CDI, 63% were suicidal, though of those who were suicidal, only 34% were also depressed. These authors also found that 71% of subjects with suicidal ideation and high depression scores on CDI met criteria for depressive disorders. However, they discovered that the majority of subjects with suicidal ideation but low depression scores had behavior disorder diagnoses and only 3 of these had depressive disorders. Also, children with high depression scores but no suicidal ideation had schizophrenia or behavior disorders, but only 2 met criteria for depressive disorders. Actual suicide attempts were variable and did not reflect a continuum of suicidal ideation. Those subjects whose suicide attempt did not lead to psychiatric hospitalization appeared to feel less depressed and did not meet criteria for depressive disorders; most of the subjects whose suicide attempt led to hospitalization met criteria for affective disorders. Only 20% of the sample indicated feeling hopeless, and these feelings did not distinguish attempters from nonattempters. Also children reported feeling hopeless as often as adolescents in the study.

Garfinkel and Golombek (1974) report that while suicide may often be linked to a seemingly trivial event that triggers the child's self-destructive behavior and although this event produced the impulsive response in the the child, there has been an ongoing depressive process that has usually been expressed episodically and behaviorally. The child often has a history of appearing to be sad, withdrawn, and inhibited.

Connell (1972) found it surprising that most adults did not notice depressive symptoms in their children. Of the 15 children in his study, 9 of their families reported a history indicating that their children were showing signs of clinical depression several weeks or months before they attempted suicide. These 9 children showed increasing social withdrawal and expressed feelings of rejection, loneliness, a loss of interest in friends and hobbies, and "falling off" in school performance before their attempts. Two refused to attend school, and their bouts of weeping and negative self-concept were common; 7 of the children had vocalized their suicidal thoughts, and 3 had made previous attempt(s) at suicide;

8 children showed behavior patterns of overeating, stealing, and hostility; 3 had sleep disturbances; and somatic symptoms such as headaches and abdominal pain were common. They seemed to have a postinfluenzal depression.

Those who did not show signs of clinical depression were irritable and withdrawn and they showed explosive, angry behavior if provoked. Only one family had sought psychiatric help. Others with children who had somatic complaints visited a family doctor, but the matter was dropped when the illness had no organic basis. Even after the suicidal attempt, the parents were often unresponsive to their child's distress.

Depressive symptoms exhibited by these 15 children and the number showing each symptom are listed by Connell (1972) below.[9]

| | |
|---|---|
| Underfunctioning in school | 12 |
| Change in mood observed by others | 9 |
| Social withdrawal | 9 |
| 'Compensatory symptoms' (stealing, overeating) | 8 |
| Thoughts of suicide communicated to others | 7 |
| Previous attempts at suicide | 3 |
| Bouts of weeping | 6 |
| Sleep disturbance | 3 |
| Somatic symptoms (headache, abdominal pain) | 12 |

The most frequent cause of depression in the suicidal children in a Lawler, Nakielny, and Wright study (1963) was the loss of a love object. Several patients had lost a parent through death or separation, a few had lost teachers, one had lost a family pet, and several had lost prestige through failure in school. In one case the suicidal attempt appeared to be an appeal for help as a means of escaping an intolerable living situation.

Haider (1968) reported that the child in his study exhibited depression with restlessness, school refusal, crying without reason, sleep disturbance, isolation, boredom, antisocial activity, compulsive hyperactivity, running away from home, and behavioral difficulties at home.

Gould (1965) notes that it is difficult to imagine that a child experiencing the chronic loss of a loved object will not show depression in some form. However, because these factors are often expressed by impulsivity, hypermotility, and other disguised forms, this depression is less likely to show up as "pure" depression. Gould feels that depression is common in children and adolescents, that it is overlooked by therapists in both pure and disguised form, and that it is almost always a part of the psycho-dynamics of the "suicidal personality" of children and adolescents.

Extreme parental control was associated with high depression scores equated with repressed hostility in McIntire and Angle's (1973) study.

Hendin (1975) describes depression in suicidal children thus:

> For many young people, life is a grueling war of attrition in which depression is the best available accomplice, the only way to ward off the impact of their daily lives. Such students experience death daily in their attempts to bury their anger, rage, and pain deep within themselves. As the lives of students who are severely depressed and made suicide attempts suggest, the fascination with death is often the climax of having been emotionally dead for a lifetime.

Both Winn and Halla (1966) and Shaw and Schelkun (1965) note that depression in children is often difficult to identify. Winn and Halla noticed that often the children who appeared to have the most reasons to be depressed appeared to be the least depressed and children who continued to look sad after hospital admission were often schizophrenic children who were overreacting to a relatively minimal stress. Shaw and Schelkun (1965) observed that depression in children is often masked by denial.

The following case study describes a child who is depressed:

> A typical patient in group one [with parents who totally reject the parental role] is a 14-year-old boy. As a child he was unplanned for and unwanted. He was the second and last child of a middle-class family. His mother was cold, withdrawn, and depressed. She showed little interest in him as a child. She ran the household and her own life in a mechanical way. His father was a little, frightened, passive person who submitted to the authority of his wife. The patient referred to his father

as a small, dark, fearful, ugly "mouse-like" man. He felt he looked and acted like his father. The boy felt there was no hope for himself and expressed constant depression with suicidal preoccupation. His depression was punctuated by periods of acute anxiety most marked in dreams in which he saw himself 'sweating over an exam for which he had failed to study,' or dreams where he was caught in a quagmire and was unable to move despite his desperate struggling. His closest tie was to his only sibling, a brother two years older than he. Though both were withdrawn, the two boys together struggled to maintain themselves in their friendless environment, finding in each other some slight companionship and meaningfulness in an otherwise empty world.

Occasionally, the two boys together climbed a high fence surrounding the electric company near their home. The area was full of croaking birds and pigeons who scattered when they came. One day the elder boy lost his grip, shrieked, and fell. The patient climbed down to find his moaning brother dying, the croaking birds fluttering about. The croaking pigeons haunted him one year later as he spoke of them; he was unable to do his school work because he could still hear them fluttering about, making their awful sounds as he sat in the classroom. His parents stated he wept frequently 'without reason.' He had to be withdrawn from school at the time of the first anniversary of his brother's death, when his depression mounted into psychotic proportions and he threatened suicide. (Schrut, 1964)[10]

## Low Self-Esteem

Self-destructive, battered children assume that they are to blame for the punishment they receive (Green, 1978). The child's self-hatred and low self-esteem increase and become the focus for subsequent self-destructive behavior. This acting out of the battered child of parental hostility directed toward the child may be an important factor in suicidal behavior.

Parents who exert extreme control as well as rejection by requiring impossibly high expectations of their child convey the message that the child is incapable or "no good." The repressed hostility that results is often expressed as a suicidal gesture or a suicidal attempt (McIntire and Angle, 1973).

Two case studies show how impossible expectations cause guilt reactions in two girls:

> One seventeen-year-old girl had given bone marrow to her sister who was dying of leukemia. She had witnessed the last phase of her sister's tragic and prolonged suffering but was whisked away before her death 'to spare her the emotional upset.'
>
> This girl had been jealous of her sister and, without being able to express it, had harbored hostile wishes for her. When her marrow did not succeed in saving her sister, she felt responsible for her death.
>
> The other girl, age fourteen, was the daughter of a demanding mother in good economic circumstances who had not progressed far in her own education. She wished to give her daughter every opportunity which she herself had not experienced in her own youth and expected high performance and grateful appreciation. The young lady was never able to reward her mother sufficiently for 'everything mother had put into her,' and considered herself a disappointment to her parents. (Glaser, 1965)[5]

## Loneliness

Children in Connell's (1972) study exhibited their need for dependent relationships and their failure in finding support within their families. An 11-year-old boy said, "Nobody cares for me. Dad's only mad at me. I meant to die. I don't want to see him again." A 14-year-old girl said that if she couldn't live with both parents, she didn't want to live at all. These children often complained that they could not talk with their parents who were either too busy or too remote to reach.

## Hopelessness

In addition to viewing death as pleasant and temporary, the chronic depression and anxiety, frequent incidents of suicidal behaviors seen in her or his parents, and states of hopelessness and

worthlessness may increase a child's vulnerability to suicidal behavior, according to Pfeffer, Conte, Plutchik, and Jerrett (1979).

The following is a case study of a girl who feels hopeless in the
situation in which her family has placed her:

> E. was a fourteen-year-old girl when seen because of fainting
> spells and unhappiness. She had run away from home, leaving
> notes indicating that she saw herself as stupid, dumb, and
> "Why do you need me?" Her IQ was reported as 77 and 84
> on separate tests one year apart. Her parents were intelligent,
> and she had a brother, three years younger, who was a very
> good student. The family lived in a well-to-do suburban neigh-
> borhood. At first she went to a regular class in public school
> where she could not do the work but was promoted 'out of
> compassion.' When placed in a special education class later she
> felt degraded. The parents had taken her to many consultants
> and were unable to accept her mental retardation which, even
> though mild, put her in sharp contrast with the bright brother
> and children in the neighborhood.
>
> One evening she acted withdrawn and stated to her
> brother, 'Don't be upset if I am not here tomorrow.' In the
> early morning hours she was found lying on a road. She claim-
> ed that she had heard voices or dreamed that she should get
> up and be run over by a car. She thought that if she ran away
> everybody would be better off. She admitted to thoughts of
> suicide on other occasions and also that she would repeat her
> attempt if the 'voices would tell her very loudly.' (Glaser,
> 1971)[11]

## Sense of Being Different

Shaffer's (1974) study of children between the ages of 12 and
14 who completed suicide indicates that a large proportion of them
were of above average intelligence. Ten of the 30 had an IQ above
115. Of the 20 children whose height was known, only two were
below the 50th percentile for height, but a disproportionate number were tall or very tall for their age.

Such factors as premature social and psychosexual development
may appear to be an insurmountable obstacle to children approaching puberty (Glaser, 1971). Causes may be endogenous, such as

early sexual maturation (with visible secondary sex characteristics and accelerated growth) or exogenous factors produced by family imbalance. Delayed development also may produce severe obstacles, but it is usually recognized as a cause for disturbance.

If a parent dies, the oldest or only child may be placed in the position of a quasi-spouse with the remaining parent, and that adult's thoughts and worries may be shared with the child. The child, who is too young to understand issues in the proper perspective, may have a sense of failure, inadequacy, and overwhelming guilt feelings because of an inability to adequately assume the role of a spouse. This situation may be complicated by the parent's vacillation by talking to the child as an adult on the one hand but by putting the child back in her or his place with such statements as, "You should not worry about such things—you are just a child," on the other hand (Glaser, 1971).

The following case study demonstrates a situation in which a child has been placed in a difficult situation by her mother:

> P., a twelve-year-old girl, was seen by the author because of suicidal threats made to mother and at school. She had difficulties getting along with the mother, her nine-year-old sister, and her peers. Her father had died when P. was seven years old, and the mother began to discuss financial matters, including future economic security, with her daughter, and allowed her to baby-sit for her sister who was only three years younger. Yet mother complained that P. was never a child, always acted more mature but was strong-willed and fought with her younger sister. P. complained about the silly interests of her peers and felt as though she were sixteen, but older teenagers did not accept the pudgy little twelve-year-old. 'I don't consider myself a child but an unfortunately degraded half adult.' P. talked in the interview about inadequacy of the school curriculum, pressure of regimentation, and the confused state of national and world affairs. Sometimes she felt like playing in the stream with water and sand but was ashamed. The child had difficulties in falling asleep, spoke about hating herself and about wanting to escape by institutionalization or suicide. (Glaser, 1971)[11]

## Hostility and Anger

Suicidal children exhibit depression, hostility, and bitter lone-liness that the families and associates may notice. These children may have superficial relationships and may even appear popular in some cases, but they seem to derive little emotional satisfaction from this contact. Affections may be displaced to animals. An un-usual attachment to a pet may at times point out a child's estrange-ment from human relationships (Shaw and Schelkun, 1965).

Paulson, Stone, and Sposto (1978) report that there is no sex-significant difference in the ideational violence between boys and girls, and children as young as five years demonstrate both in fan-tasy and verbalized threats that physical assault upon family mem-bers and hostility displaced to siblings is equally common in boys and girls. Almost every suicidal attempt by children involves a pat-tern of self-abuse that usually results in body mutilation. Behavior that included stabbing, cutting, scalding, burning, purposeful run-ning into moving vehicles, and jumping from high places far ex-ceeded relatively "nonviolent" suicide attempts by a medication overdose in latency-age children. There is a significant association between this assault upon the child's body by the child and the disorganized, chaotic state of the family. From the perspective of modeling theory and social learning, the suicidal child is acting out the family violence. The child is making a plea for love and affec-tion in a situation in which the norm has been rejection and isola-tion; she or he is demonstrating a wish to die because there is no emotional bonding within the home.

## BEHAVIORAL FACTORS

When Shaffer (1974) asked teachers to describe the 30 children who had completed suicide in his sample, they produced the fol-lowing list of behavioral characteristics:

1. "Chip on the shoulder—felt people didn't like him (her), felt people were unduly critical of him (her)"    9 cases
2. "Impulsive—no self control—volative-erratic"    6 cases

3. "Quiet—difficult to get through to—uncommunicative"                                        9 cases
4. "Perfectionist—high standards—neat—tidy, method-
   ical—self-critical—afraid of making mistakes"      6 cases
5. "Insufficient information" or none of the above    6 cases

Children in Shaffer's sample had presented a combination of antisocial and emotional symptoms. Those symptoms, separated by sex, are presented in Table 3.

McIntire and Angle (1973) noted that 88% of the 50 subjects seen at poison control centers had a history of significant personal-social difficulties. These included the following:

| | |
|---|---|
| Immaturity | 38% |
| School dropout | 18% |
| Loner | 16% |
| Behavior problem | 15% |
| Delinquency | 14% |
| Prior suicide gestures | 26% |

Self-destructive battered children (Green, 1978) showed aggressive and destructive behavior at home and at school. They often

Table 3   Symptoms Shown by Children Who Committed Suicide

| | Boy | Girl | Total |
|---|---|---|---|
| Antisocial | | | |
| Bullying and fighting | 7 | 2 | 9 |
| Stealing | 6 | 3 | 9 |
| Truancy | 7 | 2 | 9 |
| Running away | 3 | 0 | 3 |
| Emotional/Affective | | | |
| Depressed mood or tearfulness | 7 | 6 | 13 |
| Hypochondriasis | 2 | 2 | 4 |
| Excessive fears | 4 | 0 | 4 |
| School refusal | 4 | 0 | 4 |
| Ideas of reference or self-denigration | 2 | 2 | 4 |
| Morbid preoccupations | 4 | 0 | 4 |
| Boredom | 2 | 0 | 2 |

From Shaffer (1974). Copyright 1974, *Journal of Child Psychology and Psychiatry and Allied Disciplines.*

were described as hyperactive with minimal frustration tolerance. They expressed themselves more frequently with motor activity than verbally, and because of inadequate superego models and faulty internalization, they lacked the usual superego restraints normally found in latency-age children.

Of the 30 suicidal patients studied by Haldane and Haider (1967), the majority had been abnormally intolerant of frustration from their preschool years and had shown unusual dependence on parents; they were aggressive, demanding, and noticeably jealous of their siblings. Of the 10 boys, 6 had run away from home at some time; 5 of the boys had shown overt anti-social behavior in some form. Four of the girls had run away from home, and 1 had been involved in several episodes of theft. One boy and 2 girls had had previous psychiatric treatment, and two boys and two girls had made previous suicide attempts. Three girls made additional suicide attempts after the attempt that led to referral; 1 girl and 1 boy made an attempt while under treatment.

Table 4 reports the diagnosis of the children included in Haldane and Haider's (1967) study.

Mattsson, Seese, and Hawkins (1969) found that 28% of the suicidal patients in their study had shown behavioral disorders such as impulsiveness, defiance, assaultive behavior, delinquency, truancy, and promiscuous behavior accompanied at times by suicidal gestures for a year before their suicide attempts. There were also "neurotic" symptoms such as withdrawal, fears, and somatic complaints in 46% of the patients.

### Table 4  Diagnoses of Children

| Diagnosis | Boys | Girls | Total |
|---|---|---|---|
| Character disorder | 6 | 13 | 19 |
| Reactive behavior disorder | 1 | 1 | 4 |
| Depressive state | 3 | 3 | 6 |
| Schizophrenia | – | 1 | 1 |
| Totals | 10 | 20 | 30 |

From Haldane and Haider (1967). Copyright 1967, *British Journal of Clinical Practice.*

The following case studies demonstrate some of the behaviors seen in suicidal children.

J.Y., Male (11). Referred a year before to another department of Child Psychiatry because of truancy, stealing and 'malicious mischief.' Because of the unsatisfactory family situation, he was placed in a Children's Home where he made three attempts to strangle himself, one almost successful.

After 9 months' inpatient treatment he was placed with foster parents, father maintaining contact, but gradually relapsed into antisocial behavior and the prognosis is thought to be poor. (Haldane and Haider, 1967)[1 2]

W.S., Male (13). He was referred with a 4-5 year history of running away from home, truancy and theft. He had been in a Remand Home; on Probation; under treatment at Child Guidance Clinic and in a Children's Home. He had, inappropriately, been recommended for admission to residential school for maladjusted children. He took an overdose of phenobarbitone and aspirin, to prevent having to leave home.

After 8 months' treatment in an adolescent unit with little improvement he was referred, but before he was seen the family moved to another area. (Haldane and Haider, 1967)[1 2]

J.M., Male (15). Eldest of three boys. Brought up in an atmosphere of rigid religious righteousness and sexual repression. His first attempt followed a charge of indecent exposure and fear of parents' discovery of masturbation; the second after being involved with other boys in a charge of theft. Both attempts were made by cutting wrist.

He improved after a period in an adolescent unit. But about two years later he was referred to adult psychiatry service suffering from schizo-affective illness. (Haldane and Haider, 1967)[1 2]

## Behavior and Character Disorders

The largest diagnostic group in Haider's (1968) study of 64 suicidal children was composed of children with character and behavior disorders. They were immature, impulsive children who reacted strongly and excessively to minor stresses. Children who had character disorders attempted suicide as a spite reaction. These children were in constant conflict with the environment, were hostile in their feelings toward others, and often suffered from depression. Most of the younger children were considered to be suffering from behavior disorders.

## Aggression

Shaw and Schelkun (1965) say that suicidal behavior is often interpreted as a sign of aggression toward the self. This aggression turned inward may involve suicidal tendencies in children who have lost someone close to them through death or abandonment. The child may see death as a form of voluntary desertion and, therefore, as a rejection. It has been shown that children who commit murder often have a history of previous suicide attempts.

In the majority of the 30 cases in Haldane and Haider's (1967) study, the suicidal attempt was dramatic, impulsive, and aggressively toned and accompanied by feelings of revenge after a long series of home difficulties and with a lack of emotional satisfaction for both child and parent. The child was aggressively rebelling against a hostile, rejecting world, and the suicidal act expressed infantile omnipotence. It also was an attempt to gain love of which she or he had been deprived.

For many, when a child's parents wish that she or he does not exist and feel they would be happier without children, their child may "pick up" these clues (which may be communicated to the child in nonverbal or verbal ways and unconsciously as well as consciously) and try to follow the parents' wishes by attempting suicide, if this seems to be the only way to gain their parents' approval and love (Gould, 1965).

The following case studies present examples of aggressive behavior in suicidal children.

> J.B., Male (12). The second of 7 children of an anxious submissive mother and an aggressive father who had a history of juvenile delinquency, adult crime, drunkenness, sexual infidelity and unwillingness to work. J.B. was referred one year before because of excitable, aggressive behavior and outpatient treatment had been started. He had spent two periods

in a Children's Home during the same year. Episodes of verbal and physical aggressiveness alternated with periods of tearfulness and despair. He attempted to gas himself in school after a quarrel with a teacher, who unjustly accused him for some misdemeanor.

Later, after a period in an adolescent unit, he returned to maternal grandparents; then from a Children's Home to a boys' hostel; and eventually to an Approved School following a charge of manslaughter. (Haldane and Haider, 1967)[12]

A 14-year-old boy was a product of a mother who was chronically angry and rejecting, showing him little affection. At age 14, Stuart attempted suicide with barbiturates and was brought to the Suicide Prevention Center. He took all the capsules that his mother had in her medicine cabinet and said he would have taken more if she had them. He indicated this also in the presence of his mother. Fortunately for the boy's life, she had only six capsules. He was surly, angry, and resentful. At a superficial level, he displaced upon the world the unconscious complex that had originated in his parental relationships and took from society whatever he could get. Stealing, lying, and cheating, he attempted to wrest from life that which was due him and repay life with the contempt which he felt was its due.

He demonstrated an explosive, uncontrollable aggressiveness and impulsiveness which represent the ego's adaptational mode of dealing with his problem of hating his mother. At age 12 years he attempted suicide by hanging himself with some kite string, but the kite string broke.

He used his mother's guilt and anxiety by threatening suicide to manipulate her and laughed at all her attempts to help him. He also reacted in the same manner with the personnel at the Suicide Prevention Center who, like mother, he felt unconsciously really wished his behavior to continue. He constantly injured himself as a small child, sustaining several fractures from automobile accidents in which he ran into the street. In one instance, as a child, he burned himself while playing with matches. Despite all warnings, his self-destructiveness continued unabated. Now, in his early teens, the mechanism which previously had been an unconscious one was being consciously employed to obtain a reaction from his mother. The mechanism, begun in childhood in an unconscious struggle, was now a consciously manipulated behavior.

His mother stated she could do nothing with him and asked for help in managing the child. She threatened suicide herself, thereby reinforcing her unconscious suggestion to him to follow suit. She described life with him as a running battle of constant duration and recalled their fights when 'he was so small he had just begun to walk.' The father, a laborer, tried to control him by alternately bribing him with more allowance and gifts and by punishing him, all to no avail. After several interviews, the mother reluctantly admitted that her only sibling, a much despised younger brother, acted 'just like my son when he was a child.' Somehow she knew her son would be 'just like him.' (Schrut, 1964)[10]

## Impulsiveness

In children, suicide may include an impulsive element. When this is an only or main factor, children may have higher suicide rates than adults because their egos or defenses have not developed to a point where their impulsiveness is as controlled as it is by adults. However, this impulsiveness may also work against completing suicide because a hasty and ill-conceived plan will probably not be successful (Gould, 1965).

Impulsive suicide attempts, such as suddenly jumping from a window, are similar to impulsive behavior in aggressive children, such as their pushing or shoving another child in a potentially lethal situation (Shaw and Schelkun, 1965).

## Sadism and Masochism

Some suicidal children may display cruelty to both themselves and other children. In contrast to most suicidal children who act from despair and unhappiness, these children seem to derive pleasure from their behavior, which is often sexual in nature. This happens most often with adolescents (Shaw and Schelkun, 1965).

## Modeling

Self-destructive battered children imitate their parent's aggressive and impulsive characteristics (Green, 1978). These children also learn to regard themselves with the same hostility and criticism that the parents express for the child.

When aggressive behavior occurs in suicidal children, the aggression may not be provoked by rejection. However, many children have extremely aggressive families and have identified themselves with aggressive parents and siblings, rather than reacting with aggression to a rejecting parent. This aggression, which may not be permitted to be expressed against others, is then directed toward the self (Bender and Schilder, 1937).

Glaser (1965) noted that in 3 cases of the 15 he studied, mothers had told their children prior to their suicide attempt about suicides in the immediate environment. One mother told her distressed daughter, "Don't do what Joe did" (Joe had completed suicide). One girl had a close friend who had taken an overdose of aspirin. One girl claimed she felt depressed after hearing a song titled "What Am I Living For?" on the radio.

## SEX DIFFERENCES

There is some disagreement about whether boys or girls attempt suicide more often. Pfeffer (1981) and Pfeffer, Conte, Plutchik, and Jerrett (1980) report that in their samples more boys attempted suicide. However, Bakwin (1957); Jacobziner (1960); "Suicide and Suicidal Attempts in Children and Adolescents" in The Lancet (1964); Lawler, Nakielny, and Wright (1963); and Otto (1966) report that statistical findings on large samples in general indicate that girls outnumber boys in suicide attempts, usually by 2:1. Also, Haldane and Haider (1967) and Morrison and Collier (1969) report that their small samples show more girls attempting suicide than boys.

Bakwin (1957) reports that while attempts are more frequent by girls, completed suicides are more common for boys. Mattsson, Seese, and Hawkins (1969) found that girls outnumber boys in their sample by 3:1, but indicated that male patients appeared to be "in general, sicker" than female patients. In both their attempts and their threats, boys tended to be judged as more associated with a depressed state and as more continual suicidal risks than girls.

Rosenberg and Latimer (1966) noted that of 163 girls admitted for suicidal behavior, 22.6% had made serious attempts prior to admission. Of 209 boys admitted, 6.7% had made serious suicidal attempts.

Shaffer (1974) found a marked difference in methods used, with proportionately more girls taking an overdose of drugs and only boys hanging themselves. All the children who shot themselves lived in rural areas where guns were kept for sport or for shooting vermin, and there had been no attempt to conceal or secure the firearms they used. Winn and Halla (1966) noticed that while boys often ran in front of cars in suicide attempts, only girls seemed to regard subway trains as a method for attempting suicide.

While Shaffer (1974) found in his study that only boys hanged themselves, Bergstrand and Otto (1962) found that girls also used hanging or strangulation as a means of suicide attempt. Haider (1968), in his study of 64 suicidal children, found that the majority of the 42 girls took drugs, which contrasted with the 22 suicidal boys, who preferred violent means. However, Mattsson, Seese, and Hawkins (1969) did not find this difference. The boys in their study did not employ more lethal methods than girls, and drug ingestion was equally prominent in children of both sexes. Paulson, Stone, and Sposto (1978) also found no sex-significant difference in the ideational violence between boys and girls in their suicidal children of ages 4 to 12. (See Chapter 7 for more general information on methods of suicide used by children.)

Gould (1965), who indicated that he found girls attempted suicide more frequently than boys but the boys were generally sicker, felt that the culture was a major factor in these statistics. He indicated that girls in the Western culture have fewer outlets for aggression than boys. For example, a girl may be sent to court for promiscuity, but a boy behaving in like manner would never come to the attention of the court. Fighting, aggressive behavior, and disobedience to parents and to authority figures are tolerated more often in boys than in girls.

Girls, therefore, with fewer chances for release for aggressive and hostile feelings to the environment, may turn these feelings inward. This enhances the possibility of suicide. Girls, partly due to the culture, show more hysterical features than do boys, and this may lead to suicidal behavior such as impulsive actions following frustration or disappointment. Suicide is less of a cultural taboo for girls but is considered "weak," "cowardly" and "chicken" in boys.

## SUMMARY: CHARACTERISTICS AND PRESENTING SYMPTOMS IN SUICIDAL CHILDREN

Children may warn others in their environment either verbally or in another fashion before engaging in a suicide attempt. Glaser (1965) classed these warnings into four categories: just talk (with suicide mentioned as a possibility by the child); gesture (a suicidal act planned by the child so it will be noted by important people in the child's life); threat (more serious suicidal behavior); and attempt (a desperate warning involving a definite risk).

Children may be genetically at high risk for suicide. Such factors as hypersensitivity, suggestibility, psychological or physical pathology, and developmental disturbances may put some children at higher risk for suicidal behavior than children who don't have these constitutional factors. Such factors as slightly depressed IQ scores which may predict school difficulties and low stress tolerance may also cause some children to be higher suicide risks. Abused children may find themselves in such a stressful environmental situation that suicide may appear to be the only way out.

Suicidal children often demonstrate such affective characteristics as depression, hopelessness, worthlessness, and distorted death concepts. Depression and suicidal ideations are often (but not always) correlated in children, and suicidal behaviors which appear impulsive on the surface may be the result of an ongoing depressive process. These depressive signs often go unnoticed by the child's parents. Low self-esteem, loneliness, and hopelessness are also common affects of suicidal children.

The child who feels different from peers, either because of

physical or psychological characteristics (too tall, unattractive, lower IQ than family or peers) or because the parent has placed the child in an unusual position (requiring the child to take on adult responsibilities at an early age, for example) may feel overwhelmed by such differences and react by becoming suicidal.

Suicidal children often have a variety of negative behavior characteristics. Among them, aggression may be the most predominant. This may be reflected as either aggression turned inward or as aggression, hostility, and anger directed at others. Suicidal children also often display impulsiveness and may be sadistic or masochistic. Modeling appears to be a factor in the suicidal behavior of some suggestible children.

There is a great deal of disagreement about whether girls or boys attempt suicide more frequently. Some authors report that in large samples girls attempt suicide more frequently but boys are more likely to complete suicide, and Mattsson, Seese, and Hawkins (1969) report that, while girls attempt suicide more frequently, boys who do attempt suicide are generally "sicker." Girls have been reported to use poison and drugs as the suicidal method more frequently than boys, while boys often chose what may prove to be more lethal methods such as hanging and shooting themselves. Gould (1965) reports that these differences may have a cultural basis. Girls are not allowed aggressive outlets open to boys (such as promiscuity, disobedience to parents, and fighting) without a great deal more public censure, and thus are more likely to turn aggressive and hostile feelings inward, and such behavior may be more likely to result in suicidal behavior.

# 6

# Precipitating Factors and Underlying Reasons

## PRECIPITATING FACTORS

The most common factors triggering a suicide attempt, according to Mattsson, Seese, and Hawkins (1969) were the following:

| | |
|---|---|
| Acute conflict between the child and his parental figure | 40% |
| Grief reactions or loss of heterosexual love object | 20% |
| School problems (failures, peer clashes) | 14% |
| Sexual conflicts related to masturbation, menstruation, or homosexual contacts | 14% |
| Pregnancy | 10% |

Often, suicide attempts are efforts to alter an intolerable living situation or to punish significant people in the environment. They are attempts to resolve or escape from a disturbing situation that appears to be beyond the child's capacity to manage (Garfinkel and Golombek, 1974).

Both Haider (1968) and Haldane and Haider (1967) noted that a quarrel with parents or parent figures was the most common precipitating factor in suicide attempts. Anxiety regarding a sexual relationship (in 7 of 64 cases), detection of truancy (7 in 64 cases), the strain of family problems (6 of 64 cases) and anxiety about examinations, mother's health, and the loss of a friend were also mentioned by Haider (1968).

McIntire and Angle (1973) say that the stress factors, coupled with parental reactions and extremes of parental control and expectation, left subjects with so few options that threatening to take their own lives was the only apparent way these children felt they could solve the problem.

In young children, fear of punishment, remorse, shame, guilt feelings, and anger are prominent factors in suicide attempts (Bakwin, 1957). Jacobziner (1960) found that disciplinary measures, emotional upsets, and depression were the chief causes in his study.

Of those children who gave a reason for their suicide attempt in Winn and Halla's (1966) sample of 70 New York City children who attempted suicide, 50% said they had a hallucination telling them to kill themselves; 20% said the threat or attempt was motivated by a loss or separation from the parent or parent surrogate or other love object. Only 15% listed feelings of inadequacy or failure as the motivating factor. There were 40% who either gave no reason or mentioned a quarrel with a parent or sibling.

## UNDERLYING REASONS FOR SUICIDAL BEHAVIOR

Mattsson, Seese, and Hawkins (1969) list the following reasons for suicidal behavior in children in their study of 75 children and adolescents:

> Group 1: Loss of a Love Object Followed by Acute or Prolonged Grief (3 boys; 14 girls)—These patients had sustained death of or desertion by a parent or a peer of the opposite sex. They were overtly depressed and stated their wish to die or join the deceased person; a pervasive state of loneliness and despair was characteristic rather than guilt and self-deprecation.
>
> Group 2: "The Bad Me," Markedly Self-Deprecating Patients (9 boys of whom 3 were under age 12; 11 girls)—Much hostility turned inward and a loss of a sense of well-being charac-

terized these children; quotes such as "I'm good for nothing," "I must die," and references to sexual sins and "bad" behavior toward their parents filled their records. The common diagnosis was neurotic reaction with emphasis on rigid super-ego inhibitions, incapacitating guilt reactions, and a view of death as a solution (rebirth).

*Group 3: The Final "Cry for Help" Directed Beyond the Immediate Family* (1 boy; 14 girls)—Overwhelming external stress was the primary factor among this group; family chaos, maternal scarcity, physical illness, etc., had been present for a long time. In most instances, these patients responded rapidly to postemergency intervention as their signal of distress was finally heeded.

*Group 4: The Revengeful, Angry Teen-ager* (3 boys; 10 girls) —These adolescents clearly stated the manipulative aspect of their suicidal gestures; "This will teach father a lesson" or "I was mad as hell" were typical quotes. They denied any serious intention and had frequently also made homicidal threats when irate.

*Group 5: The Psychotic Adolescent* (2 boys; 5 girls)—For these patients suicide appeared more as a desperate means to relieve increasing tension and confusion than the result of an acting on a delusional belief; actually, repeated threats were more common than attempts.

*Group 6: "The Suicidal Game"* (1 boy; 2 girls)—For these three adolescents, flirting with death was thrilling ("death isn't so bad") and the reaction of their stunned peers rewarding. Rarely were there any changes (spontaneous or therapeutically induced) in their extreme denial of fears of death, injuries, etc., which might have modified their dangerous counterphobic attitudes.[13]

Mattsson, Seese and Hawkins (1969) further state that the children in these six groups gave outward signs of their inner distress before the attempted suicide.

Connell (1972) indicates that punishment by parents is not far from punishment of self for children. A child may see death as reversible and may attempt suicide in an effort to teach parents a lesson; a child may not be aware of the outcome of some suicidal attempts (i.e., the dosage of drugs); and, while most suicidal acts are multidetermined, there is generally an overriding factor. Among the 15 children he examined, the following motives were indicated:

| | |
|---|---|
| Signal of distress (cry for help) | 6 |
| Escape from an intolerable situation | 3 |
| Manipulation of family | 2 |
| Self-punishment | 2 |
| To join a deceased mother | 1 |
| "Testing God out" | 1 |

Otto (1966), in a large sample of Swedish children, reported the following reasons for their suicide attempts:

| | |
|---|---|
| Home and parental problems | 69.0% |
| Love problems | 14.3% |
| School problems | 16.7% |

In a study of 62 children drawn from his sample of suicidal children and adolescents who said school problems were the reasons for their suicidal attempt, Otto (1965) found that the most frequent cause was poor school results followed by adjustment difficulties and a desire to quit school that was prevented.

Bender and Schilder (1937) mention the unwillingness to face a difficult situation as a major motivation in child suicide, adding that spite often plays a role. They say that it is doubtful that children expect to succeed in committing suicide, and they need to be assured of love and care when their attempt is thwarted. They add that one cannot understand the unconscious motives for suicide in children without considering the family situation.

## SUMMARY: PRECIPITATING FACTORS AND UNDERLYING REASONS FOR SUICIDAL BEHAVIOR

Children exhibiting suicidal behavior may react to an immediate precipitating cause which often appears trivial on the surface (but which may be a kind of "last straw" effect). Further exploration may uncover deeper underlying reasons which may be more serious and/or more ongoing.

Typical precipitating causes expressed by children include fear of punishment, remorse, guilt feelings, and anger. Disciplinary actions, emotional upsets, and depression were also factors for some children.

Underlying reasons often include reaction to loss, attempts at self-punishment, an attempt to obtain help in an intolerable situation, revenge, and flirting with death (the last two are more common in adolescents, however). Suicide attempts may be used to manipulate parents and as a reaction to home, school, or romance difficulties.

Often, precipitating causes and underlying reasons are the same, but frequently they are quite different.

# 7

# Methods of Suicide in Children

It had been reported previously that young children often have limited access to lethal weapons or drugs and so are prone to use methods of suicide that are familiarly dangerous behavior to children, such as jumping from heights and running into traffic (Shaw and Schelkun, 1965). It was also pointed out by Winn and Halla (1966) that children who lived in New York City and comprised the population of their study were taken on the subway since infancy and lived in houses that emptied directly onto the street, except for the sidewalk. The mothers must warn these children from an early age about the real dangers of falling off a subway platform, running into traffic, and falling from roofs and fire escapes; the children are aware of the lethality of these dangers from early childhood.

In fact, in Winn and Halla's (1966) study of these low-socioeconomic city children, 57% of the boys threatened to jump from a height such as an open window, the roof, or a fire escape; 33% threatened to cut or stab themselves; 15% threatened to run in front of a car or train; 12% threatened to choke or hang themselves; and 10% threatened to take poison. Among the girls, many more threatened to take drugs; 47% of the girls threatened to take poison or sleeping pills; 43% threatened to cut or stab themselves; 33% threatened to jump from a height; 20% threatened to run in front of a car or train; and 17% threatened to choke or hang themselves. Percentages equal more than 100% because some children threatened with more than one method.

However, a number of authors (Bergstrand and Otto, 1962; Connell, 1972; Haider, 1968; Mattsson, Seese, and Hawkins, 1969; Rosenberg and Latimer, 1966) discovered that drugs of various kinds were the most common methods used for suicide and suicidal attempts. The availability of barbiturates and other drugs seems to be a major factor. In his study, Connell (1972) points out that drugs taken by all those children who attempted suicide were drugs that had been prescribed for them or their families and had often been in the home for months or even years.

Garfinkel and Golombek (1974) suggest limited prescribing of barbiturates; more frequent prescriptions for smaller quantities of drugs; use of larger pills, which are more difficult to swallow; and packaging certain drugs individually in aluminum foil to ensure extra time for thought while the pill is being unwrapped. A means of deterring suicide in Britain in use at the time of Garfinkel and Golombek's study was the combining of a small amount of emetic with barbiturates.

In Haider's (1968) study, 50 of 64 suicidal children took drugs alone or in combination. The breakdown was as follows:

| | |
|---|---|
| Barbiturates | 26 |
| Salicylates | 4 |
| Combination of drugs | 6 |
| Nature of drugs not known | 14 |

Mattsson, Seese, and Hawkins (1969) reported the following breakdown of drugs in their study of suicidal attempts in children:

| | |
|---|---|
| Aspirin compounds | 25 |
| Sedatives and tranquilizers | 10 |
| Other drugs | 6 |

Mattsson, Seese, and Hawkins also reported ingestion of bleach, inhalation of natural gas, superficial wrist-slashing, and an intentional auto crash as suicidal methods. They also report that the lethality of the suicidal method appears to have little correlation with the psychiatric disposition of the suicidal emergency. Of those suicidal children whose attempts were considered potentially lethal by the emergency room staff, only a few were admitted (in this study sample), while patients who were referred because of physically harmless suicidal gestures were often considered seriously disturbed and admitted to the hospital.

Connell (1972) reported only one boy who attempted suicide by the use of physical violence. He attempted to jump from a high veranda but was restrained. The other 14 children in this study took drug overdoses.

Table 5 presents the information obtained by Bergstrand and Otto (1962), using a large sample of Swedish children and adolescents, regarding methods of suicide attempt.

Narcotic drugs were used by 86.9% of the sample, while all other methods were used only by 13.1%. While hanging is the next most common method after narcotics of suicide attempt among boys (24), cutting oneself is the next most common method for girls (51). According to this sample, more violent methods (all other methods listed except for narcotic drugs) seem to be used

### Table 5  Methods of Suicidal Attempts

| Method of Suicidal Attempt | Male | Female | Total number |
| --- | --- | --- | --- |
| Narcotic drugs | 269 | 1,232 | 1,501 |
| Hanging and strangulation | 24 | 17 | 41 |
| Shooting | 4 | 1 | 5 |
| Gas poisoning | 14 | 18 | 32 |
| Leaping from height | 8 | 10 | 18 |
| Throwing self before vehicle | 1 | 6 | 7 |
| Drowning | 5 | 13 | 18 |
| Cutting self | 15 | 51 | 66 |
| Swallowing sharp object | 6 | 1 | 7 |
| Other methods | 5 | 27 | 32 |

From Bergstrand and Otto (1962). Copyright 1962, *Acta Paediatrica Scandanavica.*

more frequently by boys (110 of a total sample of 351 boys, or 31%) than by girls (144 of a total sample of 1,376 girls, or 10%). Other authors (Haldane and Haider, 1967; Shaffer, 1974) have found that girls use overdoses of drugs more often while boys use violent methods.

Young children often perceive death in a different way than older children and adolescents. Ackerly (1967) observed that a 3½-year-old child was heard saying, "I will put your eye out and kill you." To this child, loss of a body part was equated with death. To the Oedipal child, castration is associated with death, and a 3-year, 11-month-old boy said, "If my penis came off, I'd die." When children begin to be threatened with severe harm or death if they go out into the street, get too close to a window, or come too close to electrical outlets and fires, death to them becomes associated with both violence and punishment for disobeying parents. By about age 4, children also begin to associate dying with growing old.

Death threats in latency-age children arise from: (1) aggressive drives (primarily oral sadism); (2) narcissistic expectations; (3) archaic superego; (4) withdrawal of libido from objects; (5) altering ego by identification (often with a suicidal mother); (6) disappointment at not achieving an ego ideal; (7) loss of a sense of well-being; (8) the struggle with the emerging concept of death; (9) an attempt to overcome a state of helplessness; and (10) a wish for rebirth or reunion with the all-giving mother (Ackerly, 1967). Methods in school-age children (6 to 14) may be taken from television, radio, movies, comics, fairy tales, mythology, the Bible and newspapers, but original ideas are also common. Ackerly found that in his sample, 100 children with emotional problems reported that they had thought of killing themselves by swallowing paste, ink, feces, sea water, alcohol, dirty handkerchiefs, and certain flowers and by smoking too many cigars and putting on too much lipstick. Ackerly also reports that suicidal preoccupations in children are as common at age 6 as they are at age 14.

## SUMMARY: METHODS OF SUICIDE IN CHILDREN

Some authors feel that children, who are less able physically to use and have less access to more lethal means of suicide attempt such as shooting, hanging, and poison, often use methods available to them in their environment such as jumping from a high place and running into traffic. Urban children, particularly those in low-socioeconomic areas, are warned frequently about the dangers of rooftops, streets, and subway platforms, and they are aware of the lethality of these things.

A number of authors, however, have found that drugs and poisons are the most common method of suicide attempt by children, and the availability of these drugs may be a major factor in their choice. Connell (1972) found that all children in his study who used drugs had those drugs prescribed to them or to their families and the drugs had been in the home for months or years. Precautionary measures are noted.

Children's perception of death often affects the way they believe death occurs with loss of a body part considered a major reason for death. Ackerly (1967) offers a psychoanalytic perception of death threats in latency-age children. These young children's suicidal methods may be taken from accounts and fantasies available to them in their environment, but they often produce creative methods for attempting suicide on their own.

# 8
# Treatment

## ASSESSMENT

If children are to be protected from the risk of suicide, the following preventative measures must be taken:

1. Accepting that suicidal behavior can occur in (children and) younger adolescents and that it is serious
2. Detection of vulnerable children (lending a ready ear to hints before the cry becomes imperative), and recognition of depressive symptoms in childhood
3. Ensuring that as doctors we do not provide too ready a means for the impulsive act (care in prescription, and warning to parents of potential dangers is essential)
4. Care in packaging, so that a large number of tablets are not immediately available to the impulsive child (individual presentation in aluminum foil wrapping may act as a deterrent by giving the child time to consider, as s/he unwraps). (Connell, 1972)[9]

In determining the likelihood of future suicide attempts by children who have threatened or attempted suicide, it is necessary to evaluate the degree of the environmental stress, the degree of individual psychopathology of the child, and the reaction and potential support in the child's environment (Shaw and Schelkun, 1965).

Shaw and Schelkun (1965) offer the following list for evaluating risk behavior in potentially suicidal children[8]:

### Check List for Evaluating Risk of Suicidal Behavior

Depression
Hostility, aggression or inhibited aggression
Loneliness
Self-deprecation
Schizophrenia
Psychoneurosis
Difficulty in communication
Serious conflict
Unsympathetic environment
Sadomasochistic tendencies
Death of parent or sibling (or parent-surrogate)
Broken home
Impulsive acting-out
Recent loss of love object or separation
Previous suicide attempts
Morbid fantasies, dreams
Hypersensitivity
Hypersuggestibility
Low frustration tolerance
Accident-proneness
Chronic or painful disease or deformity
Magical thinking
Age 14 or over
Male
Seasonal change (especially spring)

The authors suggest that if several of these factors are present, they must be regarded as a dangerous sign.

Suicidal behavior of any kind should be considered an emergency (Shaw and Schelkun, 1965). Adults responsible for the child's care should be interviewed when the child first sees a therapist. Hospitalization will depend on the home climate and the amount of support the child has there. When a child has responsible people who care for her or him but feel helpless in the situation, guidance and advice must allow those responsible to care for the child at home. If responsible adults are overprotective, rejecting, defensive, paranoid, rigid, punishing, moralistic, or helplessly dependent, little help can be expected from them.

Pfeffer, Conte, Plutchik, and Jerrett (1979) have developed a Child Suicide Potential Scale, which may be used to assess suicidal behavior in children. This scale is divided into eight categories, with an explanation of the purpose of each category. Information on this scale includes: (1) spectrum of suicidal behavior (with a classification of suicidal behavior along a 5-point spectrum of severity which ranges from nonsuicidal children to children making a serious suicide attempt); (2) precipitating events (which documents environmental stress for the six months preceding the child's psychiatric evaluation, and may include such areas as school problems, household changes, quality of friendships, and losses); (3) affects and behavior (which documents emotional states and symptomatic behavior of the child during the six months preceding the child's psychiatric evaluation, and may include anxiety, sadness, hopelessness, temper tantrums, defiance, running away, and fire-setting; (4) family background (which documents family events and psychopathology, if present, of the parent. These factors may include separations, deaths, severe discipline, parental depression, and alcohol and/or drug abuse by the parents); (5) past affects and behavior (which is similar to number 3, but documents the period occurring before the six months preceding the child's psychiatric evaluation); (6) concept of death (which records the child's preoccupations and experiences with death and view of death); (7) ego functioning (which records the qualities of ego functioning with regard to intelligence, affect regulation, impulse control, and reality testing); and (8) ego defense mechanisms (which documents the child's utilization of ego defenses such as denial, reaction formation, and repression). These authors then have constructed a 5-point scale determined from the above information which can be used as a guide to determine the seriousness of the child's suicidal behavior. This scale provides the following information: (1) non-suicidal (determined when there is no evidence of any self-destructive behavior or no suicidal thoughts or actions by the child); (2) suicidal ideation (determined when the child has thoughts or verbalizations of suicidal intentions, such as stating "I want to kill myself" or having auditory hallucinations to commit suicide); (3) suicidal threat (which includes verbalization of impending suicidal actions and/or a precursor action which, if implemented by the child could result in harm to the child. Examples of suicidal threat might include verbalizations such as "I am going to run in front of a car," or actions such as the child putting a knife under his or her pillow or standing near an open window and threatening to jump out); (4) mild attempt (which implies an actual self-destructive action which realistically would not endanger the child's life or require intensive medical attention, such as swallowing a few pills); and (5) serious attempt (which is an actual self-destructive act which could endanger the child's life and may necessitate intensive medical care, such as if the child jumped from a height).

## HOSPITALIZATION

Lawler, Nakielny, and Wright (1963) feel that any child who makes a suicidal attempt, no matter how minor it seems to be, is giving evidence of trouble and a need for help. They feel that virtually all of these children should be admitted to the hospital for a period of observation and investigation and treatment for repair of any self-inflicted wounds or other physiological problems. Precautions in the hospital should include having the child near a nurse's station on the ground floor of the hospital and under close supervision, particularly if the child has been depressed.

Lawler, Nakielny, and Wright (1963) offer the following information about immediacy of treatment[14]:

Immediate
    Hospitalization
    Detailed history from parents
    Psychiatric assessment of patient

Psychological tests
Social service assessment of home situation if necessary
  (a) Antidepressant drugs
  (b) Phenothiazine drugs in schizophrenic group
Psychotherapy
  (a) Supportive type in schizophrenic group
  (b) Insight psychotherapy in depressions and grief reactions

Follow-up care
Correction of noxious environmental factors
Psychotherapy and antidepressant or antipsychotic drugs
Placement if necessary

Hospitalizing the child offers immediate release from the pressures that precipitated the suicide attempt (Gould, 1965). The child feels she or he is in a setting that is designed for support, protection, care, and help. It is important not to reassure the patient without understanding the dynamics involved in the suicide attempt (words that do not convey meaning or understanding to the patient, such as "Everything will be all right," are to be avoided). Instead, it is necessary to pay attention and listen to the patient, to take her or him and the suicide attempt seriously, and to avoid any procedure that further diminishes the patient's self-esteem. It is important for hospital personnel to make themselves available.

Hospitalization does not need to be for prolonged periods (Shaw and Schelkun, 1965). When the hospitalized patient is removed from the conflict-producing situation, then the patient can be more easily observed and evaluated, and she or he is reminded that help is being offered; that problems are being taken seriously; and that she or he can be more carefully supervised. Thus, the child is more likely to cooperatively accept a therapeutic relationship.

Pfeffer (1977) says that hospital admission is indicated if: "(1) the child is unable to withstand stress, (2) the child is unable to utilize diagnostic interviews as an incentive to delay further self-destructive actions, and (3) the family is unable to provide sufficient environmental stability for the child."

However, Glaser (1971) says that because the child under 10 years of age is not as likely to complete suicide as older children, adolescents and adults, hospitalization as a safety measure is not usually necessary. It only leads to forced separations from parents, which may be interpreted as rejection or abandonment. It also means forced and increased dependency, regimentation, and depersonalization and removes the child from the security of the home and known environment.

## DRUG THERAPY

Tranquilizers and antidepressants may be used for agitated and depressed patients (Gould, 1965). Lawler, Nakielny, and Wright (1963) suggest antidepressant drugs for vegetative signs of depression, such as anorexia, weight loss, constipation, and insomnia. Specifically, imipramine was used most often; phenothiazine drugs were used for schizophrenics; and chlorpromazine and trifluoperazine were the antipsychotic drugs used (phenothiazine for the control of agitation and chlorpromazine for suppressing frightening hallucinations).

## PSYCHOTHERAPY

Lawler, Nakielny, and Wright (1963) say that all patients in their group received individual psychotherapy, for support in the schizophrenic group and as insight therapy for the neurotic group.

Therapy should be used to gain insights into the child's unsatisfied needs, to work through the actual or threatened loss of a loved object, and to strengthen the child's object relations (with parents or therapist) (Gould, 1965).

Pfeffer (1977) describes therapy for the hospitalized child as occurring in three phases: the initial phase, the working-through phase, and the termination phase. In the initial phase, a therapeutic alliance is established with the child and the family, the seriousness of the child's suicidal behavior is emphasized, the concern for the welfare of the child and the family is expressed, and the suicidal symptoms as a sign of family distress are discussed. Also, it is stated that the therapy is available to provide relief for the child.

During the working-through phase, the repetition of important transference issues for the child is observed in therapy sessions and on the ward, and the child's behavior is discussed openly with the child. Family members work with the therapist to gain insights into the family dynamics that were emphasized by the child's suicidal behavior. In the termination phase, feelings of object loss, rejection, and abandonment stimulated by the approaching separation from the hospital are discussed with the child, and the family's hopeful anticipation and increased anxiety at the approaching release of the child from the hospital are discussed with the family.

The following case study illustrates the phases of psychotherapy described.

*Initial Phase.* Martin was a seven-year-old boy who threatened to jump off the roof at school. Threats to run away and to kill himself began several months before admission at the time that his brother was born and when Martin entered first grade. He had a severe learning disability, which made him frustrated, angry, and humiliated. His parents ignored this and punished him harshly for his difficulties at school. He felt no one loved him and no one wanted to protect him from the anxiety and humiliation at school. As a result, he often thought he would jump off the roof.

Martin lived with his mother, stepfather, and two younger siblings. His stepfather, who was rarely home, would often provoke arguments with his mother. Martin's mother was a quiet, depressed, and passive person. She denied the severity of her son's problems as well as her own family problems. Martin was increasingly frightened of punishment from his stepfather for his temper tantrums.

At admission, Martin was verbal, bright, and complained that other children did not like him and that his teacher was mean to him. He told a story of a boy he knew who died by jumping off a roof because his mother would not buy him anything. Initially, Martin stayed by himself. He appeared depressed and frightened of the other children. When angered, Martin withdrew and seldom spoke to others. He was delighted to see his therapist regularly and felt comforted by having a warm consistent adult who listened to him. His individual sessions had a positive effect upon his interactions on the ward. He became more verbal, animated, and even initiated fights with other children, who he felt did not like him. He told his therapist frequently that he wanted to go home because the other children did not like him, but he also warned of his past threat to jump off the roof.

*Working-Through Phase.* As he continued to meet with his therapist, Martin spoke more openly about his feelings of being the victim of other children and of his family. On the ward, he spoke about killing himself whenever he did not get his way. It was upsetting to him that his mother came to see his therapist erratically.

As his relationships to his therapist intensified, he asked her to help him to learn to read. As a result, his school work improved, and he became competitive academically with other children. Fights with other children decreased as he felt a sense of security, self-esteem, and concern from the staff. Plans for discharge home were considered, but he reminded the therapist about the roof. Further confirmation of his fears about returning home were obtained by his allusions in his play to secrets and family problems which he could not openly talk about. All staff felt that he needed a comprehensive day program with intensive psychotherapy and a special education class for his learning disabilities. Although his mother showed increased awareness of his needs, his family could not be relied on to be sufficiently sensitive to his anxieties. It was necessary to provide a network of concerned adults who would respond immediately if his suicidal thinking recurred. A day treatment program in the nearby state children's hospital accepted him.

*Termination Phase.* Martin was happy about leaving the hospital although anxious about having a new therapist. Talking about this change with the ward staff helped him realize that he would still be protected. His transition to the day treatment program was aided by his knowledge that some of his hospital friends were also attending that program. At this time no suicidal ideas were expressed, and he was hopeful about the future. His family was relieved to know that he would return home. They felt accepting of the treatment plans. (Pfeffer, 1977)[15]

Haldane and Haider (1967) say that 27 of their 30 patients were offered treatment that included psychotherapy with the child or with the parents; casework with parents; pharmacotherapy; and work with other agencies, including the adult psychiatry service, general practitioners, general hospital departments, children's and probation departments, hostels, approved schools, and voluntary agencies. A breakdown of the results of that treatment of the patients is given in Table 6. Haldane and Haider (1967) indicate that if there is to be a more effective response to family disorganization that results in attempted suicide by children, there needs to be more effective coordination among services designed to promote and maintain child life and health. They add that no service acting alone including a psychiatric service can offer effective help to children attempting suicide.

Physicians, and particularly psychiatrists, should declare themselves available at all times for the suicidal patient (Glaser, 1965). Once contact has been made with the psychiatrist, it must be maintained either by regularly scheduled therapeutic sessions with the

Table 6    Results of Treatment Using a Variety of Methods in Combination

| Results of Treatment | Boys | Girls | Total |
|---|---|---|---|
| Improved | – | 7 | 7 |
| Did not accept or withdrew from treatment | 3 | 4 | 7 |
| Moved to other areas | 1 | 1 | 2 |
| Still in therapy | 1 | 1 | 2 |
| Treated and later referred to adult department | 1 | 1 | 2 |
| Committed to Approved School or local authority care or put on probation | 3 | 4 | 7 |
| Not improved | 1 | 2 | 3 |
| Totals | 10 | 20 | 30 |

From Haldane and Haider (1967). Copyright 1967, *British Journal of Clinical Practice*.

child or by the psychiatrist's remaining available to the family in times of renewed crisis or stress.

Resistance to treatment is common in both the child and the family (Shaw and Schelkun, 1965). The therapist must take full advantage of the initial interview, when family anxiety is likely to be heightened and denial is least likely to be effective. In addition to relieving conflict and stress in the child, the therapist should try to remove dangerous suggestive elements in the child's life. Lethal weapons should be removed from the home, drugs should be kept in the medicine cabinet and out of the child's reach, and strong attachments to dead relatives or pets should be discouraged.

The goal of psychotherapy for suicidal children is improved adjustment (Shaw and Schelkun, 1965). The child should be encouraged to talk out her or his feelings (without insisting on morbid preoccupation with the child's troubles and conflicts), and play, art, and humor should be used as techniques. Psychodynamics may be utilized as a guide for treatment (inward aggression may be rechanneled, grief and mourning may be sublimated, fear of abandonment may be explored and lessened). Sometimes, the psychodynamics are not understood, but the child may improve. Sometimes, the job of the therapist is not to help the child work through conflicts but to help the child live with them.

The long case study by Aleksandrowicz (1975) which follows demonstrates the use of psychotherapy with a suicidal 7½-year-old girl.

> Daphna was a beautiful girl with long black hair, but she did not think of herself as beautiful [Daphna had attempted suicide by jumping from a third story window and had fractured her pelvis in the attempt]. She tearfully said, 'I am retarded.' 'Why?" I asked her in surprise. 'Because I need psychotherapy.' 'But,' I said, 'I don't know how to treat retarded children, and the problems we will try to understand here are so complicated that they will require a lot of brains.' The tears disappeared and the words came gushing out. She talked about her fears, described some of her symptoms, and expressed self-hatred. She complained of always being tired, sleepy, and

bored. While talking she restlessly walked around, changed seats, lay on the couch, asked for sweets, or rocked on the swing in the yard.

After the first session Daphna refused to come. The parents brought her, and we discussed resistance. From then on throughout the fourteen months of treatment, resistance was never insurmountable. In the first few months Daphna mostly expressed her ambivalence toward mother and other authoritarian figures, consistently blaming others for all her troubles. One day she told me the following daydream: 'I want to be a prehistoric man because the prehistoric man lived alone in a cave and had only his immediate family, no uncles. He also had a fire in order to chase away the animals of prey. He constructed everything with his own hands and therefore it was *really his*, and nothing could be taken away from him. So, I am a caveman, wandering from place to place until I finally find the proper clay from which I make a clay pot, and I am satisfied. Now if I live in modern times, look what happens to me. I come to buy a clay pot and pay with a bracelet. The bracelet breaks and then the shopkeeper comes to me and wants the pot back. I refuse to return it because I have paid for it. Then he steals it and I steal it back. Then he reports me to the police. I am arrested and put on trial. But they won't give me justice and I am sentenced to two weeks in prison. Then they put him (the shopkeeper) in prison and I am freed, but his wife, who happened to meet me in the grocery store, screams at me. We fight and she kills me. No, no, she does not. I exaggerate. We only fight.'

We approached this fantasy as we would a dream. None of the associations brought to light dealt directly with the attempted suicide though the daydream is obviously related to it. The contents of the 'prehistoric man' were analyzed along three main lines of thought: (a) the wish to be an only child, and to return to the womb; (b) the anal component, i.e., possessiveness and control; (c) the reality of growing up, and the mistrust.

Daphna began to understand that actually it was she who

wanted to hurt and to kill, thereby provoking guilt and self-punishment. After this fantasy had been worked through, Daphna showed improvement in symptoms, particularly in her relationships with her siblings and with the neighborhood children. The mood swings also decreased.

The fluctuating relationship with her teacher did not change and was reflected in Daphna's grades. The tension between Daphna and her mother remained high, and was expressed by a strong negative transference to me; she was suspicious and at times accused me of preferring other patients.

During the daytime Daphna would become bored, restless, or tired and would sink into deep sleep with depressing dreams. During the night the sleepwalking episodes and sweating persisted.

A new turning point in her behavior occurred when she brought to the hour the following dream (whose manifest content was influenced by a television movie): 'A she-elephant . . .two hunters killed her. Then the she-wolf also came to eat the elephant but the little boy with the *long black hair* did not allow the she-wolf to eat the (she) elephant. . .he lay over her body and cried.'

In discussing the dream, Daphna realized that the 'hunters' were her father and brother, the she-elephant her mother. The little she-wolf was the sister sucking her mother's breast and '*eating the mother*,' and the little boy with the *long hair*, protecting the dead mother, was Daphna.

The dream reveals Daphna's penis envy and her wish to be a boy. She expressed both a fantasy that her mother had a hidden penis (trunk) and the anger against the mother who 'deprived' Daphna of a penis—a fact perceived by the patient as endangering her life. She spoke about her mother's mysterious bleeding. I supplied the information concerning menstruation; she became tense, breathing heavily, and finally burst out screaming, 'Tell me exactly how man and woman copulate and *don't lie to me like everybody else*.' I explained, but there was little need for it. She already had accurate information of her own. During this stage of the treatment, she told me about incestuous games with her siblings, spoke about her masturbation and about pornographic literature she obtained from different sources. She gave full expression to her voyeurism, telling me how one night she came to her parents' bedroom and saw her mother lying naked, eyes half-closed 'as if she fainted or was dead'—the dead elephant from the dream.

The parents informed me about a change in Daphna's behavior: Sleepwalking and nighttime sweating disappeared and during the daytime she was less tired and more relaxed.

I then became ill and could not see Daphna for a whole month. When I returned to work with Daphna, she told me she missed me and remembered a dream: 'I dreamt that I am dead and I am a pile of dried-up bones, and I deserve it because I am too haughty.' For the first time she began to talk about her attempted suicide. She remembered only the sheet in which she was wrapped when she fell. During this therapeutic hour she expressed the fear that her angry wishes had made me sick and that she could have killed me. She was also able to discuss her guilt feelings resulting from the ambivalence toward her mother. Daphna firmly believed in her ability to curse and kill her mother and me. As one expression of her omnipotence she told the following story:

Her father and his brothers played poker and the father was winning. It was hot and stuffy in the room and Daphna went out. A short while afterwards, the father called her back into the room since he was losing money. Daphna returned and the father began to win. 'You see,' Daphna said with a frightened voice, 'if I can bring good luck, I can also bring bad luck.'

It was difficult for me to explain to her that the grandiose omnipotent thoughts belong to the preverbal stage and to convince her that they are not part of the reality since the culture, through the father, had encouraged Daphna's narcissism and belief in her omnipotence. Daphna's reaction to my interpretation was very stormy and lasted several sessions. She did not want to give up thoughts of omnipotence but, at the same time, she was terrified of herself and wanted to be 'a girl like the other girls.'

During the months that followed there was a gradual but

consistent decrease in symptoms. Daphna became more even-tempered and more relaxed. Her bitter clashes with mother stopped and her relationship with her siblings improved considerably. In addition, she was doing well in school and got along with other children. She seemed to have more control over her impulsiveness and of all her old symptoms; only the headaches and eye-blinking remained.

The parents were satisfied with Daphna's improvement and fourteen months after the beginning of treatment decided to terminate it. I had doubts about terminating Daphna's treatment, feeling that neither her infantile narcissistic fantasies nor her oral aggressive impulses had been dealt with adequately. However, I reluctantly accepted their decision. (Aleksandrowicz, 1975)[3]

## ENVIRONMENTAL INTERVENTION

Changes in the environment prevent the patient from returning to the same stressful setting in which the suicidal attempt occurred. The parents are the main environmental factor, and they should learn what their roles have been in interacting with the suicidal child and how they have contributed to the problem. If the parents will not learn about their own problems, they may be willing to understand the child's needs and alter their behavior and attitudes in relation to those needs. Changes in activities, friendships, and school curriculum for the child may improve the situation. If active intervention in the home environment is not possible, it may be best to send the child to a residential treatment center where treatment is available in a nonstressful environment (Gould, 1965).

McIntire and Angle (1973) suggest that foster placement with supportive therapy may be necessary to alter the environment sufficiently for the suicidal child. Lawler, Nakielny, and Wright (1963) also mention placement away from home when the environment cannot be modified, along with individual psychotherapy.

Lukianowicz (1968) mentions that it is important to treat the parents along with the children and that an educational psychologist may approach teachers about the child's problems and difficulties.

A family life that is harmonious with parents who provide nurturance, support, and guidance and who present good male and female identification figures to the child are of primary importance, and the child needs to develop her or his own sense of individual personality and worth in the parent-child relationship. To help provide such a situation, Rosenberg and Latimer (1966) suggest counseling for the parents, interaction with teachers, and the school, and contact with religious organizations. They express the need for more adequate placement resources in the form of special foster homes and small institutions and the development of comprehensive mental health centers.

An informed community that will act when the child needs help is a valuable resource. Paulson, Stone, and Sposto (1978) discuss the UCLA Neuropsychiatric Institute that offered multiple intervention resources, including behavior modification training for the parents; individual, family and/or private psychotherapy; inpatient treatment; and foster placement and adoption for 34 children seen from 1970 to 1974.

## OTHER INTERVENTIONS

Mattsson, Seese, and Hawkins (1969); Morrison and Collier (1969); and Pfeffer (1981) mention psychiatric clinics and Morrison and Collier report on child psychiatry emergency service. Therapeutic teams that include a child psychiatrist, a social worker, and perhaps others can deal with crisis situations with suicidal children.

Mattsson, Seese, and Hawkins (1969) show the following breakdown of children referred to emergency services for suicidal behavior:

| Disposition | Disposition made | Disposition effected |
|---|---|---|
| Child psychiatry clinic | 13 | 5 |
| Referred to social agency | 17 | 11 |
| Referred to court | 6 | 5 |

In addition, 44% of suicidal children were admitted to inpatient hospital facilities and included mainly the overtly psychotic, markedly depressed, and assaultive children. However, as can be seen, a large number of families failed to effect recommendations.

The public health nurse may be recommended to make home visits in child suicide-attempt situations (Jacobziner, 1960). The public health nurse has the advantages of knowing existing community resources and being able to establish easy rapport with families. Families tend not to consider the nurse's visit a threat and will usually cooperate and give information.

Poison control centers can serve as "the gate-keeper of suicide prevention" (McIntire and Angle, 1971). Because accidental poisoning is socially accepted, many self-destructive children may appear at these centers. The poison control center can afford a different perspective on self-destructive behavior from that obtained at psychiatric clinics and suicide centers.

## SUMMARY: TREATMENT

Authors have produced risk scales and suicidal potential scales in an effort to predict which children will attempt suicide.

Some authors recommend that a suicidal child should be evaluated, even when the suicidal attempt appears minor, because the child is issuing a cry for help. Hospitalization may be used, not only to treat those children who have attempted suicide, but as a means of having the child available for evaluation and of protecting the child from a dangerous environment. Drug therapy, psychotherapy, and environmental intervention are also means of aiding the suicidal child.

# Part II
# Suicide in Adolescents

# 9

# Introduction

## ADOLESCENT DEVELOPMENT

The adolescent mind is essentially in a state or moratorium, a psychosocial stage between the child and the adult and also between the moral code of the child and the ethical code of the adult (Erikson, 1950). The adolescent experiences an increase in egocentrism similar to that of a much earlier stage of development, when she or he goes through a phase in which each "attributes an unlimited power to his own thoughts" (Inhelder and Piaget, 1958).

This uniquely adolescent cognitive development is "characteristically and boldly, even brazenly, universal and expansive in scope, taking as it does nothing less than the cosmos for its range. It is abstract while simultaneously concrete in its treatment of abstractions, like the edge of the universe or time. It stretches human thinking to some of its loftiest possibilities, but does it in so cumbersome a way as to immediately betray the facts of its youthful rawness, novelty, and inexperience. It bears numerous earmarks of being a newly found tool or toy, not yet fully mastered by its owner, and while it flexes new muscles, it also leads to some embarrassing falls and losses of balance" (Erlich, 1978).

The growth at this stage is no less affective than cognitive. A series of conflicts emerge between parents and adolescents, especially among those youngsters who have lived in circumstances that were insecure or lacked love. A need for immediate satisfaction often places these adolescents in difficult situations, with frequent disappointments (Otto, 1972). The sex drive that accompanies physical and social changes for the adolescent causes adjustment problems that may be overwhelming to some adolescents (Miller, 1975). Adolescents who are insecure may react to what appears to be a "trivial situation" with a suicide attempt when they find themselves in the border zone between childhood and adulthood. For adolescents whose relationship with their parents was not positive, relationships "broken off" with friends of the opposite sex may cause an intense reaction that may be expressed in suicidal acts. Love conflicts are often the most common reason for adolescents' suicidal attempts (Otto, 1972).

## ESCALATION STAGE

When children's relationships with their parents have been negative, behavioral problems increase as adolescence approaches. The parent's attempt to control the adolescent plus the ambivalent feelings toward the child produce continuing provocative behavior, changeable moods, periods of withdrawal and secretiveness in the child, who experiences feelings of helplessness, frustration, and being shut out by the parent. Reasoning and understanding break down, and the parent and child become estranged from each other. A parent's nonverbal message that the adolescent is no longer wanted and that the parent wants to be rid of her or him often is what is now being communicated (Sabbath, 1969).

## GENERAL INFORMATION ON SUICIDE IN ADOLESCENTS

Jacobs (1971) feels that when the adolescent suicide's and suicide-attempter's accounts are taken seriously, the conclusion can be only that the adolescent has made a conscious, rational choice. He adds, "Indeed, it is difficult to imagine a definition of suicide that does not acknowledge intentionality." Jacobs observed that the suicide attempt either leaves things essentially unchanged for the adolescent or, more often than not, adds to the adolescent's problems.

Rabkin (1978) quotes Diane Syer, director of a crisis-intervention unit at Toronto East General Hospital, as saying that the "typical" suicidal patient is a person with a series of problems, with emotional resources strained, and with coping becoming more and more difficult. Suicide is seen more and more clearly as the way out of the desperate situation, which has left the adolescent feeling confused, angry, and frightened.

## STAGES AND STEPS PRECEDING SUICIDE

Both Jacobs (1971) and Teicher (1970) describe the following three stages that progress to the social isolation that results in the adolescent's suicide attempt:

1. A long-standing history of problems from childhood to early adolescence;
2. A period of escalation during which many new problems associated with achieving adolescence are introduced; and
3. A final stage, the weeks and days immediately preceding an attempt, characterized by a chain-reaction dissolution of the adolescent's few remaining primary associations.

Jacobs (1971) further notes that it was not a particular incident in the lives of adolescents that caused them to attempt suicide, but the nature, number, and ordering of events that were the crucial factors. It was the context also that gave any particular occurrence its significance.

Teicher (1970) noted the following list of longstanding problems of adolescents admitted to the Los Angeles County-USC Medical Center:

1. 20 per cent of all adolescent suicide attempters had a parent who attempted suicide.
2. 40 per cent had a parent, relative, or close friend who attempted suicide.

3. 72 per cent had one or both natural parents absent from home (divorced, separated, or deceased).

4. 84 per cent of those suicide attempters with step-parents felt that they were contending with an unwanted step-parent.

5. 58 per cent of all cases had a parent who was married more than once.

6. 62 per cent had both parents working (or one parent at work when there was only one parent present).

7. 50 per cent of the suicide attempters' families had a net annual income of $3600 or less, and 52 per cent of those families with annual income of $3600 or less had net annual income of $2700 or less.

8. The average number of serious problem-making environmental changes experienced by the adolescent suicide attempter was 10.42 (e.g., parents remarrying, family members in hospital, death in family, changing schools, sibling leaving home, foster home placement, being in Juvenile Hall, etc.).

9. 74 per cent of the suicide attempters viewed their family conflict as "extreme."

10. 16 per cent had serious problems with a parent due to alcoholism of the parent.

11. Large numbers lived with persons other than parents (foster home placement, left with relatives for prolonged periods).

12. There was marked residential mobility, an abnormal number of school changes, and siblings leaving the home.[16]

The following case study (Jacobs, 1971) of a 15-year-old girl who swallowed a large number of pain pills she had received for treatment of a backache illustrates a history of long standing problems.

1. Carla was left alone at home for the weekend while her mother and new boyfriend went off for a trip to Mexico. (From the mother we learned that Carla felt lonely and called a girl friend and asked her to come over. The friend refused.)

2. Carla had a fight that week with her mother that revolved around Carla's desire to return to her Aunt and Uncle's home in Oregon where she had spent six months (about one and a half years ago). Her 12-year-old brother still resides there. (From the mother we learn Carla and the brother were sent to the Aunt's home at that time because the mother had a breakdown resulting from the loss of a child at birth.)

3. Last week Carla had cut classes for two and a half days staying around the house trying to intercept a letter the Aunt was supposed to send which contained travel money for Carla to come to Oregon. (The Aunt finally wrote saying Carla couldn't come.) At that point Carla's mother said, "If you leave home, you can come back for my funeral."

4. As a result of cutting classes, Carla was sure she would be asked to return to her old high school which she hated. This would of course mean leaving behind her new friends. (She had just completed a move, her 13th, and was at the new school on a "temporary permit.")

5. Also during that week her gym teacher and confidant had been killed in an auto accident. (From the mother we learn that Carla was "unusually easy-going" that week even though she was being punished for forging a letter of excuse to the school principal and signing her mother's name to it. The punishment consisted of being put on "total restriction," i.e., no phone calls, dates, seeing friends or going anywhere for a week's time.)

6. Her mother had married twice before and was preparing to marry soon for a third time to her current boyfriend.

7. Carla's real father left home 13 years ago when she was 2 years old.

8. Carla hates her mother and stepfather.

9. Her mother stated that Carla was aware that she (Carla's mother) had previously attempted suicide and that the stepfather's mother and grandmother were both suicides. Carla sometimes chided her mother on her attempt.

10. Carla used to belong to many clubs, had close friends, and was very happy while with her aunt in Oregon. Since her

return to Los Angeles (and to her mother) a year and a half ago she has been unhappy, has only one close friend (whom she didn't confide in) and belongs to no school or outside social groups or organizations.

11. She used to be an A student when in grammar school. Now Carla gets just "average grades." Her school attendance (according to the mother) has also suffered recently.

12. All of her "behavioral problems" and the resulting "disciplinary techniques" used by the parent to counter them, and all that cycle implies also began upon her return from Oregon, i.e., within the last one and a half years.

13. Monday morning Carla woke up, and having decided the night before to kill herself, went to school, and took a bottle of assorted pills in an attempt to take her life. (From the mother we learn that before going to school she called her boy friend and told him of her plans to take the pills. He didn't believe her and did nothing about it.) [A school attendance officer found the empty bottle of pills, followed her from school, and took her to the hospital]. (Jacobs, 1971)[17]

Two other authors have mentioned steps preceding the suicide attempt. Barter, Swaback, and Todd (1968) say that the child has often made a previous suicide attempt that was unrecognized or ignored and the adolescent may continue suicidal behavior after hospitalization for an attempt. Also, those who continue with suicidal behavior have an associated living condition that contributes to the behavior. Teicher (1970) indicates that, in the early history of the adolescent, the mother was angry, depressed, or withdrawn before and after the child's birth; the child has experienced a significant loss, usually of the father, before or during the Oedipal phase of development; the child has been made to reverse roles with the mother; and the mother is preoccupied with her own depression at the time of the adolescent's suicide attempt.

## SUICIDE AS THE ONLY SOLUTION

*Level A*

Jacobs (1971) lists the events that must occur before the adolescent may "overcome the moral and social constraints against suicide and appear a trust violator" (of her or his own life). He or she must:    *Level 3*

1. Be faced with an unexpected, intolerable, and unsolvable problem;
2. View this not as an isolated unpleasant incident, but within the context of a long biography of such troubled situations and the expectation of future ones;
3. Believe that death is the only absolute answer to this apparent absolute dilemma of life;
4. Come to this point of view by way of,
   a. an increasing social isolation whereby he is unable to share his problems with the person or persons who must share it if it is to be resolved, or
   b. being isolated from the curse of some incurable disease which in turn isolates him from health and the community, thereby doubly insuring the insolubility of the problem;
5. Overcome the social constraints, i.e., the social norms he has internalized whereby he views suicide as irrational and/ or immoral;
6. Succeed in this because he feels himself less an integral part of the society than the others and therefore is held less firmly by its bonds, i.e., is less constrained;
7. Accomplish step 6 by applying to his intended conduct—suicide—a verbalization which enables him to adjust his conceptions of himself as a trusted person to his conceptions of himself as a trust violator;
8. Succeed in doing this by defining the situation in such a way that the problem is,
   a. not of his own making,
   b. unresolved not from any lack of effort on his part to deal with it and
   c. not given to any resolution known to him excepting

death (he doesn't want it this way, but. . .it's "the
only way out");

9. In short, define death as necessary by the above process
and in so doing remove all choice and with it sin and im-
morality; and

10. Make some provision for insuring against the reoccurrence
of these problems in the afterlife.[17]

Jacobs (1971) noted that only one suicide-attempter in his
study seemed to use the "maladaptive" technique of attempting
suicide before resorting to other behaviors to solve the problem
first. He adds that a "maladaptive" way for the suicide-attempter
to behave would be to stop trying to solve the problems by whatever means seemed to possibly offer any hope of success. Another
way of adapting to the situation, Jacobs suggests, would be to deny
one's reality and thus be rid of the problem. He notes, however,
that only one of 98 suicide-attempters interviewed in his study exhibited such a denial of reality. He says, "In general, one was im-
pressed by the attempters' 'adult' and accurate assessment of their
predicament. If anything, they were too much 'with it.' "

Teicher (1970) says the suicide attempt is usually thought of
in advance and weighed rationally against other alternatives before
it is chosen. Other methods tried first include rebelling, withdrawal,
running away from home, and lying. After these methods have been
tried and have failed, suicide or a suicide attempt is tried as the
only other solution to the problem. Teicher adds that it is not surprising that suicide attempts often result later in suicide because
the adolescent often finds that the attempt also failed to solve the
problem. Such a solution "does not necessarily constitute an arbi-
trary or irrational conclusion on the part of the adolescent. It is
based on the adolescent's very real experiences with life and a biography characterized by a progressive social isolation from meaningful social relationships. They would, if they could, choose to
live. The potential suicide felt he had no choice."

Such questions as how many problems were present, the nature
of these problems, under what circumstances they occurred, what
was their sequence, to what extent did the adolescent feel there
was a possible resolution to the problems, and how the parents re-

acted to the problems are all significant in determining the suicidal risk (Teicher, 1970).

## INCIDENCE

In 1962, Tuckman and Connon reported that suicide was the sixth leading cause of death in the 15- to 24-year-old age group. In 1978, Rosenkrantz reported that suicide is the second most common cause of death in this age group (topped only by accidents), with college students and nonwhites being particularly vulnerable. Suicides are much more frequent among teenagers than in later life (Bakwin, 1966), and adolescents also make many more attempts per successful suicide than do adults (anywhere from 20:1 to 120:1 has been estimated; the adult ratio is 8:1) (Rosenkrantz, 1978).

McIntire and Angle (1980) report that in the age group of 15 to 24 years, suicide rates have increased from 4:100,000 in 1957 to 13.6:100,000 in 1977. Firearms, poisoning, and hanging are reported to be the major causes of death in both the 5- to 14-year-old and 15- to 20-year-old age groups. While poisoning accounts for only 25% of completed suicides, it is by far the most common method used for suicide gestures.

Eisenberg (1980) has tabulated suicide rates by age and sex for the years through 1977 (see Tables 7 and 8).

Table 7    Male Suicide Rates in United States (per 100,000)

| | Age group (years) | | |
|---|---|---|---|
| | 10-14 | 15-19 | 20-24 |
| 1950 | 0.5 | 3.5 | 9.3 |
| 1960 | 0.9 | 5.6 | 11.5 |
| 1970 | 0.9 | 8.8 | 19.3 |
| 1975 | 1.2 | 12.2 | 26.4 |
| 1977 | 1.6 | 14.2 | 29.9 |

From Eisenberg (1980). Data from the Mortality Statistics Branch, National Center for Health Statistics, US Department of Health, Education and Welfare. Copyright 1980, *Pediatrics*.

Table 8    Female Suicide Rates in United States (per 100,000)

| | Age group (years) | | |
| --- | --- | --- | --- |
| | 10-14 | 15-19 | 20-24 |
| 1950 | 0.1 | 1.8 | 3.3 |
| 1960 | 0.2 | 1.6 | 2.9 |
| 1970 | 0.3 | 2.9 | 5.7 |
| 1975 | 0.4 | 2.9 | 6.8 |
| 1977 | 0.3 | 3.4 | 7.3 |

From Eisenberg (1980). Data from the Mortality Statistics Branch, National Center for Health Statistics, US Department of Health, Education and Welfare. Copyright 1980, *Pediatrics*.

Holinger (1978) reports that the 15-to-24-year-old age group experienced an increase rate of 131% from 1961 to 1975, and the 5-to-14-year-old age group had an increase of 150% in the same time period (though there are many fewer total suicides for the younger age group). The rate of suicides rises rapidly following puberty (Finch and Poznansky, 1971).

Eisenberg (1980), Holinger (1978) and Miller (1975) report that statistical data for child and adolescent suicides are unreliable and represent undercounts. Reasons for this include the facts that: (1) data are based on reports by local coroners, who do not always report a child or adolescent death as suicide because of social, religious, and legal taboos; (2) physicians facing families of a suicide victim may list the cause of death as "accident" to avoid further grief for the family; (3) there are differences in reporting at the state level; and (4) accidents are the leading cause of death in children and adolescents, and there is no way to know how many of these accidents may be unreported suicides.

Suicide rates reflect such factors as: higher rates for male adolescents than female adolescents; and higher rates for whites than for blacks; more suicides in the spring months than in winter; more suicides in urban communities than in rural communities; more suicides among professional groups than among manual workers; and higher rates among Protestants than among Catholics and Jews. Lower rates for Catholics have been attributed to the strong stand of the Church on self-destruction and among Jews to the close-knit character of Jewish society and cultural aversion to physical violence (Bakwin, 1966). Catholicism does not always provide a powerful deterrent against suicide. For example, the predominantly Catholic Puerto Ricans in New York City have a high suicide rate. Also, suicide rates among the black population and among female adolescents are rising rapidly (Finch and Poznanski, 1971).

Societal and cultural influences are reflected in national suicide rates. Japan, Switzerland and Finland, for example, have high rates, while Norway, Scotland and Ireland typically have lower suicide rates. San Francisco has reported more than four times as many suicides as Boston. These statistics seem to reflect an outside force other than the individual that exerts a strong influence on the frequency of suicide (Bakwin, 1966).

## ATTEMPTED AND COMPLETED SUICIDE

Jacobziner (1965a) reports that in his study, the ratio of attempts to completed suicide was 100:1. He adds that attempts are grossly underreported. He feels that the ratio of attempts to completed suicides is much higher than the figures indicate, and that attempts, particularly among female adolescents, are far more frequent than estimates have indicated.

Otto (1972) found that children and adolescents who had attempted suicide were more likely to have completed suicide 10 to 15 years later than a control group of nonsuicidal children and adolescents. These completed suicides were more frequent among male than among female adolescents, and the greatest risk of a completed suicide was during the same year or the year after the suicide attempt. Otto's statistics indicate that there are 3 to 4 attempts by male adolescents, and 25 to 30 by female adolescents for every one completed suicide. Both boys and girls who later complete suicide use active methods (such as hanging, strangulation, and shooting) more often than passive ones (such as ingestion of drugs or other chemical preparation and gas poisoning). Adolescents who complete suicide have been sick-listed more frequently for mental reasons. Three-quarters used the same method to complete suicide as they used for the attempt, a fourth changed from passive to active methods, and 5% changed from active to passive methods. Girls who used active methods typically are younger and have character disturbances and neuroses.

## SUICIDE AND HOMICIDE

From 1961 to 1975, suicide and homicide rates for adolescents doubled, but accident rates have changed only slightly. The death rates for accidents for adolescents as a whole are higher than homicide rates, and homicide rates are higher than suicide rates (Holinger, 1979). Among white adolescents, accidents (two-thirds of them vehicular) are the leading cause of death, while among nonwhite adolescents, deaths from homicides surpass deaths from accidents (Eisenberg, 1980).

Because homicide and suicide rates are often negatively correlated, it has been speculated that the combined suicide-homicide rate may really express the amount of aggression and violence in a particular area or cultural group. It is not unusual, however, for individuals to express both suicidal and homicidal impulses. Psychiatrists and mental health workers often work with individuals who discuss killing someone while at the same time mentioning their own suicidal thoughts (Finch and Poznanski, 1971). The following case studies illustrate this kind of hostility.

> On September 22, 1975, a 15-year-old boy named L.E. committed a vicious murder. The crime started out as a simple bicycle theft, but by the time it was over the thief had stabbed another teenager four times and left him for dead in a deserted Bronx, New York, park. Nine months later, L.E. himself met death. His body was found suspended from a noose. (Lee, 1978)[18]

> Minutes after a jury convicted J.P. of armed robbery, the 19-year-old crashed through a courtroom window on the 10th floor of the Criminal Court Building, reports the *Los Angeles Herald Examiner* (March 4, 1976, p. 2). (Lee, 1978)[18]

The records of the Chicago police show that on April 2, 1976, an 18-year-old, who had lost his job three weeks earlier, beat his sweetheart and their two-month-old daughter to death with a baseball bat. Then he hanged himself. (Lee, 1978)[18]

Helen was a 17-year-old girl when first seen by the psychiatrist. The history revealed that she had been adopted at age two by American parents when they were in a foreign country. On the surface it would have appeared that their motives for adopting this youngster were entirely altruistic. A more thorough evaluation revealed serious, neurotic factors contributing to the adoption. Both parents were extremely strict and unloving although they considered themselves model parents. They thought they had made a great sacrifice to adopt this child from a "bad background" and give her all their "love and attention." Needless to say the youngster became aware of their basic hostility early and much difficulty developed between her and her parents. By the time she was fifteen she made a suicide attempt by taking half a bottle of aspirin. During the psychiatric interview following this, it became evident that she had a strong antagonism to her parents but that aggression and hostility had never been permitted in the household. She had been expected to be grateful to her adoptive parents for having rescued her. She was really struggling with an intense desire to find an outlet for her hostility. Perhaps the most clear indication of the inability she had in determining the direction of her hostility came when she talked of the relationship with the family physician. On the one hand, she was extremely attached to and fond of him and in a sense had an adolescent "crush" on him. However, in her more disturbed moments she was bothered by an intense impulse to kill him. (Finch and Poznanski, 1971)[19]

# 10
# Family Factors

## GENERAL INFORMATION

Several authors (Bigras, Gauthier, Bouchard, and Tassé, 1966; Jacobziner, 1965a, 1965b; McAnarney, 1979; Otto, 1972; Tuckman and Connon, 1962) mention family disorganization as a component of the families of suicidal adolescents. Tuckman and Connon (1962) mention that at the time of the attempt, 47% of their sample were from homes broken by separation, divorce, or death of one or both parents. They feel this may be an underestimation as some data were not available. Jacobziner (1965a) found that of 597 confirmed reports of suicide attempts among adolescents in New York City, 21% of their families were missing a parent. In 12% of the cases, the father was deceased; in 2% of the cases, the adolescent lived with relatives; and in 2% of the cases in which the father was in the home, he was an alleged alcoholic. Divorce was reported in 6% of the families. McAnarney (1979) went further to say that, "In societies where family ties are close, suicidal rates are low and conversely, where families are not close, suicidal rates are high."

Otto (1972), in his study of Swedish children who have attempted suicide, reports the following: "Mental illness, personality disturbances, alcoholism and other signs of mental and social disturbance have also been recorded amongst the parents [in addition to broken homes, illegitimate birth or the early loss of parents through death]. It seems that childhood conditions like these produce a fragility in the individual, who can, in a situation of intense strain, take refuge in something as self-destructive as a suicide act."

Bigras, Gauthier, Bouchard, and Tassé (1966) report that in 15 of the 21 cases they studied, the fathers were described as passive, inefficient in their father role or physically absent, and 9 of the 21 mothers were described as cold and rejecting.

In adolescents manifesting suicidal behavior, the pattern of family control and demands is often an extreme. Most of these adolescents come from homes marked by indifference, low expectations, and sporadic control (Jacobs, 1971). While parents of suicidal adolescents used "talking it over" only slightly less and "withholding privileges" only slightly more than control parents as a means of dealing with problems, parents of suicidal adolescents were about twice as likely to use methods such as "criticizing," "nagging," "yelling," "withholding approval" or "whipping and spanking." "Withholding privileges" was characterized by parents of suicidal adolescents as the discipline "most often used" for "most serious" problems and by the adolescents as the "worst" form of discipline. What ultimately occurred between these adolescents and parents was an admission that they no longer were capable of understanding each other and that any attempts at a meaningful exchange of ideas and any possible resolution of problems by this exchange would have been futile.

Jacobziner (1965a) reports that in 52% of the attempts in his study, either one or both parents were present at the time of the attempt. However, the following case study looks at what this sometimes means.

(Doreen, 16). Right now I seem so composed and so together that you find it hard to believe that I ever attempted suicide. Well I did, and not that long ago, either. I guess it was just a point in my life where I was sort of depressed and had a lot of things to work out. It was a turning point about a lot of things. There was a lot of conflict with my family. Afterwards I had to sort out what I wanted to do as opposed to what they wanted me to do. When I thought about it, it made me more determined to get things together the way I wanted to, rather than die.

The circumstances around the attempt had to do with a boyfriend of mine that I had been dating for a long time, who my family didn't like but who I was really serious about. My family didn't like him or his family because they felt I was being corrupted by them with evil ideas. Like my family is quite religious.

The way I was going with all the pressure building up it wasn't long before I made a suicide attempt. What triggered it off was when my family just flatly told me that I couldn't see him anymore, which I thought was ridiculous. Here I was sixteen years old, and they just said, "You can't see him anymore." We'd been having a lot of conflicts at home. I'd been kicked out a few times, and had left by myself a few times, but I'd always come back. And when they did that I just decided that I'd show them and really make them pay. So I took a whole bunch of pain killers, and I really thought I was going to kill myself.

They were my pills prescribed for me because I had a lot of sinus problems. I'd get really severe sinus headaches. I had quite a storehouse of them, because I didn't take them very often. They really wiped you out! So I took a whole bottle full of them. Then I called my boyfriend and I was talking to him, and he started to suspect something. I wouldn't say for sure, but probably I phoned him deliberately, because I don't think I really wanted to die. At the time I just wanted to make my family pay. I was really mad at them. I guess it was about the only thing I could do so that they couldn't control my life at that point—other than to leave. So I was really showing them. It's sort of stupid.

So my boyfriend figured it out. Apparently he phoned his mother and told her, and then he phoned me back and just talked to me over the phone. He found out how many of what I'd taken, that kind of thing. My parents were home at the time, but they weren't aware of what was going on because my bedroom was downstairs.

My boyfriend told his mother, and she and her husband came over to my place, much to my surprise. By this time I was quite groggy. They told my family, and my family took me to the hospital. The people there gave me the stuff to make you throw up; and everybody at the hospital gave me shit, which I thought was really weird. They made an appointment for me with a psychiatrist for the next day. They didn't take the trouble to find out what the matter was then. They figured they'd let the psychiatrist do it.

My parents were shocked at first. Nobody will ever talk about it in my family. Matter of fact, I think my mother might not even remember it. I think she's completely blocked it from her mind. At the time I know they talked to their minister and sought some help themselves. But my mother was worried about what the neighbours would think if they actually found out. She really said that!

When I made the suicide attempt I didn't really think about wanting to die. It didn't even occur to me that it could happen until after I did it. Then I got scared. At the time I just had this one purpose—to get back at my parents. I did it so impulsively. And the one thing that triggered it was when they said, "You can't see him anymore."

After my attempt, my parents figured I'd been under a lot of stress, so they just thought I should go to bed early. They didn't really see their involvement in my stress. They felt I was too involved with my boyfriend, which I might have been. But if you ask me, they handled it all wrong. They could have done something before, but not at that point. They just said, "Go to bed because you're under a lot of stress." We didn't talk about it again. They never sat down and had a heart-to-heart talk with me. But I don't know if I would have wanted them to. It really would have opened up a whole new can of worms and I don't know if I would have wanted that. Things had gone too far. We didn't talk about the emotions between us that much. There was so much to be covered there, it really would have been too hard.

I think it did make a difference in our relationship. After that we either didn't talk or we quarrelled. I didn't stay around much longer. It was really tense. I left home when I was seventeen. I didn't have much respect for them anymore. (Rabkin, 1978)[20]

The guilt and shame of survivors of those who complete suicide can be overwhelming, because suicide represents the ultimate rejection. The suicidal person is letting his or her friends and family know they were not able to help with the adolescent's problems and that the adolescent does not value them enough to live (Rabkin, 1978).

## THE EFFECT OF LOSS

Suicide risk increases in adolescents who have experienced the death of a parent, guardian, or significant relative during their early years. In younger patients, the suicide or suicide attempt may be a means of trying to establish a reunion with the lost person (Finch and Poznanski, 1971). In some cases, the loss is not a person, but a pet, a career aspiration, or the loss of a feeling of being wanted or needed (Lee, 1978; Sabbath, 1969). Loss of the intact family by the death of a parent or as a result of divorce, separation, or changing family status may inhibit an adolescent's ability to identify with an adult model. This may cause impulsive, self-destructive behaviors which adolescents may use to avoid confronting their failures (McAnarney, 1979).

Otto (1972) notes that as compensation for a lack of love during childhood, adolescents often become involved in intensive, emotion-charged relationships. This may be a liaison between two immature individuals. If such a relationship breaks up, the result may be a regressive reaction of an intense and deep nature.

Jacobs (1971) said that it is not the loss of a parent in early childhood per se that predisposes someone to suicidal behavior in later life. This loss is part of a process that must be viewed in terms of when the loss occurred and/or recurred. Also, it is not the loss of the love object that is so distressing—it is the loss of love. Jacobs also indicates that an object need not be physically absent to be lost; alienation from parents, for example, may produce similar results.

The following case study deals with loss in adolescent suicide-attempters.

[This is the case of a] 17-year-old girl, admitted to an intensive treatment program in a hospital in the United States. She was referred by her therapist, with whom she had worked for more than one year, because of escalating conflicts (temper tantrums and physical fights) with her family, particularly her mother; increased sexual acting out of her conflicts; and ruminative and progressive suicidal preoccupations heightened by her therapist's approaching vacation.

Shortly after her admission, she scratched her wrists, insisting that she had done this because of the staff's lack of concern. Her ward administrator wrote, "In her indirect manner, she did indicate she was frightened of losing control as much as she felt she needed to let feelings out; she seemed in particular to yearn to be held and contained. . .It was the staff's job to take care of her." She talked about a depressed inner experience of emptiness, which appeared, at least in part, to be a defense against rage and unmet dependency needs. While "she had shown no manifest thought disorder, she presented a circuitous cognitive style which was vague and inexplicit."

The girl was the second child of her mother's first marriage to a man of different ethnic background, a marriage characterized by violence, beatings, and wild suspiciousness. The mother left her first husband when she was two months' pregnant with the patient, moved in with her parents, and subsequently had a significant depressive episode, requiring outpatient treatment. She remarried when the patient was 3 years old. After enjoying an initial period of loving attention from her new adoptive father, the patient experienced another loss when after one year a shift occurred in his affections with the birth of his own first daughter. Her early experiences of loss and deprivation, especially in quality of maternal readiness for love and engagement (implicit in the mother's depression following the breakup of her stormy first marriage) are briefly captured in these few highlights from the history. It should also be borne in mind that she was hospitalized as a result of her increased suicidal behavior in response to her therapist's anticipated vacation. Despite the therapist's great uneasiness that led her to hospitalize the patient, she was not able to focus this concern. Interestingly, the same vague feeling of uneasy concern continued to mark the information communications of staff people involved in her care. (Erlich, 1978)[21]

## THE EXPENDABLE CHILD

Sometimes there is a parental wish, conscious or unconscious, spoken or unspoken, that the child sees as the parent's wish to be rid of her or him and for the child to die. This relationship reaches a critical point in the context of the stresses associated with adolescence (Sabbath, 1969). The adolescents who see themselves as expendable children are often from families whose divorced parents continually fight over them and from financially marginal families with the parents blaming the teenager for their monetary problems, or they may be adolescents who have "failed" the family by becoming pregnant, failing in school, or getting in trouble with the law (American Academy of Pediatrics, 1980). The following case study excerpts illustrate this situation:

Mannon, in the beginning of her treatment, talked only of her father, whom she described as a pervert, a coward and a hypocrite. In fact, an open incestuous relationship had existed between her and her father over a period of three years. She felt that it was his fault that she had become no good and socially depraved. Gradually she realized though that her mother was an accomplice to this incestuous relationship in that she had never protected her. She realized that all during her childhood, her mother had rejected her. Even now the mother often repeats: "I would have been rid of you if you had succeeded in your suicide attempt." Actually this suicidal attempt had been an attempt to find again the tranquility, quietness and peace which had been so lacking ever since her father had been erotically pursuing her. But she particularly wanted to return to the good and serene mother which death symbolized for her. (Bigras, Gauthier, Bouchard and Tassé, 1966)[22]

I first knew I was cracking up when I was fourteen. I bit my hand as hard as I could and I drew blood. I called my mom and said, "Look! I need help." And she said, "There's a good movie on downstairs and we have company." At the time I really felt like a fool. But now, looking at it from a different perspective, I could boot her ass for her reaction.

It wasn't long after that I made my first suicide attempt. I remember I was going with my mother and sister to a roadside stand to buy some corn. I had taken two bottles of sleeping pills before we left and I told my mother what I had done a few minutes after we got into the car. She said, "I hope you're happy. Now we can't go to get corn. We'll have to go to the hospital to have your stomach pumped." I said, "Well just forget it then." And she forgot it. I went home and slept it off. I guess the pills weren't too powerful. (Rabkin, 1978)[20]

## BROKEN HOMES

Dorpat, Jackson, and Ripley (1965) report that of 114 subjects in their study who completed suicide, 50% came from broken homes. Of 121 subjects who attempted suicide, 64% came from broken homes. The death of a parent was the most common cause of the broken home in those adolescents who completed suicide, and a home broken by divorce was the most common cause in those who attempted suicide. Almost half of those who had come from broken homes and had completed suicide had lost both parents, and almost two-thirds of those who had broken homes and attempted suicide had lost both parents.

However, Jacobs and Teicher (1967) feel that there is a continuing process rather than a specific instance of "broken home" or "lost love object," in which the adolescent in question is subjected to conditions that result in a suicide attempt.

## ROLE REVERSAL

In one-parent homes, unresolved and unsatisfied dependency needs in the parent often cause a role reversal with the favored child. These attempts may be partially successful because an adolescent child on her or his way to maturity may feel positive about the role. However, anxiety, pain, frustration, and hostility are often produced in the adolescent, and negative feelings may be directed inward for any inabilities in the role. Suicidal behavior may be the result (Kreider and Motto, 1974).

## SIBLING POSITION AND FAMILY CONSIDERATIONS

Cantor (1972) examined records of a suicide-prevention clinic to determine sibling position and family constellation for adolescents who had attempted suicide. It was discovered that of 12 girls 1 was an only child, 9 were firstborn and 2 were in other birth positions. Of 5 boys, 2 were only children, 2 were firstborn and 1 was later than firstborn, making a total of 14 firstborn and 3 adolescents born in other positions. Of the 10 firstborn girls, 7 had younger brothers as their next closest sibling, and 2 had younger sisters (1 was an only child). They speculate that not only birth order, but sex of siblings must be a factor in suicide attempts.

## AGENCY CONTACTS

Barter, Swaback, and Todd (1968) found that adolescent suicide-attempters had significantly higher rates of contact with social service agencies (such as a welfare agency, a mental health

Table 9    Percentage of Unduplicated Agency Contacts by Type
of Agency and by Family Composition

| Type of agency | Adolescent | Other family members | Family as a unit | Total contacts |
|---|---|---|---|---|
| Delinquency | 33 | 18 | 0 | 51 |
| Domestic relations | 1 | 0 | 37 | 38 |
| Counseling | 10 | 6 | 16 | 32 |
| Protective | 0 | 0 | 29 | 29 |
| Economic | 0 | 0 | 28 | 28 |
| Health | 9 | 15 | 1 | 25 |
| Psychiatric | 14 | 3 | 0 | 17 |
| Other | 3 | 9 | 2 | 14 |

From Tuckman and Connon (1962). Copyright 1962, American Psychiatric Association.

clinic, or a mental hospital) than do controls. Bigras, Gautheir, Bouchard, and Tassé (1966) found that in 20 of 21 cases they studied a social worker was involved with the family.

Tuckman and Connon (1962), over a two-year period, studied 100 Philadelphia children and asolescents under 18 years of age who had attempted suicide and come to the attention of the Philadelphia Police Department. These authors found a correlation between suicide attempts in the child and adolescent populations and family disorganization. Table 9 summarizes the information they discovered about social service agency contact among families of suicidal adolescents. Each type of contact is reported only once per person (unduplicated).

## SUMMARY: FAMILY FACTORS

Among those factors associated with suicidal adolescents, loss, broken homes, mental, personality, and alcoholic disturbances of the parents, and extreme family patterns of control and demand are commonly found. Parents of the adolescent often make it clear that the child is unwanted and is expendable.

Some authors point out that it is not the specific instance of homes broken by death, divorce, or separations that cause adolescents to make a suicide attempt, but a continuing process of loss.

Other factors which interact with the adolescent to produce suicide potential include role reversal, in which the parent may force the child into an adult role and the parent assumes the role of the child; sibling position and sex; and family disorganization of a magnitude that contact with social service agencies is common.

# 11

# Social and Environmental Factors

## SOCIAL ISOLATION

Barter, Swaback, and Todd (1968) found that 68% of adolescents admitted to the hospital after suicide attempts had a minimal or no social life compared with control adolescents not showing suicidal behavior, who had an active social life [defined as at least one date per week or some other type of organized group activity] in 88% of the cases. Otto (1972), in a follow-up study of suicidal adolescents 10 to 15 years later, found that more were still single or had been granted divorces than normal controls. He speculates that there may be some common hidden factor between the single state and suicide attempts that results in social or mental isolation.

Jacobs (1971) reports that adolescents who are sent to Juvenile Hall experience a serious physical illness, are hospitalized, drop out or are suspended from school, have a romance culminate abruptly and/or discover pregnancy, and experience isolation from meaningful social relationships. Most of these events occurred abruptly and unexpectedly. The suicide attempter not only experienced a greater number of such disruptive events more often; these problems tended to escalate, compared to controls. The events suicide-attempters experienced also tended to be more serious in nature than for the controls.

## SOCIETAL FACTORS

Societal pressures of which youth are aware include economic instability, potential fuel shortages, population problems, and pollution. These may present an insecure world to the adolescent. The United States is also undergoing changes in the family, the role of women, minority status, formal religion, mobility, achievement, and expressions of aggression. While some adolescents may welcome changes in society, others may feel insecure and frightened. Such reassurances that previously were elicited from family and religion may be absent. Because the adolescent is in a transitional stage of development before entry into the adult world, the adult world of uncertainty may prove too frightening for an increasing number of adolescents, who then attempt or commit suicide (McAnarney, 1979).

## SOCIAL ALIENATION

Alienation of the adolescent will set in motion a process that leads to a breakdown of interpersonal relationships, communication blockage, isolation, and powerlessness. All cause the person to withdraw from further social contact with others. Such a process may lead eventually to a suicide attempt or completed suicide (Wenz, 1979b). Adolescents may feel particularly isolated from the decision-making process at school, where they may complain that coursework is not relevant to contemporary society and the job market (Lee, 1978). Adolescent suicide may be viewed in terms of an extreme behavioral response to the general condition of alienation that characterizes contemporary technological society (Miller, 1975).

The following poem, written by a 16-year-old boy who later committed suicide, illustrates this alienation:

He always wanted to explain things
But no one cared.
The teacher came and spoke to him.
She told him to wear a tie like all
    the other boys.
He said it didn't matter.
After that they drew.
And he drew all yellow and it was the
    way he felt about the morning
and it was beautiful.
The teacher came and smiled at him.
"What's this?" she said. "Why don't
    you draw something like Ken's drawing
Isn't that beautiful?"
After that his mother bought him a tie.
And he always drew airplanes and rocket
    ships like everyone else.
And he threw the old picture away.
And when he lay out alone looking at the
    sky
It was big and blue and all of everything.
But he wasn't anymore.
He was square inside and brown
And his hands were still
And he was like everyone else.
And the things inside him that needed
    saying didn't need it anymore.
It had stopped pushing.
It was crushed.
Stiff
Like everything else.
(Miller, 1975)[23] *

---

\*Previously published as "Poem About Our Society," *Toronto Daily Star*, July 9, 1969,
p. 7.

## MOBILITY

Groups in transition have higher rates of successful suicides than stable groups. Groups who experience the most mobility in today's society are those people living in central and disorganized portions of cities, immigrants, and people who are transferred every few years by large companies. Adolescents are more mobile than ever before as improved transportation and acquisition of a driver's license encourages movement from place to place. Adolescents and others may feel isolated and lonely as they move into unfamiliar surroundings (McAnarney, 1979).

## ACHIEVEMENT PRESSURE

Suicide rates tend to be higher in societies in which achievement is a major priority and lower in cultures in which there is less pressure to achieve. The pressure to achieve academically may be felt particularly during adolescence. Failure at academic achievement is particularly painful to adolescents whose families place heavy emphasis on academic achievement and success in a vocation. Some adolescents may choose suicide rather than fail in these areas (McAnarney, 1979).

## POWERLESSNESS

Disorganized families who may differ from the usually accepted cultural and family norms may present a "normlessness" to the adolescent that can result in powerlessness as she or he fails to find a norm consensus among family members. Such an adolescent must find his or her own way by a process of trial and error and is pushed to initiate her or his own set of rules by which to live. This approach may cause social and psychological difficulties for the adolescent. A suicidal attempt by an adolescent in such a family is merely a symptom of a process that involves the entire family (Wenz, 1979a).

## SCHOOL PROBLEMS

Adolescents who attempt suicide often have a relatively poor academic record despite an average or above average I.Q., and a large percentage of them drop out of school for other than academic reasons. Many of these students are one to four years behind their classmates, and most have had long-standing school problems that have antedated the suicidal attempt by at least two years (Finch and Poznanski, 1971). Both Finch and Poznanski (1971) and Otto (1972) feel that it is unusual for school to be the direct cause of a suicide attempt. Both add, however, that at higher education levels [late high school and college], school may be the reason why adolescents find themselves unable to maintain the standards of academic work they have set for themselves and feel they are failing themselves and their parents. An unsatisfactory school result is the most common reason given for a suicide attempt by those adolescents who indicate school as the reason for their suicide attempt (Otto, 1972).

The following case studies are illustrations of suicide attempters with school difficulties:

A 15 year old girl, the only child of divorced parents. The father is an alcoholic. She attends junior high school and has to work hard in order to keep up with her school work. She has been in touch with a child psychiatric clinic earlier. She is intelligent but has pronounced reading and writing difficulties. In the middle of August, a couple of days before the autumn term started, she ingested about 20 sleeping tablets. She was admitted to hospital and gave fear of starting school again as the reason for attempting suicide. The psychiatric report describes her as an intelligent, hysteroid and infantile personality with reading and writing difficulties. (Otto, 1972)[24]

A 19 year old girl who comes from a good social environment. The mother is obviously nervous. The girl has a half brother. At the age of sixteen she took an overdose of sleeping tablets. This last year she has had sleeping difficulties. She is extremely ambitious and was to have tried her school leaving examinations a few weeks after her parents found her lying unconscious in her bed when they entered her room to wish her a happy birthday. She had taken about 75 sleeping tablets and was admitted to hospital unconscious. As a reason for her suicide attempt she said that she felt despair because she didn't feel herself to be appreciated by her teachers. She was diagnosed as an emotionally unstable, infantile personality who is suffering from reactive depression of a neurotic character provoked by exogenous factors. (Otto, 1972)[24]

## RELIGION

As children move into adolescence, they may choose to move away from their families' traditional religious beliefs. Finding themselves in transition between their own belief system and their family's belief system may make them feel isolated in times of stress. It is probably not the factor of the religious belief system, but that of transition from a religious system to none or a different one that causes the individual to feel vulnerable and isolated. An adolescent's identity may include either his or her family's belief system or not following the family's belief system (McAnarney, 1979).

## SUMMARY: SOCIAL AND ENVIRONMENTAL FACTORS

Adolescence is a time of transition. Modern society presents pressures to adolescents in the form of economoc instability, potential fuel shortages, population problems, and pollution. Interpersonal relationships and social relationships may become more difficult for some adolescents. Mobility of society may produce a sense of isolation and loneliness in some adolescents. Achievement pressures connected with school and future work training may cause those adolescents who do not do well to feel they have failed themselves and their parents. Higher education may prove overwhelming to many young people. Disorganized families may produce a sense of powerlessness in adolescents who are forced into finding life standards with no firm background for forming such standards, and forming a personal belief system apart from the family's belief system may put a great deal of pressure on some adolescents. Changing emotional and intellectual status in a changing and often unstable world may produce a crisis of suicidal proportions in some adolescents.

# 12

# Characteristics and Presenting Symptoms in Adolescent Suicide

## WARNINGS

Otto (1972) lists the following presuicidal changes in behavior that are most common with various mental states, such as neurosis, character disturbances, and psychosis:

1. Changes in social behavior with adjustment difficulties at school or work, neglect of personal hygiene, increased consumption of alcohol, vagrancy and other forms of asocial behaviour.
2. Mental changes such as increased irritability, aggressiveness, unstable affectivity and peevishness.
3. Symptoms of a more neurotic character, such as anxiety, anguish, compulsion, insomnia, problems with food and psychosomatic symptoms, etc.
4. Depressive symptoms such as reserve, depression, forgetfulness, apathy, indifference, loss of appetite, inertia, etc.
5. Symptoms of a psychotic character such as hallucinations, dissension, paranoic ideas, etc.[24]

Adaptive failures such as eating and sleeping disturbances, somatic complaints, excessive withdrawal, or rebellious interpersonal behavior may mark the presuicidal adolescent (Perlstein, 1966). Other warning signs may include a change in personality or behavior, agitation, irritability, anxiety, depression, anorexia, insomnia, frequent outbursts of temper (Jacobziner, 1965a), and other acting-out behavior such as stealing or running away (McAnarney, 1979). Adolescents who are planning suicide may give away prized possessions or write notes or poems expressing death themes (American Academy of Pediatrics, 1980).

However, as Finch and Poznanski noted (1971): "The majority of adolescents who attempt suicide do not give those people around them any signals in the form of recognizable changes in behavior that the event is forthcoming." It is impossible to crystallize a specific presuicidal syndrome that predicts if an adolescent will commit a suicidal act (Otto, 1964). Also, the adolescent's "environment" often neglects to recognize repeated threats, fails to hear hints, and does not pick up on signals. It is only in retrospect that the escalation leading to suicide is remembered or recognized (Otto, 1972).

### Cry for Help

A suicide attempt may be preceded by some form of communication, verbal or nonverbal, of great distress that acts as a cry for help. If there is no response to this communication, the suicide attempt is then made (Perlstein, 1966). The suicide attempt is used as a cry for help in many cases, with the adolescent trying to call attention to her or his condition in an attempt to change the present situation (Miller, 1975). McIntire and Angle (1980) feel that the adolescent suicide attempt or gesture should always be treated as a cry for help.

### Lethality

Lethality of an attempt may be considered high if the adolescent uses an elaborate scheme to avoid being discovered and uses an extremely lethal method such as shooting or hanging (American

Academy of Pediatrics, 1980). Suicide attempts may be classified as intentioned, subintentioned, and unintentioned, and high and low lethality may be determined on that basis (McIntire, Angle, Wikoff, and Schlicht, 1977). The more serious the suicide intent, the more dangerous the means that will be employed; leaping from a high place, shooting one's self, or running in front of an oncoming car imply serious intent (Finch and Poznanski, 1971).

McIntire and Angle (1980) used the following information to help determine risk potential in suicidal patients:

1. Circumstantial lethality—the probability of rescue
2. Prior self-destructive behavior
3. Depression or negative self-concept
4. Hostility
5. Stress
6. Reaction of parent or parent surrogate
7. Loss of communication
8. Lack of supportive resources
9. Extremes of parental expectations and control[25]

The subjects were then categorized according to:

1. *Lethality of intent* - low, medium or high (based on probability of rescue)
2. *Diagnostic category* - intoxication, manipulative gesture, depressive gesture, true attempt
3. *Functional and social incapacitation* - none, mild, moderate, high
4. *Estimated risk* - for repeated suicide behavior.[25]

Risk was rated as *high* if lethality of intent was medium or high or if a gesture of low intent was coupled with prior suicidal behavior, significant depression, or thought disturbance. A prediction of high risk was best correlated with: the lethality of intent or probability of rescue in the original event; prior suicidal gestures; and with high ratings for depression or depression-hostility (McIntire and Angle, 1980).

McIntire and Angle (1980) include the following as significant risk factors in determining lethality:

1. All attempts of marked lethality
2. A psychotic patient who has decided life is too painful to continue
3. Patients with intense physiologic discomfort
4. Patients who have established a pattern of drug abuse that shows a total disregard for their physical safety
5. Patients with a history of previous suicide attempts
6. Patients who strongly identify with a person who has successfully committed suicide
7. Patients who combine intense anger with their depression
8. Patients without a positive or potentially positive social support system
9. Patients who either verbally or nonverbally have indicated that they have made a definite plan to terminate their existence.[25]

## GENERAL INFORMATION

Jacobziner (1965a, 1965b) notes that individuals who attempted suicide were judged to be "average adolescents" by their parents, by school authorities, and by nurses who visited adolescent attempters. These adolescents were reported to be average in growth and development, physical structure, social well-being, and intelligence by their families and by the public health nurse. This report does not differ from the general population distribution.

Stanley and Barter (1970) report no difference in suicidal adolescents and a control group of those who are psychiatrically ill but not suicidal adolescents in the incidence of parent loss, amount of family conflict, the degree of social isolation, or frequency of clear crises. Members of the suicide-attempt group were younger at parent loss, however, and the parental discord was more frequently talk of separation. After hospitalization, suicidal adolescents and controls did not differ significantly in adjustment, but those adolescents who repeated their suicide attempts did differ from the controls, doing less well in school, having inadequate social lives, and being less likely to be living with a parent or parents.

In contrast to the above information, Shaffer (1974) found

that young adolescents who completed suicide were, in large proportions, above average intelligence and tall or very tall for their age.

Jacobs (1971) says that while suicide-attempters and a group of normal controls both had losses and debilitating events in their early lives, the original problems for the suicide-attempters did not tend to diminish after adolescence, and new problems were added. This produced for the suicidal adolescent an abrupt escalation of problems coinciding with the onset of adolescence.

## CONSTITUTIONAL CORRELATIONS

### Suggestibility

An adolescent with a history of suicide in her or his family is more likely to commit suicide during a period of stress than is an adolescent without such a history (American Academy of Pediatrics, 1980). Depressed adolescents respond more readily to the suggestion of suicide than do adults, and there are sometimes suicide epidemics in primitive cultures and other settings. "Anniversary suicides" indicate the suggestibility of the adolescent. The following poem, written by Harriet Moore, an American poet and editor from the early part of the century, when she was 10 years old and reacting to the death of a classmate, illustrates suggestibility:

I hear them whispering—what is it?
"Lizzie Wescott-hush."
Where is she? Yesterday she was here—
So nice, so pretty, with curly hair—
Here at her desk, like me.
It's something awful—where is she?
"Hush—Lizzie Wescott is dead."
Dead.
What is it to be dead?

It's easy—anybody might do it—
Yes, —even me!

Why do I think of it all the time,
God?

Please take the thought from me—
I don't want to!
It's too dark for a little girl down there,
And too cold.
Take it away.
If I step on that crack in the sidewalk—I'll have to do it.
Oh, awful, if I should step on that crack!
Help me over it, God—surely you don't want me to do it!
Thank you!
Oh, help me!

Why am I running so fast—
Running away!
Oh, why did I see it—
That big blue bottle with *Poison* on it, and a skull-and two
    bones!
Now I'll have to do it—
It's right there—so near!
How can I help it now?
(Miller, 1975)[23]*

The following case study (Otto, 1972) also illustrates a situation in which suggestibility played a role in an adolescent's suicide.

An intelligent youth had attempted suicide repeatedly and
was finally found lying in the forest with a tube of sleeping
tablets beside him. He had been brooding over the suicide of
a well-known author. His parents were divorced. The father,
an alcoholic, his mother had committed suicide. (Otto,
1972)[24]

## Hypersensitivity

Hypersensitivity has been discovered as another constitutional
correlation with adolescent suicidal behavior. This correlation was
found in tests made through the Rorschach method and color shad-
ing responses (Miller, 1975).

---

*Previously published in Kiell, Norman, *The Universal Experience of Adolescence*, New
    York: International Universities Press, Inc., 1964, pp. 748-791.

## Psychological or Physical Pathology

*Psychosis.* About 16% of adolescents who attempt suicide are diagnosed as psychotic. The largest number of these are schizophrenic and a small number are diagnosed as having manic-depressive psychosis (Finch and Poznanski, 1971). Psychotic adolescents are a difficult challenge because their behavior tends to be unpredictable and they tend to use more active methods in their attempts, though they are also the group most likely to give some clue to suicidal behavior ahead of time by some observable behavior change (about 50% of this group give some behavioral sign in the three months preceding a suicide attempt). They often seem to have few external and observable reasons for a suicide attempt.

Finch and Poznanski (1971) suggest that suicide in some of these acutely disturbed adolescents may be a reaction of their intact part of the personality to their own psychosis. Command hallucinations sometimes provoke psychotic adolescents to attempt suicide. This may occur during lucid periods when the teenager recognizes the depth of her or his disturbance (American Academy of Pediatrics, 1980). The psychotic teenager may have a loss of ego boundaries that distorts bonds with parents, and the adolescent feels desolate, lonely, depersonalized, and detached. Aggression may be turned outward. If turned inward, suicide may result (Schechter and Sternlof, 1970).

Wrist-slashing behavior may be a variant of the psychotic pattern. Usually, the slashing is not life-threatening but serves to reduce tension and also may serve as a source of pleasure to the psychotic adolescent (Finch and Poznanski, 1971).

The following is a case study of a daughter of a psychotic mother who, herself, was later diagnosed as psychotic (Bender, 1953).

> Helen was a 15-year-old girl who was brought to us from a child-placing agency because of recurring episodes of hysterical behavior in which she would attempt to threaten suicide. These episodes seemed to coincide to some extent with her menstrual periods, which had begun at the age of 13 years. She was the child of a psychotic mother, had been born in a state hospital and reared in her early years by one or another

relative, much of the time by her inadequate grandmother and indifferent father. She began running away from home at the age of eight when her mother was home on parole for a period. She was deeply sensitive concerning her mother's condition and felt that if she were properly understood and cared for she could be at home and the family reunited. She wrote to her mother regularly and fantasied the ideal home life which she expressed in stories, plays and poems which she wrote and pictures she painted. She had been living in boarding homes for years but repeatedly ran away in order to get to her own home. She made dramatic scenes, apparently to gain attention in the schools and homes. Her suicidal efforts included tying jumping ropes around her neck until forcibly removed, swallowing pen points, running into the road in the path of automobiles, swallowing ink, slashing her arms and legs with long scratches and smearing the slashes with ink, trying to choke herself with her hands, scratching her neck with her fingernails. Similar episodes were observed in the hospital, together with silly, annoying behavior which always brought disapproval and punishment from the other children and nurses, which seemed to please her. She considered herself very dumb, unattractive and unlovable and seemed to do what she could to act out this role. (Bender, 1953)[26]

*Neurosis.* Anxiety states and compulsive neuroses may lead to suicide in adolescents. These suicidal adolescents fear loss of control of their instinctive desires and meet severe retaliation by the superego or conscience. They may feel inner panic and attempt suicide (Schechter and Sternlof, 1970).

The following study illustrates the case of a suicidal adolescent with neurosis:

A fourteen year old youth attending elementary school. He is illegitimate and has grown up in insecure conditions. He lives with his ailing paternal grandparents. Good relations prevail in the home apart from certain conflicts with the grandfather. The boy has always presented a certain neuro-labile impression but has, on the while, behaved satisfactorily. During recent months he has had "fits" during which he turns pale, begins to shake and easily becomes nervous and excited. He was finally found by his grandparents with a leather belt around his neck; he had attempted to hang himself. The psychiatric examination revealed that this was a neurosis in an astheno-hysteroid personality with pronounced reading and writing difficulties. (Otto, 1972)[24]

*Visual/Motor Problems.* Kenny, Rohn, Sarles, Reynolds, and Heald (1979) interviewed a group of 18 adolescents who had attempted suicide and discovered that the incidence of visual-motor problems of the types associated with neurologic dysfunction and learning disabilities was more frequent among these suicide-attempters than among controls. The group of suicidal adolescents were also reported to have more adjustment problems with a higher rate of school failure than the control group.

*Menstruation.* An increase in suicide attempts before or during menstruation suggests a physiological condition that may be a contributing factor to suicidal behavior. Menstruation has also been connected with an increase in psychotic symptomatology, admission rates to mental hospitals, accidents, and criminal behavior. Premenstrual suicides are more apt not to be premeditated and are often precipitated by a quarrel. They occur more often with women living with a mate. It appears that either emotional stress escalates premenstrual tension or that premenstrual tension escalates emotional stress (Finch and Poznanski, 1971).

## STRESS TOLERANCE

Adolescence is typically considered a time of stress (Schechter and Sternlof, 1970). For many, school is often characterized by one's fear of not having the right answer, of not understanding, of being singled out, of not being singled out, or of reproach, of ridicule, and of failure (Lee, 1978). Adolescents under particular stress at school are those who are intellectually below average or borderline cases; children of retarded somatic, emotional or intellectual development; those with motoric difficulties; and children with special difficulties, such as reading or writing. Children who are ill, sensitive, or who have psychiatric disturbances are at risk. Some adolescents are forced to undertake higher education because of the ambitions of their parents in spite of the fact that they are not intellectually equipped for it (Otto, 1972).

A suicide attempt may be a sudden impulsive reaction to a particular stress situation. This impulsive quality is particularly characteristic of the adolescent. However, suicide attempts are usually the result of multiple psychodynamic factors that have been present for the adolescent for a long period of time (Rosenkrantz, 1978).

Adolescents characterized as suicidal at a poison control center reported a history of significant emotional stress listed as: humiliation, punishment, sense of failure, romance problems, pregnancy, family problems, loss of a parent or other significant relative, and "other difficulties." Precipitating stress "revolved around the five P's: Parents, peers, privation, punctured romance and pregnancy" (McIntire and Angle, 1980).

## POOR IMPULSE CONTROL

Adolescents who have poor impulse control may make a fatal suicide attempt without intending to complete suicide. These adolescents include those with minimal brain dysfunction and with episodic violent behavior syndromes. They are not as capable of controlling impulsive actions as other adolescents (American Academy of Pediatrics, 1980).

## ACCIDENTS

An adolescent who has a serious accident or burn should have a psychosocial evaluation, because some accidents may be suicide attempts that have failed (American Academy of Pediatrics, 1980). There has long been a question of the connection between automobile accidents and suicides among adolescents. If an adolescent is ambivalent about whether or not she or he wants to die, the adolescent may fortify herself or himself with alcohol or tranquilizers and perform the same act with the automobile. For those less aware of their suicidal impulses, simply driving recklessly with or without alcohol or drugs may sooner or later result in an accident, with death as the result. With the increase of teenage suicides and homicides, there has also been an increase in automobile accidents. One can speculate about a correlation among these suicides, homicides, and automobile accidents among adolescents (Finch and Poznanski, 1971).

With adolescents who have a tendency to have a number of "accidents," the physician should look for self-destructive aspects of this behavior. The adolescent may not overtly display depression, anxiety, and apparent despair (Schechter and Sternlof, 1970).

The following account is of an accident-prone adolescent whose actions eventually led to his death.

> A youth has committed repeated self-destructive actions, amongst other things he has been involved in several motorcar crashes and has been too casual in his use of tablets and alcohol for several years. In connection with violent anxiety, he committed several suicide acts of which one led to death. Both his parents were alcoholics. The mother had probably committed suicide. (Otto, 1972)[24]

## AFFECTIVE FACTORS

### Depression

Depression is the most common emotion observed by those adolescents who are suicidal. This may be exhibited as boredom, restlessness, and preoccupation with trivia; however, the adolescent may act out his feelings in delinquent, sexually promiscuous, or drug-abusing ways (Miller, 1975). Because mood swings are common for normal adolescents, detection of depression is made that much more difficult. Psychosomatic complaints, daredevil behavior, or truancy may be common instead (American Academy of Pediatrics, 1980). Adolescents who are depressed may also engage in inappropriate laughing, smiling, and a general hail-fellow-well-met demeanor, as when someone close to them dies (Schechter and Sternlof, 1970). Other masked symptoms of depression in the adolescent include social withdrawal, loss of initiative, a decrease in appetite, and difficulty in sleeping (Finch and Poznanski, 1971).

In severe depressions, the adolescent has suffered the real or imagined loss of another person or a concept of self about which feelings may be intense or ambivalent. Anger against the negative aspects of the self may be turned inward and, when such a person attempts suicide, she or he may choose an extremely violent means (McIntire and Angle, 1980).

It appears that the greater the parental involvement with an adolescent, the lower the depressive scale rating, and the less involvement with the parents, the higher the depressive scale rating. It also appears that increased community involvement can reduce an adolescent's depression (McIntire and Angle, 1980).

Manic-depressive illness seems to have some hereditary elements. Neurotic depression has been linked to an increased risk of manic-depressive illness in relatives, which suggests the possibility of some relationship between endogenous and neurotic depression (Finch and Poznanski, 1971).

The following case studies are of adolescents diagnosed as being depressed.

> A 17-year-old girl who was born in Finland but brought up in a foster home in Sweden. Both the foster parents under the influence of alcohol. Lives in lodgings near her foster parents' home when attending high school. She has to work alongside school and is therefore permanently tired and overworked. She made one suicide attempt a year before the case in question after a conflict with a friend. During recent months she has become more and more depressed, irritated, tired and apathetic. She has been prescribed tablets to combat her tiredness by her doctor. She was found unconscious by a friend and taken to the hospital. The attempted suicide was interpreted as a short circuit reaction due to her remarkable social conditions. Diagnosis: Depression of neurotic character. (Otto, 1972)[24]

> This 16-year-old sophomore at a parochial high school had been having problems with depression for most of the second

semester of his sophomore year. Being quiet, shy, thin, and gangly, he was unable to find a comfortable position in either heterosexual or athletic roles. His primary interests included piano playing and he was seen by his classmates as being a "jerk." Academically he was a B+ student, but this placed him only in the upper third of his class, not high enough for the honor role which was an important achievement for his family. On the last day of spring vacation he made a suicide attempt with 100 500-mg acetamimophen tablets. After less than 10 minutes he announced the fact to his parents, who took him to the closest emergency room. He was given an emetic and kept for observation to rule out potential liver damage.

*Family History.* The patient is the fifth of five children, all of whom are male and independent. Except for the patient, all the older siblings are either very successful students or are working and already have degrees. The father is a successful professional with rather obsessive-compulsive features in his personality. The mother is a relatively warm obsessive-compulsive.

*Medical History.* The patient is in good health, but has had multiple psychophysiologic complaints.

*Impression.* Depressive neurosis, compulsive personality. (McIntire and Angle, 1980)[25]

## LOW SELF-ESTEEM

Many of the girls in a study of suicidal adolescents by Bigras, Gauthier, Bouchard, and Tassé (1966) either appeared to assume obvious masculine behavior or appeared to have abdicated all sexual identification. The first group in particular appeared to be disappointed at being girls. These adolescent girls seemed to feel isolated and to have sad and painful memories of their childhoods without having the feeling that they belonged to anyone in particular.

Some adolescent suicide-attempters have a self-depreciating

attitude, seeing themselves as "bad." This type of adolescent often wants to prove her or his goodness by self-punishment. These adolescents are often very hostile, and the hostility is often thinly disguised or apparent (Finch and Poznanski, 1971).

## MAGICAL THINKING

Magical thinking was discussed for children under Death Concept (Chapter 11). Adolescents engage in "magical thinking" in terms of their suicide and also in terms of their own potential deaths. Some seem to think that if they punish themselves for a misdeed or even escape punishment entirely through death, they will escape the punishment and anger of a parent (Schechter and Sternlof, 1970). McIntire and Angle (1980) feel that "the adolescent has a sense of personal immortality no matter what his or her stated concepts are, because during adolescence, one's own death is so remote in time; one enjoys the invincibility of youth."

Adolescents sometimes think their suicide will radically transform the world. Many may not have a realistic view of the finality of death (Rabkin, 1978).

## LONELINESS

An adolescent experiencing grief over a loss may experience pervasive loneliness as well. Another type of loneliness may be produced by the size and impersonal operations of many large high schools and universities (Finch and Poznanski, 1971).

## HOPELESSNESS

The following case study illustrates the situation of a suicidal adolescent who feels hopeless, as is described by her psychologist (Rabkin, 1978).

When I first met Greta I saw her as an anxious, depressed teenager. She was able to talk about her depression, but she couldn't go into the reasons for it. She felt she was a misfit at home. She had some general ideas about the causes. She had suicidal thoughts that I found frightening, because there was something very desperate about her that made me feel it wasn't just idle talk. I just had the feeling that she would do it because there were no other alternatives available. Greta said that she had always felt that she wasn't cut out for life, there wasn't really that much doing in life that made her happy or wanted, or that gave her a good feeling about what she was doing. She seemed to me to be a very bright girl who had not utilized her potential. I could see her in university, for example: that could have happened very easily for her. But her family didn't direct her that way; they just didn't care.

Greta's background was very middle class. The predominant feature was that basically the marital situation was very bad—the parents just hated each other and admitted it. Mother was a very bright, very put-together person. Dad was passive. Mother was able to say that they were completely different and that she had no respect for him. She felt his involvement with her and the children was non-existent. She referred to him as a visiting uncle. But despite all that hostility the marriage persisted—not only for the sake of the children, but they just seemed unwilling to dissolve it. Father was too passive to take any action and Mother contented herself with the fact that he had a good management job.

I think Mother may have resented Greta right from the start because she was an unplanned pregnancy. She also felt that Greta was a child you couldn't get close to or cuddle because of her size [she is very tall]. That's stunning when you think about it. In a retrospective fashion, Mother felt that Greta demonstrated signs of emotional difficulty early on. Once when her mother was entertaining other kids at a birthday party, Greta just flew out of the room and slammed the door in a rage. She was about five at the time. Generally she found Greta snarky, unlikable and unlovable, somewhat temperamental, and a pain to have. All this seems to me to suggest that Greta was different from the other kids in her family in that she demanded more than she got. When her mother didn't meet these demands through inability, it triggered off the enormous problems that Greta has today.

Greta got thinly disguised messages from her mother about her position in the family, which is, "Frankly, my dear, you're a pain in the ass." So what can a kid do? They have to grope with those terrible feelings of inadequacy. It's sad that parents find it hard to compliment kids and bolster their self-esteem, but they are just so tied up in their own problems. The parents who are supportive usually produce kids who are more intact emotionally and socially.

To be fair, I don't think all the blame should go to Mother. Father gets his share, too. In many ways he was more of a problem. He was very cold and distant. One of the ways a girl grows to feel that she is a woman is by the way her dad pays attention to her. Because Greta wasn't getting that from her father, what feelings was she getting about growing into womanhood? A girl who wonders about her womanhood wants to know what Dad thinks and maybe rates herself on that. And if her dad is giving her cold messages, then she's going to start feeling guilty, unfeminine, and maybe a lot of other things, too. What was reinforcing Greta's feelings of worthlessness was a father saying, "I'm not even noticing you." That's pretty hard for a kid to accept.

Greta hates her father. Maybe it's good that she does, because before she realized that she had a right to hate him she was internalizing that anger towards herself, and that's one of the big things that was making her so damned depressed. Depression is anger turned inwards. One of the goals in therapy is to make her see that it's okay not to like Dad. Sometimes a parent isn't always together either.

When you look at teenagers, one of the most important things to look at is their relations with peers. Do they have any good friends? You find that kids who don't relate well are the ones who usually have trouble, then and in later life. Greta never seemingly had good peer relationships. Her so-called best friend on whom she was extremely reliant really abused her and kept adding to the negative image she had of herself. She became very jealous when this girl would do something with another girl. Greta just couldn't let go because she was so unsure of herself.

I can never tell Mother anything that goes on in therapy because that's one of our ethics, so she's never been told explicitly that Greta has strong suicidal thoughts; but she knows it anyway. She treats it in a very simplistic way. She thinks that everybody has those thoughts, and she plays them down. She doesn't ever really worry about it. If Greta ever makes an attempt, Mother will be desperately upset and guilty.

It's difficult to say whether or not Greta will make it. She's got a lot of strikes against her. Nothing is going to help until she starts getting out and doing things, but how can a person who's feeling so low get out and do things? I don't know what will happen. You must realize that a lot of adolescents work things out for themselves if they have the resources, but does Greta have the resources? She's bright. She's got a fair degree of insight. I think she's starting to realize that just because Mom and Dad maybe weren't the most loving, caring parents didn't necessarily mean that she wasn't lovable. As long as that issue is reinforced with her, I think she has a chance to succeed. (Rabkin, 1978)[20]

## BEHAVIORAL FACTORS

### Behavior and Character Disorders

Jacobs (1971) found in his study that suicidal adolescents had 50% more behavioral problems than did normal controls. While both groups felt they were being inappropriately disciplined about a third of the time (disciplined for either something they did not do or not disciplined for something they did do), suicidal adolescents, having identified more behavioral problems, were thus disciplined inappropriately more often than controls. Parents of suicidal adolescents saw the behaviors as exclusively behavioral problems, while the adolescents saw them both as behavioral problems and as adaptive techniques, and they hoped their parents would share their dual perspective and recognize their activities as a demonstration that a problem existed. However, the parents persisted in viewing these behaviors as simply behavioral problems.

Jacobs (1971) further indicated that 30 of 50 suicide-attempters in his study had gone through all categories of adaptive techniques: (1) rebelling; (2) withdrawal; (3) running away from home and; (4) attempting suicide. Of the 30 suicide-attempters, 27 who used all the above categories had used the less drastic forms of adaptive behavior before making a suicide attempt, using the order from least drastic to most drastic in all cases.

Character-disordered teenagers comprised the largest group of suicidal adolescents. Most only attempt suicide, but some do complete suicide. The degree of their psychopathology "covers a broad range and varies from the adolescent whose development has not been particularly successful and who becomes overwhelmed by adolescent sexual drives to the teenager whose failure to develop emotionally is so marked that the older label of 'psychopathic personality' seems fitting. All of the youngsters in this group demonstrate an inability to find adequate solutions to a large number of psychological and sociological problems" (Finch and Poznanski, 1971).

The angry, revengeful adolescent who attempts to punish those who interfere with him or her and who is inept at managing her or his strivings for independence are typical of this group. These adolescents may make homicidal as well as suicidal threats. They will usually deny a serious motive for the suicide or that they have any emotional problems, but their emotional problems become more evident with additional crises (Finch and Poznanski, 1971).

The following is a case study of a girl who was diagnosed as having a character disorder:

> Sarah was a tall, attractive girl seen in consultation just a few days after her sixteenth birthday following an attempted suicide, in which she had taken approximately fifty-five aspirin. After emergency treatment at a local hospital the family physician urged the parents to have Sarah see a psychiatrist. At the time of the consultation her attitude about her attempted suicide was quite casual. As she said, "It happened."

She gave the impression by her evasive and shifting answers that she easily distorted information to suit her own purposes.

Sarah was the oldest of four girls and her father's favorite. He felt possessive of her, complained about her social life which frequently absented her from the family. Sarah herself did not get along well with other members of the family and complained to the psychiatrist about all of them. She was a junior in high school and did average work academically. While seeming to be very active socially she really was a fringe member of a "fast" group of youngsters. Most of them were much more experienced in heterosexual matters than she was.

On Sarah's sixteenth birthday she was allowed to date for the first time. The youngster with whom she went out was a boy whom she had secretly admired for a long time and who was much more sophisticated than she. During this date he attempted to "French kiss" her, to which she reacted by biting him. He swore at her and took her home. Her comments about the boy indicated she had been sexually aroused by him but she attempted to deny it. She said "sex" made her sick to her stomach.

The next day Sarah's parents left on a trip and it fell her lot to be the babysitter for the younger siblings; a job she detested. It was the morning the parents left that Sarah swallowed the pills. The younger children in the family called a neighbor who contacted the parents. When the parents returned, Sarah complained about the behavior of her boyfriend on the date, describing it in some detail to her father, which, of course, mitigated some of the parental anger at having to give up their trip.

Further inquiry into Sarah's background revealed that while her adjustment looked relatively good on the surface, it was basically quite immature. She had always been a youngster who had gotten her own way in one fashion or another. Not infrequently she had turned to her father and he had always been a ready ally. She had never been prepared to stand any sort of frustration and when faced with the turmoils of adolescence she was unprepared to meet their challenge.

Sarah's own sexual arousal during the date which caused panic and the wish to retreat from adult sexuality was then compounded by being left in a parent surrogate role. The result was a rise in emotional tension to the degree that attempted suicide appeared to be her only relief. The manipulative aspects of this attempt are easily seen in that it caused her parents to return home, producing a good deal of secondary gain for her. (Finch and Poznanski, 1971)[19]

## Aggression

Both Finch and Poznanski (1971) and McAnarney (1979) describe suicide as aggression turned inward and say that the expression of aggression is learned in society, but children are taught early that violent behavior is punished by society. Aggression is present in every human because it is necessary for survival, and the amount of aggression can be increased by both frustration and exposure to repeated aggression in the environment. At adolescence, aggression drives usually increase. Adolescents who are filled with pent-up rage because of their earlier upbringing appear to have several options of dealing with this rage, and among these choices are becoming psychotic, or becoming suicidal or homicidal, according to Finch and Poznanski (1971). These authors feel that some adolescents appear to be experimenting with these methods of adjustment.

McIntire and Angle (1980) describe four adolescent personality types: aggressive independent, aggressive dependent, passive independent, and passive dependent. They say aggressive adolescents have energy for taking overt actions while the passive individuals may be less likely to carry through with their threats. The independent adolescents are nonapproval-seeking and set less store by the expectations and desires of others, while the dependent adolescents are more aware of expectations and more conscious of the negative aspects of a suicidal threat or act. In the combinations described above, the aggressive independent adolescent is more likely to follow through with a suicidal threat regardless of the actions of those in his or her environment while the aggressive dependent adolescent might follow through or not follow through depending on the actions of significant others. The passive independent adolescent may threaten suicide regardless of the actions of others, but with little likelihood of following through with the threat. The passive dependent adolescent also is not likely to act on suicidal threats, but his or her actions are more environmentally dependent.

Male adolescents find it easier to direct aggression either toward others or themselves and so are more successful at completing suicides. Blacks commit fewer suicides than whites, but they commit more homicides (Toolan, 1962).

The following is a case study of a girl with hostility turned inward:

Lucie R., whose suicidal attempt came as the mother wanted her to break up with a 20-year-old boy, was constantly occupied in her day-dreams with imagining that she was in a castle where she dominated everybody particularly her boyfriend whom she loved and admired for his strength and determination.

"I don't know why in these day-dreams I kill many people. I kill everybody." It was gradually easy to understand that it was the mother that she killed in such day-dreams, the mother who had always dominated her in a tyrannical fashion and impeded her freedom.

A year earlier, this girl had met a young man whose attentions and tenderness had touched her very much. She wanted to live only by him and for him. With him she did not have as much the feeling of being the idiot her mother thought her to be. She attached herself to this man as to a life-buoy, as she had lived under the constant danger of being destroyed by her mother. But the mother pursued her even to that point: she forbade this relationship because her daughter was too young, she said. The megalomanic and vengeful fantasies leading to the suicidal attempt were then Lucie's ultimate means of defending herself against the despotic manoeuvres of the mother. (Bigras, Gauthier, Bouchard, and Tassé, 1966)[22]

## Hyperactivity

Children with an attention deficit disorder are characterized as children as having little ability to sit still or maintain concentration even for a brief time period. As adolescents, the hyperactivity usually disappears, but many continue to behave impulsively and have poor judgment and others develop tendencies to be withdrawn, anxious, or delinquent. Most will be diagnosed as having a personality disorder, psychosis, or neurosis by the time of a suicide attempt (McIntire and Angle, 1980).

## Withdrawal

Adolescents who are classified as withdrawn, who won't talk and who have a "flattening of affect" are in an advanced stage of alienation from parents and others. An effect of this is that, while 70% of adolescents who attempt suicide do so in their homes, often with their parents present, only 20% of those who reported their attempts reported them to their parents. This often means that the adolescent may call a friend living miles away who then calls the parents in the next room to inform them of the attempt (Jacobs, 1971). The case study of Doreen (Family Factors, Chapter 10) illustrates how this can happen.

## SEX DIFFERENCES

While male adolescents complete suicide more frequently, female adolescents more often attempt suicide (American Academy of Pediatrics, 1980; Holinger, 1978; Jacobziner, 1965a and 1965b; Otto, 1972; Toolan, 1962). Toolan (1962) reports that this is prevalent throughout the world, and Otto (1972) notes that this difference appears at about age 13. Jacobziner (1965b) reports that 75% of the suicide-attempters in his study were females.

Hankoff (1979) reports that dangerous activities and excursions into violence that meet a youth's needs to confront death are largely restricted to boys, leaving suicide attempts the only available and culturally accepted encounter with death for adolescent girls. Otto (1972) says that boys have to break through a stronger cultural barrier to commit suicide and, therefore, are more mentally disturbed than girls when they attempt or commit suicide.

## SUMMARY: CHARACTERISTICS AND PRESENTING SYMPTOMS IN ADOLESCENT SUICIDE

Some suicidal adolescents, particularly those with such abnormal mental states as character disorders, neuroses, or psychoses, may give warning signs before a suicidal act. However, the majority of adolescents either do not give such a warning signal or those in the child's environment do not pick up on the hints that are given.

A suicidal act by an adolescent in most cases serves as a cry for help when other, less serious efforts to gain assistance go unheeded. McIntire and Angle (1980) have produced a series of categorizations in an attempt to determine the lethality of the suicidal adolescent's behavior.

Some authors have noted no physical or psychological differences between suicidal adolescents and controls. Others, however, found that suicidal adolescents are above average intelligence, tall for their age, and encounter more losses and debilitating events in their lives than nonsuicidal controls.

Hypersensitive and suggestible adolescents are at greater risk for suicidal behavior than those not falling into these categories. Also, adolescents who experience psychoses, neuroses, visual/motor problems, and symptoms related to menstruation emotional stress appear to attempt suicide more frequently than those not facing these circumstances.

Adolescence is a stressful time, and suicidal acts may be a reaction to the long-term stress experienced by many adolescents or to a particular stressful situation. Those adolescents with poor impulse control are more likely to fall into the category of suicide attempter.

When an adolescent seems to be having a series of serious accidents, this may be a sign of conscious or unconscious self-destructive behavior. Automobile accidents are increasing in adolescence along with suicide and homicide rates.

Depression is the most common affect present in suicidal adolescents, though this may not be present as clinical depression but may appear masked as boredom, restlessness, or delinquent behavior. Depressed and suicidal adolescents also usually have low self-esteem. They may engage in magical thinking with regard to their suicidal attempt and their possible death, and may experience loneliness and hopelessness.

Behavior and character disorders are common in suicidal adolescents, as are aggression and impulsiveness and poor judgment. Many suicidal adolescents may appear withdrawn, particularly from their parents.

Males are more likely to complete suicide than females, but females are more likely to attempt suicide.

# 13

# Precipitating Factors
# and Underlying Reasons

## PRECIPITATING FACTORS

The most common precipitating factors listed for a suicide attempt involved areas of concern that are common in homes with adolescents, such as household chores, keeping of hours, personal appearance, school attendance, homework, choice of friends, visiting relatives, etc. However, about 1 of 5 adolescents reported difficulties with the opposite sex as a reason for the suicide attempt, while only 1 of 10 parents reported this as a precipitating factor (Tuckman and Connon, 1962).

Otto (1972) offered a table summarizing causes of suicidal attempts in his study (see Table 10).

Jacobziner (1965a) reports that the precipitating cause of a suicide attempt is most often a reaction to a stressful situation that is the result of frustration, depression, overt or masked anger, or suicide may be a rebellious act, usually against a love object. Toolan (1962) lists anger, attempts to manipulate another, signal of distress, and reactions to feelings of inner disintegration (often as a response to hallucinatory commands or a desire for peace) as the major causes of suicide attempts. The American Academy of Pedia-

147

Table 10    Indicated Causes of Suicidal Attempts

|  | Boys | | Girls | | Total | |
| --- | --- | --- | --- | --- | --- | --- |
| Cause | N | Percent | N | Percent | N | Percent |
| Love conflicts | 46 | 26.9 | 281 | 39.2 | 327 | 36.9 |
| Family problems | 37 | 21.6 | 251 | 35.1 | 288 | 32.5 |
| School problems | 10 | 5.8 | 50 | 7.0 | 60 | 6.8 |
| Mental illness | 61 | 35.7 | 101 | 14.1 | 162 | 18.3 |
| Military service | 17 | 9.9 | 0 | – | 17 | 1.9 |
| Pregnancy | 0 | – | 33 | 4.6 | 33 | 3.7 |
| Total | 171 | 100 | 716 | 100 | 887 | 100 |

From Otto (1972). Copyright 1972, *Acta Psychiatrica Scandanavica.*

trics (1980) reports that an adolescent's attempt to resolve a difficult conflict, escape an intolerable living arrangement, or punish an important individual in her or his life are major causes. Jacobziner (1965b) reports the following list of causes found in suicide and suicide attempt reports in New York City:

Disturbed about school work; argument with parents because of lateness of work; argument with boy friend; emotional involvement with boy of questionable background; parental objections; parental objection to love affair; argument with common-law husband; struck by aunt; quarrel with an older sister; argument with father after coming home late from a party; argument with mother because of a boy friend; fight with boy friend; failed French in school; emotionally upset because mother tried to break up friendship with older man; was depressed; planned to kill herself; was punished by mother in presence of boy friend; reprimanded for coming home late; argument with parents, social behavior was criticized because she stayed away from home overnight; an argument with her mother because of her pregnancy; family difficulties; disagreement with girl friend; father refused to let her go to party; jilted by boy friend; despondent over school difficulties; mad at mother because she refused to give her permission to join the "gang" in the neighborhood candy store.

# UNDERLYING REASONS

Otto (1972) says that it is not unusual for underlying reasons for a suicide attempt to emerge several days after the event. He stresses that it is important not to accept either the given apparently trite precipitating factor nor what appears to be a rational explanation for the attempt immediately after it occurs. He adds that a suicide attempt appears to be an effective way of changing a socially and emotionally strained situation, and the use of passive methods (such as drugs) that carry a relatively small risk of death point up the fact that the suicide attempt is directed at involving the environment rather than in leading to death.

## Disadvantaged Adolescents

Suicidal, deprived adolescents showed an absence of any warm adult parental figure with whom to identify, a lack of investment in the future, an absence of future goal orientation, and a lack of control over their environment. They had a high activity level, a low level of school involvement, low impulse-control, an active parental conflict, and negative attitudes expressed toward the parent. These suicidal adolescents were more likely to have a history of suicide within the family and a history of overt suicidal threats as compared to a control population of disadvantaged nonsuicidal adolescents. However, the suicidal adolescents were not different from the control group in respect to: presence of a history of a recent loss of a significant love object; social isolation; absence of strong religious affiliation; and a low communication level with significant others in their environment (Corder, Shorr, and Corder, 1974). However, both Barter, Swaback, and Todd (1968) and Jacobs (1971) found suicidal adolescents more socially isolated than controls.

## Pregnant Teenagers

Of 105 New Haven residents who were 17 and under when they delivered an infant, 14 subsequently attempted or threatened suicide. The risk of suicide appeared higher in single girls, Catholics, those not from poverty areas, and those with pregnancy complications and venereal disease (Gabrielson, Klerman, Currie, Tyler, and

Jekel, 1970). Otto (1972) found that 75 (6.1%) of his sample of 1,226 girls who were suicidal reported that they were pregnant at the time of their suicide attempt and listed pregnancy as the cause of the attempt.

A 16 year old girl who has had an insecure childhood in a foster family. After leaving school she worked as a maid. When she was 3 months pregnant she was abandoned by the father of the child who had already infected her with gonorrhea. She attempted suicide a month before the case in question and a week before tried to perform an illegal abortion but without result. She has now got a new boy friend. The day she received the negative reply to her application for an abortion she took an unknown number of sleeping tablets and was admitted unconscious to hospital.

An 18 year old housewife who grew up in a good home. Her relationship with her husband is good. They have no financial problems. The patient has not shown any symptoms of mental deviation. A couple of weeks before the estimated date of her confinement she learned that she was expecting twins. She went straight home and took about 20 sleeping tablets. (Otto, 1972)[24]

## Adolescent Prisoners

Prison disrupts and shapes the task of adolescents to forge an identity. It is an arid human environment, when adolescents need a place where nurturing relationships can grow, and presents obstacles to adaptation and threats to self-esteem, when adolescents need social support, shared activity, and acceptance (Johnson, 1978).

Prison represents community rejection and prevents opportunities. Inmates who find themselves in trouble with other inmates have few viable options. If significant others abandon the adolescent prisoner, she or he may feel completely worthless and alone, and her or his situation may escalate from one of panic to one of hopelessness (Johnson, 1978).

## American Indian Adolescents

Teicher (1970) reports that suicide among American Indians is near epidemic proportions, with a rate ten times higher than that for the United States population as a whole. In two western American Indian tribes, half the men who take their lives do so before the age of 20.

Dizmang, Watson, May, and Bopp (1974) discovered a significant difference in individual and familial disruption for ten American Indians who committed suicide. These variables included the number of caretakers available during the early years (suicidal groups usually have one caretaker only), number of arrests and age at time of arrest, and boarding-school attendance. Those who committed suicide were sent to boarding school at an early age and more frequently than controls.

The following is a case study by Blanchard, Blanchard, and Roll (1976) of an American Indian boy who committed suicide:

*Family Background*: Juan's parents were born and reared in the Pueblo village, and both completed high school. They were married quite young and left the reservation. They had five children. For reasons not known, their once stable family relationships began to suffer and they returned to the Pueblo home. Juan's father had begun to drink excessively and was unable to maintain steady employment. He withdrew from fatherly responsibilities and had left the supervision and care of the children to the working wife. Although the parents continued to live together, a number of separations had occurred, and the family had given up hope of restoring satisfactory relationships.

*The Person*: Juan was a tall, well-developed teenage boy who had been having a difficult time in the community. He had been involved in several fights, always while drinking, had built up a reputation for being difficult, and had made some enemies. As a result of one of the fights Juan had been sentenced by the tribal judge to serve a 30-day sentence in the county detention home. The judge had also threatened to send Juan to jail for 6 months.

Soon after his release to the custody of a social worker, a case conference was conducted for Juan with participants from the Public Health Mental Health team, a psychologist from the county Mental Health Center, a Public Health Service social worker, a detention home counselor, the school principal, the school psychologist, the social worker, and Juan's mother. It was agreed that Juan would benefit from the structured environment of an off-reservation boarding school.

Part of the conference was a review of a psychological test report. A note concerning the use of psychological tests with an Indian student seems in order. We are very aware and very interested in the problems of testing and cultural differences. Still, Juan's test report will be presented here in the hope that in spite of the difficulties involved in cross-cultural psychological analysis, the test report will throw some light on the potential usefulness of such analyses.

Juan was given the Rorschach, the Impulse-Ego-Superego scales, the Bender Visual Motor Gestalt, and the Memory for Designs. According to the evaluation Juan's psychological status was as follows:

Juan sees himself as being bad and unworthy, and he sees the world as moralistic, punitive, condemning, and controlling. Juan's internal conflicts are causing him fairly high anxiety, loss of self-confidence, and disorganization in perception and thinking. Attending his alienation is a loss of control and fear of aggressive and sexual impulses, which he has difficulty in accepting as his own.

As a result of Juan's fear of his own impulses and his consequent distortion of reality, e.g., his suspiciousness of other's motives, Juan is unable to socialize, which only reinforces his sense of alienation, feelings of persecution, and poor self-image.

Juan is defending himself against his impulses by denial of sexual and aggressive urges and by rigid and near frantic attempts at rational control. When successful, such efforts at control are seen as outside of himself in the form of dominating, pressuring, and very threatening forces. These forces take the form of predominantly "feminine" control.

Further, it seems as if under the threat of loss of control and personal dissolution, Juan has developed a preoccupation with internal processes and a hypochondrical concern with physical well-being.

Juan's high level of anxiety, which might otherwise be a mitigating factor in this picture, is too high to be considered a positive sign. Should his anxiety increase and his defenses continue to fail him, his desire to escape the stress of an intolerable situation might precipitate impulsive behavior.

*Boarding School*: In light of the serious problems involved it was arranged that Juan have regular sessions with the school psychologist with the primary goal of helping Juan deal with anger and search for control in a constructive way. As the months went by and Juan developed a good relationship with one of the dormitory counselors, Juan and the psychologist decided that sessions would continue only on an "as needed" basis. Juan maintained contact with the psychologist by dropping by on occasion to say hello and chat a few minutes, on other occasions to discuss problems.

In the 7 months that Juan was at the school his behavior was characterized by the dormitory personnel as responsible and cooperative. This successful adjustment to the structured life of the school was what had been hoped for.

With permission from the tribal judge Juan was allowed to go home for weekend visits. These visits were closely observed and arrangements carefully worked out with Juan's mother. Every effort was made to build on and sustain the gains Juan was making at the boarding school. During his visits home Juan did not fight nor did he drink himself stuporous. He was pleased with his newfound controls and received support from his mother and school personnel. During this time repeated attempts were also made to involve Juan's father but without success.

Juan's maternal uncle, however, was involved. The Pueblo Indians of New Mexico have lived in tightly knit city-states for centuries. To ensure harmony in this culture, it is the maternal uncle rather than the father who is used to help control behavior in the child. This reduces chances for friction between father and son. It is also the maternal uncle who traditionally imparts to the child important and basic knowledge in relation to tribal religion and lifeways. To help Juan solidify his value base and learn self-discipline through relating to a significant other, attempts were made to strengthen the relationship between Juan and his maternal uncle. He spent several of his "home weekends" with his uncle.They hauled wood or hunted small animals together. It was thought that identification with uncle was being revitalized. During the years that Juan's family was away from the Pueblo he had not had the benefit of the uncle-nephew relationship.

Juan knew that his problems were not solved. But he now perceived that he was not alone; he had persons whom he could trust. Before school was out for the year he requested summer work in the Neighborhood Youth Corps at the school. An attempt was made to get him a job at the boarding school, but none was available for him. Consequently, Juan decided to get a job at the Pueblo. Then summer vacation came and Juan returned to the Pueblo. A few days later, Juan was dead. He had committed suicide. (Blanchard, Blanchard, and Roll, 1976)[27]

The authors speculate that Juan's decision to commit suicide may have been related to both the dissolving tribal culture and his disintegrating family and his father's alcoholism. Juan was subjected to discrimination, was alienated because of his father's seeming abandonment of his male role and Juan's own fear of losing control in social situations. He may have felt guilt because of his mother's frustration and anxiety produced by trying to keep the family together almost single-handedly. Juan's alcohol and drug abuse used in an attempt to deal with anger turned inward and the environmental circumstances described may have combined to produce an overwhelming emotional state out of which Juan made his final choice.

## SUMMARY: PRECIPITATING FACTORS
## AND UNDERLYING REASONS

Suicidal adolescents listed common everyday occurrences, such as disagreements over household chores, choice of friends, personal appearance, and school problems, as precipitating causes for their suicidal actions. However, underlying reasons for the suicide attempt often emerged several days after the event, and these were usually more serious than the precipitating causes given earlier. Some underlying reasons which occurred with some frequency and seriousness included being a disadvantaged adolescent, having an unwanted pregnancy, being imprisoned, and being a member of an American Indian tribe facing the series of problems that might arise from that situation.

# 14

# Methods of Suicide
# in Adolescents

Haldane and Haider (1967), in a study of children and young adolescents, found that tablets, mainly barbiturates, was the method employed most often by girls in the study, but not for the boys. While 16 of 20 girls used some form of drug or poison, only 4 of the 10 boys did. In 9 of the cases where poisoning was used as the method of attempt, the drug had been previously prescribed for the patient. Of the girls not using poison, 1 jumped from a window, 2 tried to choke themselves, and 1 slashed her wrists (after first trying to gas herself and take an overdose of drugs). Two boys cut their wrists, 1 tried to choke himself, 1 jumped from a window, 1 jumped under a bus, and 1 tried to poison himself with coal gas.

Barbiturates were found as the most common means of suicide attempt in adolescence in Bigras, Gauthier, Bouchard, and Tassé's study (1966). In addition to 15 cases where attempted suicide was with barbiturates (out of 21 cases), aspirin was used in 3 cases, drowning in 2 cases, and wrist slashing in 1 case.

In a report on self-poisoning in adolescents from a poison control center, Jacobziner (1965a) found that aspirin was used in 35% of the cases and barbiturates in 33%. He notes that the common use of these products is related to their degree of availability in the home. Tranquilizers were used in 12% of the attempts and nonbarbiturate drugs in 9.5%.

In a study of completed suicide in adolescence, Shaffer (1974) found that gas poisoning, the most common method of completing suicide in this study, was used by 8 boys and 5 girls (43% of the total sample). Of the boys not using gas to complete suicide, 5 used hanging, 1 used drug overdose, 1 used shooting, 1 suffocated with a plastic bag, 1 electrocuted himself, 1 drowned, and 1 decapitated himself. Of the remaining girls (after gas poisoning), 3 employed drug overdose, and 1 shot herself.

Toolan (1962) reports that male adolescents prefer firearms and hanging while female adolescents prefer poison as a method of suicide. Tuckman and Connon (1962) report that 83% of their 100 suicide-attempters used poison, 5% inhaled illuminating gas, and 12% used other methods, such as wrist-slashing and jumping from heights. Jacobziner (1965b) reports that suicidal attempts by ingesting poison were more common in adolescents than in adults in his study.

## ACCESSIBILITY OF BARBITURATES AND GUNS

Eisenberg (1980) says: "From 1971 to 1976 in the United States there has been a decline of almost 50% in the number of suicides ascribable to barbiturates; over the same interval, the number of barbiturate prescriptions written by physicians declined from 40 million to 20 million." He feels that more careful drug-prescribing practices by physicians can decrease suicides and suicide attempts with controlled drugs.

Also, Eisenberg (1980) feels that gun-control legislation will decrease the "success" rate of suicide attempts with guns and would also reduce the number of fatal assaults among family members. He states that since attempting suicide is an impulsive act and depends on methods immediately at hand, persons who use one method are often afraid to try another method and many who attempt suicide are ambivalent. For these reasons he believes gun-control legislation would help with suicide-prevention.

## SUMMARY: METHODS OF SUICIDE IN ADOLESCENTS

Most researchers report that some type of poison, most often barbiturates, is chosen as the method of suicide attempt and often completed suicide as well. Several authors report that, while poison is the most frequent choice of suicidal behavior in girls, boys are more likely to choose a variety of methods. In his study of completed suicides, Shaffer (1974) found that gas poisoning was chosen as the method of completing suicide most frequently by both boys and girls, but of the remaining girls, most chose poison while the boys used a variety of more active, and often fairly unique, methods.

Authors report that the availability of a suicidal method often accounts for its use. Eisenberg reports that, as the availability of doctors' prescriptions for barbiturates has declined, so have barbiturates as a method of suicidal behavior. He feels that gun control legislation would also lessen the rate of guns as a method used in suicidal behavior.

# 15
# Treatment

## ASSESSMENT OF LETHALITY AND ASSESSMENT SCALES

Weisman and Worden (1972) have developed a Risk-Rescue Rating Scale, which serves as a descriptive and quantitative method of assessing the lethality of suicide attempts. The underlying hypothesis is that the lethality of the method used in the attempt may be expressed as a ratio of factors influencing risk and rescue. Five risk and five rescue factors have been operationally defined, weighted, and scored. The Risk-Rescue Rating Scale is not a predictive instrument, but if it is considered along with such lethality measures as intentionality and psychosocial involvement (i.e., factors that are caused by a combination of psychological and social circumstances), it can be used for individual prognosis. Glaser (1965) identified warning signals in an attempt to assess the lethality of suicide attempts in children (see Chapter 5).

Tuckman and Youngman (1968) developed a scale for assessing suicide risk of attempted suicides with 17 factors that are objectively and readily determined. While many of these factors pertain to adult suicidal behavior, many may be used also for assessing adolescent suicide potential, though with caution, as the

161

scale was developed for use with adults. High risk factors which may pertain to suicidal adolescents are: sex, male; race, white; physical health, poor (acute or chronic condition in the 6-month period preceding the attempt); mental condition, nervous or mental disorder, mood or behavioral symptoms including alcoholism; medical care (within 6 months), yes; method, hanging, firearms, jumping, drowning; season, warm months (April-September); suicide note, yes; previous threat or attempt, yes.

A scale developed to be used primarily by physicians in their office, the emergency room, or in a general hospital setting to evaluate suicidal patients is discussed by Patterson, Dohn, Bird, and Patterson (1983). This scale, whose 10 major risk factors create the acronym SAD PERSONS, was also developed for use with adults primarily, and it shares much in common with the Tuckman and Youngman scale discussed above. The SAD PERSONS scale also recognizes that, while women are more likely to attempt suicide, men are actually more likely to kill themselves. It also places adolescents (19 years of age or younger) in a high risk category, which had not been done in the previous scale by Tuckman and Youngman. Other high-risk factors which may be considered in evaluating adolescents for suicide risk with this SAD PERSONS scale include: the presence of depression; the presence of alcohol abuse; rational thinking loss (such as occurs with schizophrenia, manic-depressive illness, and organic brain syndrome); social supports lacking (with an emphasis on the absence of supports in a number of areas, including relatives and religious support); the presence of a well-delineated, specific plan involving a lethal and available method of suicide; and sickness (with emphasis on chronic, debilitating, and severe illnesses).

## GENERAL TREATMENT INFORMATION

When an adolescent attempts suicide she or he is showing signs of emotional disturbance. A thorough investigation of the adolescent and the family is essential in order to provide protection to those adolescents who are serious suicide risks and to offer proper treatment for others who have indicated a need for help by their attempt (Finch and Poznanski, 1971).

The number of attempted suicides compared to the number of completed suicides by adolescents is an indication of their ambivalence. Those who succeed at suicide are primarily psychotic adolescents and also adolescents who did not intend to die but misjudged what they were doing, according to Finch and Poznanski (1971).

When a psychiatrist comes to see an adolescent who has been admitted to the hospital for a suicide attempt, the patient may deny her or his problem. It is urgent, therefore, that the time between the attempted suicide and the intervention of the psychiatrist be as short as possible, so that the adolescent does not have time to develop a series of defense mechanisms (Otto, 1972). There is very little information about action taken by families to prevent the recurrence of suicidal behavior. In one 6-month follow-up of suicide attempts by adolescents, only 3% of their families initiated contact with professional help (Tuckman and Connon, 1962).

In a study of 26 adolescent suicide-attempters, only 6 of the 26 improved after their attempt, and the improvement was associated with an improved environment. Psychiatric hospitalization with a return to an unchanged environment was uniformly unsuccessful (McIntire, Angle, Wikoff, and Schlicht, 1977).

## HOSPITALIZATION

During hospitalization of the adolescent suicide-attempter, the physician should look for evidence of a severe depression. The following areas should also be discussed with the patient and the patient's family:

1.  Identify the suicidal gesture as a cry for help.
2.  Identify the suicidal gesture as need for special observation.
3.  Identify the suicidal gesture as a need for immediate intervention.
4.  Identify the suicidal gesture as an indication the psychiatric intervention into the family process is mandatory.

(McIntire and Angle, 1980)[25]

Marks (1979) discussed the use of an inpatient unit of the department of pediatrics as a setting for suicidal adolescents, allowing them to participate with other adolescent patients in school and recreational programs. This nonstigmatizing setting appeared to allow the adolescents to integrate rapidly with nonsuicidal adolescents. There was no major disruption on the unit, and no suicidal attempts or self-abusive acts occurred.

Hospitalization allows the adolescent to receive support, protection, and care and relieves the pressure that culminated in the suicide attempt. Nurses should use precautions against future suicidal attempts and also establish rapport with the adolescent, who may feel quite alienated from society (Schechter and Sternlof, 1970).

Adolescents who are psychotic or actively suicidal and require constant guarding should be admitted to a psychiatric facility (American Academy of Pediatrics, 1980). If the adolescent suicide-attempter is not psychotic, the clinician should assess the risk-rescue ratio of the adolescent and the psychosocial resources of the patient's family (Eisenberg, 1980).

In a hospital setting, a multidisciplinary team (with psychiatrists, psychologists, social workers, activity therapists, teachers, nursing personnel, and child case workers) works in unison to individualize the daily treatment approach. A balance of patients should also be considered to provide the most benefits from patient interaction. Selection of patients and flexibility of the program should be prerogatives for those responsible for therapy in the unit (Glaser, 1978).

## THERAPY

Therapy should include investigatory methods and methods of treatment used in psychiatric work. The aim of the therapy is to help adolescents reestablish adequate object relationships (Otto, 1972) and permit the rebuilding of hope and reestablishing healthy family ties (Eisenberg, 1980).

## Individual Psychotherapy

Specific psychotherapy may benefit the adolescent who is suicidal, with the exploration of internal and external conflicts, depending on the diagnosis of the patient (Schechter and Sternlof, 1970). Brief psychotherapy at the appropriate time and place after a suicide attempt may help to diminish serious emotional disturbances and can serve as a basis for further emotional development. This type of crisis intervention may also prevent hospitalization. In a more long-term psychotherapy situation, the suicidal adolescent may commit herself or himself more rapidly to the therapeutic relationship because help is seen as necessary to the adolescent if she or he is to go on living. It is, therefore, important for the psychotherapist to realize the depth of commitment requested by the adolescent from the psychotherapist, with a reticent attitude by the therapist possibly seen as a rejection (Greuling and DeBlassie, 1980).

## Family Therapy

It is imperative to have parents actively involved with an adolescent's psychotherapy. This is especially true if the adolescent is living at home. The child's and adolescent's pathologic condition often arises from the parents' inability to relate to them, and both parents should be included if at all possible (Toolan, 1978). Family-directed therapy may be most useful when the suicide attempt, which is a cry for help, is directed at the parents, which is often the case. Because the patient may feel unloved and unworthy of love, one of the tasks of treatment is to convey a sense of caring and to restore faith in the possibility of a satisfying future.

## Group Therapy

Group therapy may help children to develop verbalization skills and mutual respect for other views. Inhibited and withdrawn adolescents, however, may be intimidated by more aggressive children, and some adolescents may be so disruptive to the group that they have to be removed (Glaser, 1978).

Drug Therapy

Drugs may be useful adjunct to treatment, with specific drug therapy depending on the diagnosis. The physician should be prepared to recognize the individuality of response that is especially characteristic with the use of psychotropic drugs (Schechter and Sternlof, 1970). Barbiturates, particularly phenobarbital, can produce or intensify a depression and suicidal tendencies, so it is unwise to use it with suicidal adolescents (Finch and Poznanski, 1971).

In prescribing medicine for patients who are potentially suicidal, the physician should use caution as to the amount of the drug and the ratio of the average dose (Finch and Poznanski, 1971). Because suicidal patients tend to store up drugs for later use, sedatives should be given in extremely small dosages (Schechter and Sternlof, 1970).

## CRISIS CENTER

The development of suicide-prevention and crisis centers has demonstrated that paraprofessionals with special training in suicide prevention can reliably evaluate the lethality of intent, the probability of rescue, the past history, and the current stress of the suicidal adolescent (McIntire, Angle, Wikoff, and Schlicht, 1977).

However, suicide rates do not indicate that a suicide-prevention center is effective enough at suicide-prevention to reduce suicide rates. The Los Angeles Suicide Prevention Center reports that more than 98% of the people who have committed suicide in their area had not contacted the center. About half of the people who did call this center were currently receiving psychotherapeutic aid, indicating that they were accepting, knowledgeable, and experienced in contacting mental health facilities, though most suicidal people may lack this background (Weiner, 1969).

## TEACHER'S ROLE

Because of the importance of school in the normal maturational process, the classroom teacher will always be involved in the lives of adolescents and their families. The teacher may be the confidant of an adolescent under stress or the first to know about an adolescent's problems (McKenry, Tishler, and Christman, 1980). Suicide by adolescents often occurs when they view the situation in terms of a breakdown of meaningful social relationships. School holds promise as a source of relief for anxieties and isolation, partly because school attendance is compulsory. Programs that increase and extend interaction between troubled students and their peers and teachers would help to establish meaningful social interactions and have the potential for reducing the threat of suicide and suicide attempts (Jacobs, 1971).

The following considerations may be helpful to teachers in assisting potentially suicidal students:

1. Listening is of first importance.
2. The threat (of suicide) should be taken seriously and not viewed as maneuvers of "adolescent manipulation or attention getting."
3. The degree of urgency will vary, and the teacher will have to rely on his/her own judgment. The fact that the adolescent has told someone indicates it is important someone know.
4. The teacher/school can serve as a knowledgeable resource in aiding the adolescent/parents in obtaining professional help.
5. If outside help is not forthcoming, the teacher can help and can mobilize help from others in the school (counselor, other teachers, selected students).
6. If the adolescent becomes involved in treatment, it would be desirable (though it cannot always be arranged) to have a continuing liaison between school and treatment facility.
7. If no outside treatment is possible, some consultative relationship between the teacher and a mental health professional is often helpful.
8. One of the questions most frequently asked by teachers concerns indicators that would identify a student who might attempt suicide when there is no mention of it, but when something is obviously troubling the student.

There is no formula, no infallible check list. However, everyone needs to be aware of any marked or sudden changes in attitude and behavior such as extreme moods and withdrawn behavior in contrast to previous patterns. The opposite of this is the student who rather quickly changes from an even pattern of behavior to one of excited, garrulous and frantic-like activity. (Powers, 1979)[28]

## PHYSICIAN'S ROLE

A physician may help to prevent or at least postpone a suicide attempt by acting, sometimes temporarily, as a "significant other," in the same way that a peer or a teacher may. The physician is also in a position, due to his or her status and role, to search for processes that lead to suicide and suicide attempts (Jacobs, 1971). In a study by Teicher and Jacobs (1966), 46% of adolescent suicide-attempters were seen by physicians for physical or mental complaints before their suicide attempts and all were seen by physicians after their attempts. Physicians had seen 26% before for previous suicide attempts; however, only 59% of those who had been seen previously for attempts had been treated for their suicidal behavior. Others were not seen by physicians and kept their attempts secret. These statistics point up the importance of the physician's role in contact with the adolescent in the weeks and months preceding a suicide attempt. The physician's interest in and aid to the adolescent and concern with her or his problems may mean the difference between life and death in such cases (Teicher and Jacobs, 1966).

General practitioners and pediatricians may underestimate the strain an adolescent feels in her or his home environment (Otto, 1972). Physicians often fail to recognize an adolescent's depression, which is sometimes hidden behind an attitude that is flippant, apathetic, or provocative.

Though it may be desirable to remain aloof and authoritarian in some physician-patient relationships, when dealing with a suicidal adolescent the physician is facing a person who has lost most of her or his capacity to see adult authority figures in a positive way. If a bond of trust is established with the adolescent, the adolescent's belief in being helped will be increased and the risk of suicide will be diminished. The difficulty of establishing rapport will provide important information about the adolescent's degree of alienation and sense of isolation (McIntire and Angle, 1980).

## RECIDIVISM

Of 20 high-risk subjects in a study by McIntire, Angle, Wikoff, and Schlicht (1977), 40% made repeated gestures—5 within six months, 2 more by 1 year, and 1 by the second year. Only 3 subjects had improved. Alcoholism, acting out, and delinquent behavior continued in 3 subjects and 3 persisted in having incapacitating thought disturbances. The other 11 had responses of depression and entrapment related to poverty, alcoholic parents, chronic illness, unwanted pregnancies, homosexual guilt, and a sense of chronic inability to cope with a multitude of problems.

McIntire and Angle (1980) report that recidivism is primarily related to an adolescent's failure to change her or his circumstances or the inability to respond to changes in the environment. In 6 subjects in their study who moved on to improved environments (2 in their own homes and 4 in foster homes), there were no repeated gestures. Of 9 subjects in the sample who were institutionalized, 3 were in reform school or prison at the time of the follow-up (6 to 24 months later), 1 was still in the institution, and 1 had made a satisfactory adjustment at home. Of 6 subjects who had required prolonged psychiatric institutionalization, 5 were still in the hospital and 5 had made repeated suicide attempts.

Those adolescents with a thought disturbance had a poor overall prognosis (McIntire and Angle, 1980). Recidivism was 31% overall and the relative risk ratio was highest for the severely depressed, those with a thought disturbance, and those with a deteriorating environment (McIntire and Angle, 1980).

In all cases in the study, families were known to social agencies, but the suicide attempt or gesture indicated the need for intervention; often the family situation was beyond repair. The best situation for most of these adolescents would be to move to a new environment with a relative or friend. However, these adolescents are a product of years of family and socioeconomic stress and they are often unattractive, rebellious, sullen or withdrawn. Foster home acceptance is unlikely for most of the older adolescents (McIntire and Angle, 1980).

## SUMMARY: TREATMENT

Assessment of lethality of suicidal adolescents is based on adult scales. Some factors, such as physical and mental conditions, depression, alcohol abuse, lack of social supports, and suicidal methods and plans that show a high degree of lethality create a high risk potential for suicide.

Hospitalization, individual therapy, family therapy, group therapy, and drug therapy are discussed. The role of the crisis center, the teacher, and the physician in dealing with adolescent suicidal behavior are described. The degree and reasons for recidivism in adolescent suicide are explained.

# Part III
# Comparison of Child and Adolescent Suicide

# 16

# Comparative Psychodynamics of Child, Adolescent, and Adult Suicides

The psychodynamics of suicide are somewhat different for children, adolescents, and adults (Gould, 1965). Adult suicide as an expression of internalized hate and unconscious death wishes directed at others has been well-documented (Paulson, Stone, and Sposto, 1978). The psychoanalytic formulation of the suicidal person's ambivalent feelings of hate and love for an object that is lost or seems lost to her or him, and the introjecting and incorporation of the object in an attempt to both preserve the loved object and destroy the hated object was a concept formulated essentially for adults and is more applicable to adults than to either children or to adolescents (Gould, 1965).

To understand suicidal behavior in children and adolescents, it is necessary to understand that the psychodynamic mechanisms of suicidal behavior are directly related to the child and adolescent's physical, intellectual, and psychological levels of development. The suicidal act is a symptomatic act, which may have multiple causes in varying combinations, and the suicide attempt may represent an effort to resolve several conflicts or tension states (Gould, 1965).

Separation during critical periods of development may be a primary predisposing event for suicidal behavior in childhood and adolescence. When this is coupled with the identification and a sado-masochistic, rejecting mother, these two events may comprise the major determining factors leading to suicide. Loss of love (rather than parental loss per se) and alienation of the adolescent during that developmental period are factors. Suicidal and depressed children and adolescents generally are reacting to a continuing process of deprivation of love and family disruption, rather than to a single traumatic event, and they perceive death as the final solution. This process usually includes a long-standing history of problems, an escalation stage occurring at adolescence, and a final stage character-ized by a dissolution of relationships, resulting in progressive isola-tion and alienation. Adolescents rarely seriously attempt suicide until other methods of obtaining help have been tried and have failed (Teicher, 1970).

## STATISTICAL INFORMATION

Suicide is the fourth leading cause of death in the 15-19 age group (Teicher, 1970; Toolan, 1975), with death by suicide seem-ing to generally increase with age (Perlstein, 1966). As in adult sui-cide populations, more than twice as many males as females actually commit suicide (Shaffer, 1974). However, females outnumber males in attempted suicide at every age level (Toolan, 1975).

If the ratio of attempted to completed suicides seen among children and adolescents under 21 years of age (i.e., 50:1) were to prevail among adults, there would have been 1 suicide attempt for every 200 individuals in New York City in 1958 (Jacobziner, 1960). Suicide attempt information is not as comprehensive for adults as it is for children; however, completed suicides by children and adolescents are often not reported, and many accidents in children are apparently subintentional suicide attempts. Of children under age 10 admitted to child psychiatric facilities, 1% to 5% have a his-tory of threatened or attempted suicide (Teicher, 1970).

From 1961 to 1975, the 5-14 age group experienced an increase of suicides of 150%, the largest reported increase. However, there were few actual children represented by these statistics (0.2 to 0.5

per 100,000). The next largest statistical increase in suicides occurred in the 15-24 age group, with a rate of 11.8 per 100,000 in 1975. For males, suicide rates increase with age, while for females the middle age group (35-64 years) have the highest suicide rates, while the youngest age group (5-24) and the oldest (65-84) have lower rates (Holinger, 1978). Combined male and female mortality rates in general have risen by 11% for the age group 15-24 over the past 20 years, due to increases from violent deaths (accidents, homicides, and suicides). These statistics don't provide a breakdown between adolescence and young adulthood and age categories include more ages than the breakdowns created for this book.

Though statistics show that recorded suicides and serious attempts are rare before age 10, several factors work together to lower recorded suicides among children. Methods used by children often result in deaths classified as accidents (e.g., jumping from heights and running into traffic). Young children have limited access to lethal weapons and drugs. Children do not leave suicide notes, which are often the chief evidence of a suicide, either because they are too young to write or may not be conditioned to written communication. Also, Western culture often underestimates the strength of a child's emotions, and may consider suicidal motives in children as unthinkable (Shaw and Schelkun, 1965).

Adolescents (15-19 and 20-24) use poisoning with substances as the most frequent method of suicide; poisoning by gas, hanging, firearms, and explosives follow in that order. Children 10-14 years old use hanging, firearms and explosives, poisoning by substance, and poisoning by gas, in that order (Holinger, 1978). Pfeffer (1981) reports that the most common types of suicidal methods used by children often differ from those used by adults, and she does not believe latency-age children use firearms as a suicidal technique.

Most adolescents show a preference for the period from 3:00 p.m. to midnight for their suicidal attempt, in contrast to adults, who prefer early morning hours. Most youngsters chose their own homes, with no adult present at the time of the attempt (Shaw and Schelkun, 1965).

## DEATH CONCEPT

The child has an incomplete and distorted concept of death, and death is not seen as final and irrevocable, as it is by the adult. This is partially due to the child's inability to think in abstractions. While it may be difficult for the adult to conceptualize her or his own death, it is literally beyond the child to do so. The adolescent stands conceptually between the child and adult in her or his understanding of death, depending on intellectual capacity, psychological needs, and interpersonal experience (Gould, 1965).

The child may also feel the unreality of death because the subject is taboo in Western civilization as a topic of discussion, and death is hidden from the child and talked of in euphemistic terms. Also, television and movies permit actors to be killed only to return for another appearance at another time. This may enhance the child's feeling of the lack of finality of death (Gould, 1965).

Nagy (1948) found that children developed a concept of death through successive developmental stages. In stage one (ages 3-5), death is seen as a departure, a further existence in changed circumstances, but not as a regular and final process. In stage two (ages 5-9), death is considered a person. In the third stage (around age 9), death is seen as a process that results in the dissolution of bodily life.

McIntire, Angle, and Struempler (1972) said only 20% of children in the age group 13 to 16 accepted death as total cessation, and that 7-year-old children were the ones most willing to accept death as total cessation. The persistence of belief in cognizance after death of a pet occurred in at least 15% to 25% of 13- to 16-year olds in their study.

## SUGGESTIBILITY

Adults vary widely in their susceptibility to suggestion, but nearly all children are susceptible to a great degree. Strong death wishes directed toward the child by significant others may result in a kind of "psychic homicide," with the child feeling a need to die. Suicide epidemics reported among adolescents and anniversary suicides are also examples of suggestibility of the child and adolescent (Shaw and Schelkun, 1965).

## IMPULSIVENESS

Most suicides under age 10 are impulsive acts to punish parents or as a retaliation against punishing parents (Shaw and Schelkun, 1965). Children and adolescents have not developed their ego or defenses to the point where their impulsive behavior is as controlled as that of the adult. If this impulsiveness were the only factor in suicide attempts in children and adolescents, the suicide would be much higher because of this lack of control (Gould, 1965).

The adolescent is more likely to attempt suicide as a result of impulsive behavior than is the child. The adolescent's ego and defenses are in flux because of biological and sociocultural pressures. Thus, impulsive behavior has a good chance of breaking through (Gould, 1965). However, this impulsiveness may work against an actual suicide. An impulsively conceived suicide attempt will probably not be successful. On occasion, though, an impulsive act may lead to a completed suicide and, though the adolescent may have regreted it afterward, she or he may be unable to reverse the action (Gould, 1965).

## MAGICAL THINKING

The young child may use magical thinking to conceive of death as reversible and to feel herself or himself immune to it. Magical thinking may also cause the child to feel responsible for another's death. When the child accepts the finality of death and the fact that she or he is also subject to death, the child may be no longer tempted to test fate by taking suicidal risks or may no longer punish herself or himself as being responsible for the death of a significant other (Shaw and Schelkun, 1965).

The child who uses magical thinking may also attempt suicide for spite, thinking that she or he will be around to see how the punishment has worked. Or the magically thinking child may seek a reunion with a deceased loved one, believing that she or he and the loved one will be alive together somewhere (Shaw and Schelkun, 1965).

In children, magical thinking in the form of hope of joining a lost loved one, of making a person love her or him, or as a symbolic rebirth after death and of wiping the slate clean, is not uncommon. As one grows older, increased ego strength and reality-testing replace magical thinking. Children who feel rejected and unloved may resort to magical thinking more often. Whereas a child's dependency needs are normal and such magical thinking falls within normal limits, an adult who indulges in this behavior consciously is much closer to the psychotic state. Children may use magical thinking and omnipotent feelings to mask anxiety. The adult may use a feeling of omnipotence by believing he or she is in control of a situation and can use suicide as a way out if things get too bad. Such thoughts may allow many people who consider suicide to keep going without making any further suicide attempts; this option of controlling the situation may not be as readily open to children, who may have more difficulty separating their magical thinking from reality (Gould, 1965).

## AGGRESSION

Suicidal behavior is often interpreted as aggression turned inward. The young child and immature adolescent may see the death of a loved one as a form of voluntary desertion and as rejection. The child may hate the loved object for deserting her or him, but repress hatred at the parent or significant other, because the child would prefer to consider herself or himself bad than to consider the significant other as bad. The hatred, aggression, and guilt that develop as a result of the real or fancied desertion of the child by the significant other is difficult for the child to control and may lead to self-destructive behavior. In adolescence, hostility and aggression previously directed toward a significant other becomes introjected and may lead to depression, self-deprecation, and self-destruction (Shaw and Schelkun, 1965).

## DEPENDENCY NEEDS

Dependence is essential for proper growth and development in the child and adolescent. Children and adolescents may turn aggression against themselves rather than direct it against those upon whom they are dependent. There are parents who wish their children did not exist, and this may be communicated to the child in either verbal or nonverbal ways. The children may attempt to fulfill the parents' unconscious or conscious wishes and attempt suicide in what they perceive as the only method available to them to win the parents' love. The core factor in forming a "suicidal personality" in children and adolescents is the felt loss of love. All other factors are superimposed upon a basic feeling of deprivation through the loss of love and support (Gould, 1965).

For some adolescents, emotional death is the price they pay for domestic peace with their parents. Suicide may be a way of life for adolescents who kill their enthusiasm, their hope, their freedom, and finally themselves in an effort to win acceptance by the parent (Hendin, 1975).

Dependency needs in both parent and child are central to a parent-child role-reversal situation. When unresolved dependency needs exist in the parent, this can lead to a parent-child role reversal, and the dependency needs in the parent can conflict with the child's own dependency needs. This conflict may result in suicidal behavior in the adolescent (Kreider and Motto, 1974).

## PSYCHOLOGICAL AND
## DEVELOPMENTAL DISTURBANCES

Young children with suicidal behavior are more likely to show serious pathology than are adolescents and adults. Adolescents who are self-destructive often have character disorders, depressive reactions, and adjustment reactions (Shaw and Schelkun, 1965).

The increase in suicides at puberty suggests that this time of sexual, physical, psychological, and social changes produce such adjustment problems in the adolescent that self-destruction may seem the only alternative. Young children, too, often undergo upsetting and rapid changes during the course of development, and these changes, combined with other factors, may result in suicidal behavior (Shaw and Schelkun, 1965).

## DEPRESSION

Depression is the single sign most often observed along with suicidal behavior at all age levels. But young children and adolescents react differently to depression than do adults. Adults may fail to assess the extent of a child's or adolescent's misery, especially when depression is masked by denial, as often occurs with children (Shaw and Schelkun, 1965).

Depression may go unrecognized in children and adolescents because it is less frequently observed in a "pure" state as described in adults, but it may be present in masked form. Impulsivity combines with depression in children and adolescents and obscures the depression, which may appear as temper tantrums, boredom, restlessness, rebelliousness, and defiance, somatic and hypochondrial preoccupation, accidental injuries, running away, and delinquent and antisocial acts. Because any "active" state is more tolerable to the child and adolescent, impulsivity and hypermotility are more relevant to the depressed child than to the depressed adult (Gould, 1965).

## ENVIRONMENT

Suicidal behavior in children and adolescents is more likely to occur in homes where the parent is physically absent either because of death or desertion of the family. An absent parent deprives children and adolescents of any hope of gaining love and support (Gould, 1965).

Suicidal behavior in children and adolescents may occur as a cry for help. The child or adolescent may warn of a suicidal attempt or may tell others that she or he has just made an attempt, so that others in the environment may intervene. A child who attempts suicide as a cry for help usually moves toward a social group. Often, though, repeated suicide attempts, which may result in fatality, are the result of the human environment's failing to react in a quick and effective way to prevent the completed suicide. The youngster who actually completes suicide may in fact be goaded into the final successful attempt by taunts of family or friends who fail to take the suicidal threats seriously (Shaw and Schelkun, 1965).

# 17

# Comparison: Attempted and Completed Suicide

Very few young children actually commit suicide, but in contrast to successful suicides, suicidal threats and attempts are common in psychiatric practice (Shaffer, 1974).

It is often difficult to distinguish between an accidental death and a suicide, particularly in the case of children and adolescents. Many suicides are denied by the family and classified as accidents. Unless there is a note left by the suicide victim or other indisputable evidence, death is not classified as due to suicide (Jacobziner, 1960). Young children are less likely to leave a note, as they may be too young to write or may not be conditioned to written communication. Also, young children usually have limited access to lethal weapons or drugs, and therefore use such methods as jumping from heights or running into traffic, methods that may be easily classified as accidents (Shaw and Schelkun, 1965).

The dynamics of suicide would be better understood if the individual's background were known. However, reconstruction of the life experiences of a suicide is difficult. Persons knowing most about the deceased may be unreliable sources because of their defensiveness resulting from guilt feelings about the death (Tuckman and Connon, 1962). Most data on suicides are based on reports of local coroners, and a large number of suicides go unreported because of social, religious, and legal taboos (Miller, 1975).

It is unclear how many attempted suicides later end in completed suicides. While many suicides have made previous attempts, many have not (Eisenberg, 1980). Also, many adolescent suicide deaths are unintentioned. For example, an adolescent did not intend to die, but was unaware of pharmacologic dosage and took an unintended lethal dose of a drug (McIntire, Angle, Wikoff, and Schlicht, 1977).

## STATISTICAL INFORMATION

The percentage of completed suicides generally increases with age, and some researchers report a psychological continuum from the suicide-threatener through the suicide-attempter to the suicide-completer (Perlstein, 1966).

In completed suicides, males predominate over females 3 to 1. In suicide attempts, females predominate over males by a ratio of 10 to 1. Suicide attempts occur from 7 to 100 times as frequently as completed suicides. Suicide threats appear to be more common prior to a completed suicide than are suicide attempts (Perlstein, 1966).

In one study of children aged 10 to 14 who committed suicide in England and Wales, it was discovered that only 0.6% of suicides are from this age group. However, 7% to 10% of all referrals to child psychiatric clinics are for threatened or attempted suicide (Shaffer, 1974).

About 12% of suicides are in the 15- to 19-year-old age range (Perlstein, 1966). Impulsive suicides are more frequent at adolescence than at other ages (Eisenberg, 1980).

Suicide attempts in children and adolescence may have an adaptive value. As reported above, the ratio of suicide attempts to completed suicides is high. Children and adolescents may attempt suicide to call attention to their condition in an effort to change their present situation. However, the cry for help may be ignored, and the attempt may end in a completed suicide. Threats and attempts may be shifted in children's and adolescent's efforts to gain help over a period of years or minutes, with the final act ending in a completed suicide (Miller, 1975).

## METHOD

In suicide attempts, ingesting drugs and slashing the body are more commonly used methods, while in completed suicides jumping, hanging, and strangulation are common as are inhalation and ingestion of poison (Perlstein, 1966).

Otto (1972) reported that ingestion of drugs, usually barbiturates, was the most common method in suicidal attempts and completed suicides, employed by 76.3% of boys and 89.7% of girls in his study. Boys are more inclined to use active methods (hanging, strangulation, and shooting) than are girls, who more often use only passive methods (ingestion of drugs and gas poisoning). He also reported that most children and adolescents used the same method to complete suicide that they had used in previous suicide attempts, while 31.3% of boys and 20% of girls switched from a passive to an active method to complete suicide. Girls who used active methods in suicide attempts belonged to the youngest age group in the study (10-13 years old).

Shaffer (1974) reported in his study of completed suicides that proportionately more girls took an overdose of drugs and only boys hanged themselves. He also reported that the three children who shot themselves lived in rural areas where guns were kept for sporting purposes, and in none of these homes had there been an attempt to conceal or secure the firearms. More unusual and complicated methods used, such as self-electrocution and drowning using weights, were used by boys of very superior intelligence.

## PERSONALITY CHARACTERISTICS

Adolescent males who have completed suicide have been described as difficult to reach, introspective, or angry. There is a conspicuous lack of interest in extracurricular activities at school, and academic performance is often below that of students with comparable intelligence quotients. In attempted suicides, high mobility of the family and lower socioeconomic status, or families that are bound together, with all the members living within a short distance of each other, seem to be factors. In all cases, the adolescent feels alienated from the parents, and the incidence of impulsive personality disorder is high in adolescent attempters (Perlstein, 1966).

In Shaffer's (1974) study of children and adolescents who completed suicide, it was found in half of the notes left that hostile affect was expressed. Shaffer also found that there was an excess of children with above average intelligence in the completed suicide group, and that a disproportionate number of the children were tall for their age. Of the 31 children, 9 in the study were either seeing a psychiatrist or were on a waiting list to see one. However, only 2 had been referred for attempted suicide. There were 2 who had a chronic illness (one with a chronic heart disease of a handicapping degree and the other with infrequent epileptic seizures). The children were described from school, psychiatric, and probation records, and by teachers, as: having a "chip on her/his shoulder"; impulsive; no self-control; quiet; difficult to get through to; uncommunicative; a perfectionist; self-critical; afraid to make mistakes; and volatile and erratic.

Shaffer (1974) described two distinctive personality types of children in his study who completed suicide: One group of children lived a solitary and isolated existence, were of superior intelligence, and were culturally different from their less-well-educated parents. Their mothers were often mentally ill. They hinted of internal conflict in suicide notes, and may have appeared depressed and withdrawn before their suicide, but may also have been found stealing or staying away from school. The second group of children, including several of the girls, were impetuous and prone to aggressive or violent outbursts, and were unduly suspicious and sensitive to and resentful of criticism, and they were frequently in trouble at school.

Otto (1972) found three connections for those children and adolescents who complete suicide: there is a predominance of boys over girls, the number of weeks spent on the sick list for psychiatric reasons is predominant among both boys and girls who complete suicide, and those girls who use active methods when attempting suicide are more likely to commit suicide than those who use passive methods. Those girls who use active methods in their suicide attempt belong to a special risk group.

Perlstein (1966) reports that the school performance of children who completed suicide was often poorer than in other children with comparable intelligence. Completed suicides often occurred among children retarded in reading ability who were isolated from extracurricular activities.

## PRECIPITATING FACTORS

The most frequent precipitating event in Shaffer's (1974) study of completed suicides was a "disciplinary crisis," present in 11 of 31 cases: Four children had had a fight with another child, 3 had a dispute with one of the parents, and 2 had been dropped from a school sporting team. One suicide took place after the child read about the suicide of a public figure; one child was found lying dead near an open copy of a novel in which an adolescent boy committed suicide. Fourteen of the children had previously discussed, threatened, or attempted suicide, eight within 24 hours of their death. Eight of the boys were not at school on the day they committed suicide. Most of the children committed suicide while at home alone (in contrast to attempted suicides, which often occur with others in the house or near friends). Seven of the children were from broken homes (six of these homes were broken by divorce and in two of these the child's mother had died sometime after the divorce. At the time of Shaffer's investigation, which occurred between one and four years after the child's death, six additional sets of parents had separated from one another or had gotten a divorce. Thirteen of the children were the eldest in the family and 11 were the youngest.

The death of a parent in childhood predisposes the child to later completed suicide. Significantly more children and adolescents in the completed group studied by Dorpat, Jackson, and Ripley (1965) as compared to the attempt group lost a parent by death. Most children who attempted suicide seemed to be reacting to a threatened or temporary separation, and their attempt could be interpreted as an effort to bring about a reunion with the love objects in their environment. Those in the attempt group had a significantly greater percent of parental loss due to divorce or marital separation than those in the completed group. Those in the completed group appeared to be reacting to irrevocable losses, such as the death of a love object.

Suicide may be rare in young children because successful suicide requires prior planning, and young children may not be able to do this; this aspect of cognitive development does not appear until late childhood. Children in Shaffer's (1974) study in most cases planned to have access to an empty house. Certain methods, such as hanging, require a certain technical sophistication and careful selection of an appropriate site. Few of the deaths in Shaffer's report appeared to be impulsive. Evidence of prior planning was evident in most.

# Part IV
# Analysis of Case Studies

# 18
# Analysis of Case Studies

In an effort to collectively assess the information available in the literature on child and adolescent suicide, a statistical analysis of 167 case studies occurring in the literature reviewed here is presented. Both Statistical Package for the Social Sciences (SPSS) and Statistical Analysis System (SAS) were used. Frequencies and Chi squares were the statistical methods most often used since virtually all the data presented is nominal, and these tests are most useful with this type of data. Cluster analysis was used in a few instances.

## METHOD

After an extensive literature review of child and adolescent suicide, we developed a list of variables considered important in the study of suicidal behavior (i.e., threat, attempt, and completed suicide) in child and adolescent populations. Based on these authors' research and clinical findings an 81-item questionnaire was developed which encompassed those variables (see Appendix B). This questionnaire was then administered to each of 167 case studies of child and adolescent suicide behavior occurring in the literature we reviewed. In order to be included in the statistical analysis of data obtained from administering the questionnaire, the case study had to at least report the age and sex of the child or adolescent and enough information to allow us to determine if the suicide behavior was a threat, attempt, or completed suicide.

## SUBJECTS

Data is drawn from subjects as they appeared at the time the case study was written by the authors. The cases are primarily psychiatric patients who are grouped together chiefly on the basis of their age range (4.5 to 20 years of age) and their suicidal behavior (threat, attempt, and completed suicide).

Of the 167 case studies of suicidal behavior, 77 females and 90 males were represented. Ages were grouped into 4 categories for easier analysis, and these categories reflect Piaget's (1960) stages of cognitive development and Nagy's (1948, 1959) age divisions based on death concept. They are: Group 1, 4.5-8 years of age; Group 2, 9-11 years of age; Group 3, 12-15 years of age; and Group 4, 16-20 years of age. There were 24 children (14.4%) in Group 1, 35 children (21%) in Group 2, 54 children (32.3%) in Group 3, and 54 children (32.3%) in Group 4. Of this sample, there were 31 children who threatened suicide, 116 children who attempted suicide, and 20 children who completed suicide. A suicide threat is defined as a suicide behavior which is limited to verbal expression of a wish to kill oneself; a suicide attempt might be of either low or high lethality, and the child may or may not have actually intended for the attempt to end in death, but an actual action was taken that might have ended the child's life. A completed suicide resulted in the child's death. There is no control or comparison group of nonsuicidal patients in this analysis of case studies.

## CONFOUNDING FACTORS

Confounding factors include (1) time span over which these case reports were presented in the literature (1953-1980); (2) method used for collecting the original case study information (including interviewing of the subject immediately or very shortly after the attempt, interviewing the subject some years after the attempt, discussing the attempt or completed suicide with family and friends, and obtaining information from public documents); (3) the secondary source from which the case studies were drawn for this analysis (that is, the case study authors); and (4) the case study authors' own biases about what to include and what to leave out of the case study.

## FREQUENCIES

Because a questionnaire was used with existing case studies, many authors did not include information for all the questions in the questionnaire; therefore missing cases will be a drawback throughout this analysis. Some questions have been excluded from analysis because of too many missing cases. Number of cases included in the analysis will be noted when it is less than 167.

## FINDINGS

### Child and Adolescent Characteristics

*Age and Sex Characteristics.* While male suicide rates based on chi square data are higher than expected from statistical analysis in the first two age group categories (ages 4.5-8 and 9-11 years) and lower than expected for the last two adolescent categories (ages 12-15 and 16-20 years), female rates show the opposite trend. There is a sharp rise in female suicide rates at adolescence, and these results are significant (p <.001). Male numbers remain much more stable across age groups (see Table 11).

*Age and Threatened, Attempted, and Completed Suicide.* Older ages are significantly more likely to complete suicide than are the younger age groups (p <.001). In fact, only one suicide completer was younger than the 16- to 20-year-old group, and this subject fell into the next youngest age group, comprising ages 12 to 15 years. The two youngest age groups threatened suicide more fre-

Table 11    Sex and Age of Children and Adolescents
with Suicidal Behavior

| Age in Years | Sex | | | |
|---|---|---|---|---|
| | Female | | Male | |
| | N | Percent | N | Percent |
| 4.5-8 | 5 | 6.5 | 19 | 21.1 |
| 9-11 | 9 | 11.7 | 26 | 28.9 |
| 12-15 | 34 | 44.1 | 20 | 22.2 |
| 16-20 | 29 | 37.7 | 25 | 27.8 |
| Totals | 77 | | 90 | |

N = 167, df = 3, p<.001.

quently than expected, while the two oldest age groups threatened suicide less often than expected. Information about age and threatened, attempted and completed suicide is presented in Table 12.

In the completed suicide group, 20% were tall for their age, and 5% were overweight. The percentages from the attempted plus threatened suicide group are much smaller: 2 (1.4%) were tall for their age, 2 (1.4%) were short for their age, 1 (0.7%) were considered unattractive, and 2 (1.4%) were overweight. No completed suicide subjects were in the short or unattractive categories. These frequencies are relative, based on the entire group of 167 subjects.

Many authors divide attempted suicide into suicide and suicide gesture. Based on the seriousness of the attempt, a fourth category of suicide gesture was added to the existing categories of threat, attempt, and completed suicide in this analysis of case studies. A suicide attempt was judged to be a suicide gesture when the lethality was low, when there was a high probability that the child would be found, or when all indications were that the child did not really intend to commit suicide. The suicide attempt was judged to be a serious suicide attempt when the lethality was high, when the child was less likely to be discovered, or when all indications were that the child really expected the attempt to end in death or had a serious wish to die. Attempt or gesture was judged on the case study authors' conclusions and the child's report of the incident. Because of the subjectivity of this classification, the attempt cate-

Table 12    Age and Suicidal Behaviors of Threatened,
Attempted, and Completed Suicide

| Age in years | Threat N | Threat Percent | Attempt N | Attempt Percent | Completed N | Completed Percent |
|---|---|---|---|---|---|---|
| 4.5-8 | 8 | 25.8 | 16 | 13.8 | 0 | 0 |
| 9-11 | 12 | 38.7 | 23 | 19.8 | 0 | 0 |
| 12-15 | 9 | 29.0 | 44 | 38.0 | 1 | 5.0 |
| 16-20 | 2 | 6.5 | 33 | 28.4 | 19 | 95.0 |
| Totals | 31 | | 116 | | 20 | |

N = 167, df = 6, p<.001.

gory will combine gesture and serious attempt in additional analysis of data and, in the case of comparison of completed suicides and attempted suicide, threat, gesture, and attempt will be combined. The following information was available about these four categories of suicidal behavior: threat, 31 children (18.5%); gesture, 76 children (45.5%); attempt, 40 children (24%); and completed suicide, 20 children (12%).

## Method of Suicide Behavior

Methods reported in the case studies for suicidal children and adolescents include poison, 69 (50.4%)*; running into traffic, 14 (10.2%); hanging, 15 (10.9%); jumping from a high place, 10 (7.3%); shooting, 1 (.7%); various methods used in combination, 13 (9.5%); gas, 2 (1.5%); slashing wrists, 10 (7.3%); and other, 3 (2.2%). Method was reported for 137 subjects.

*Age, Sex and Method of Suicide Behavior.* There was an increase with age for the use of poison and slashing wrists as the method of the suicidal behavior. There was a decrease with age for the use of: running into traffic (which was highest for the 4.5-8-year-old age group and stabilized after that); jumping from a high place (which was greatest for age 9-11 years); and for the use of various methods in combination (which was also greatest for the

---

*Frequencies are adjusted to omit missing data unless otherwise noted.

9- to 11-year-olds). Hanging remained stable across age groups, showing only a slight drop for age group 12-15 years. Only the oldest age group (16-20 years) used shooting as a method for suicide, and that only occurred in one instance, and resulted in a completed suicide. Only 12- to 15-year-olds and 16- to 20-year-olds used gas as a method of suicide attempt, with only one child for each age group (see Table 13). Suicidal method and age data were significant (p <.01).

While young children in both the 4.5 to 8-year-old and 9- to 11-year-old age groups were below the expected chi square levels for the suicidal methods of poisoning, shooting, and gassing themselves, they were above expectations for running into traffic, hanging, and jumping. Both adolescent age groups (12-15-year-olds and 16-20-year-olds) were above expectations for poison as a method. In fact, 43.1% of the total methods reported were composed of poisoning incidents among these two oldest age groups (12-15 and 16-20). Cluster analysis bears out this observation. Suicide attempters cluster with adolescent age groups and poisoning as the attempt method. Younger ages tend to use more various and more active methods such as running into traffic, hanging, and jumping from a high place. This was true for both young females and for young males.

There was a significant difference in male and female method choices (p <.001). Poisoning was the most common method of suicidal incident for both males and females, used by 69 of 137 subjects for whom method was reported (50.4%). Poisoning was used by 46 females and 23 males as a method of suicidal behavior. Poisoning and wrist slashing were the only methods used more frequently by females than by males. Only males used shooting and gas as a suicidal method. While method of attempt went very sharply down for females after poisoning, males appeared more varied in their choice of methods, and hanging, running into traffic, and various methods used in combination also appeared with some frequency (see Table 14).

When method by sex is controlled for age, only the youngest age group (4.5-8 years) of males outnumber females in poison as a method for suicide attempt, though cell size is very small. Only 12- to 15-year-old females outnumber males in using running into traffic as a method of suicide and, in fact, 9- to 11-year-old and 16- to

## Table 13  Age and Method of Suicidal Behavior of Children and Adolescents

| Age in years | Poison | | Traffic | | Hanging | | Jumping | | Shooting | | Various | | Gas | | Wrists | | Other | |
|---|---|---|---|---|---|---|---|---|---|---|---|---|---|---|---|---|---|---|
| | N | Percent | N | Percent | N | Percent | N | Percent | N | Percent | N | Percent | N | Percent | N | Percent | N | Percent |
| 4.5-8 | 3 | 4.4 | 5 | 35.8 | 4 | 26.7 | 2 | 20.0 | 0 | 0 | 1 | 7.7 | 0 | 0 | 2 | 20.0 | 1 | 33.3 |
| 9-11 | 7 | 10.1 | 3 | 21.4 | 4 | 26.7 | 6 | 60.0 | 0 | 0 | 6 | 46.1 | 0 | 0 | 1 | 10.0 | 1 | 33.3 |
| 12-15 | 25 | 36.2 | 3 | 21.4 | 3 | 19.9 | 1 | 10.0 | 0 | 0 | 5 | 38.5 | 1 | 50.0 | 3 | 30.0 | 1 | 33.3 |
| 16-20 | 34 | 49.3 | 3 | 21.4 | 4 | 26.7 | 1 | 10.0 | 1 | 100.0 | 1 | 7.7 | 1 | 50.0 | 4 | 40.0 | 0 | 0 |
| Totals | 69 | | 14 | | 15 | | 10 | | 1 | | 13 | | 2 | | 10 | | 3 | |

N = 137, df = 24, p<.01

Table 14    Method of Suicidal Behavior and Sex of
Suicidal Children and Adolescents

|  | Female | | Male | |
|---|---|---|---|---|
| Method | N | Percent | N | Percent |
| Poison | 46 | 69.7 | 23 | 32.4 |
| Traffic | 5 | 7.6 | 9 | 12.7 |
| Hanging | 2 | 3.0 | 13 | 18.3 |
| Jumping | 3 | 4.5 | 7 | 9.9 |
| Shooting | 0 | 0 | 1 | 1.4 |
| Various | 4 | 6.1 | 9 | 12.7 |
| Gas | 0 | 0 | 2 | 2.8 |
| Wrists | 6 | 9.1 | 4 | 5.6 |
| Other | 0 | 0 | 3 | 4.2 |
| Totals | 66 | | 71 | |

N = 137, df = 8, p<.001.

20-year-old females don't use traffic as a method at all. Both males and females increased in the use of poisoning as a method with age, from 1 female and 2 males in the youngest age group (4.5-8 years) to 22 females and 12 males in the oldest group (16-20 years). The number of females using all methods combined increased dramatically across age groups while males increased much more gradually. Many less young children of both sexes are involved in a suicidal incident than are older children, but the increase is most rapid for females between 9-11 years and 12-15 years, with a leveling off at 16-20 years of age, while there is a continual rise for males. These results are significant (p <.001).

Suicidal methods do not differ a great deal between attempt and completed suicide groups. Though more efficient methods seem to be chosen more frequently among the completed suicide group (poison, 45%; hanging, 20%; shooting, 5%; and gas, 5%), running into traffic (a not very efficient means as far as actually completing suicide is concerned) was used in 15% of the completed group with success. Running into traffic is typically considered an impulsive act of gesturing younger children; gesturing is a suicide attempt that is considered low in lethality and seldom results in death. Among the attempt and threatened groups, methods were poison, 40.8%; traffic, 7.5%; hanging, 7.5%; jumping from a high place, 6.8%; various methods used in combination, 8.8%; gas, 7%; wrist-slashing, 6.8%; and other, 2%. These are relative frequencies based on the 20-member completed suicide and the 147-member attempt and threatened suicide groups with method not reported for 10% of the completed suicide group and not reported for 12% of the attempt and threatened suicide groups.

## Location of the Suicide Incident

Of the 60 cases in which location of the attempt was reported, 20 children (38.3%) were at home with their parents present, 7 children (11.7%) were at home with their parents not present, 21 children (35%) were in a location where other people were present or nearby, and 9 children (15%) were isolated with no people nearby.

In the completed suicide group, 6 children (30%) were isolated and 1 child (5%) was with people at the time of the attempt; no location was reported for the rest of the sample. In the attempted plus threatened groups, 3 children (2%) were isolated, 20 children (13.6%) were with people, 23 children (15.6%) were at home with their parents present, and 7 children (4.8%) were at home with their parents not present at the time of the attempted suicide. These are relative frequencies based on the total of completed suicides (20) and the total of attempted and threatened suicides (147) with some data on location of attempted or completed suicide missing for both groups.

## Behavior Characteristics

There were nine possible negative behavior characteristics and more than one behavior characteristic could appear for an individual subject, therefore frequencies are relative, based on the total sample of 167 children and adolescents. Behavior characteristics were: hyperactivity, aggression, disobedience, withdrawal, delinquency, truancy, running away, enuresis and encopresis, and other. They were present in the following numbers and percentages:

hyperactive, 6 (3.6%); aggressive, 33 (19.8%); disobedient, 8 (4.8%); withdrawn, 18 (10.8%); delinquent, 55 (32.9%); truant, 25 (15%); run away, 18 (10.8%); enuretic and encopretic, 10 (6%); and other, 13 (7.8%). The above information is based on responses and not respondents because a child could be classified by more than one behavior characteristic. It is of interest that this information includes 42 children (25.2%) in the total sample of 167 children with a single negative characteristic and 54 children (32.3%) with more than one negative behavior characteristic, for a total of 96 children (57.5%) with negative behavior characteristics reported in the case studies.

The largest number of children with the behavior problems of hyperactivity, aggression, and disobedience fell into the first two age groups (4.5-8 years and 9-11 years). The largest number of children with the behavior problems of withdrawal, delinquency, truancy, and running away fell into the two older age groups (12- to 15-years and 16- to 20-years) though truancy and running away seemed to cluster with the ages 9-11 years and 12-15 years (around puberty). The oldest age group (16-20 years) had the lowest percentage of all behavior problems. The youngest age group (4.5-8 years) had the highest percentage of hyperactive behavior (66.7%; the other 33.3% of this behavior was in the next age group, 9-11 years). The 4.5-8-year-old group also had the highest percentages of aggressive behavior (39.4%) and disobedience (37.5%). The 12-15-year-old age group demonstrated the most withdrawal (55.6%), delinquency (49.1%), truancy (48%), and running away (44.4%).

Cluster analysis demonstrated the degree to which children in the youngest age group are aggressive. Of 22 children in the youngest age group who were reported as having behavior problems (out of a sample of 24 children totally in this 4.5-8-year-old age category), 14 were characterized as aggressive. In other words, 63% of the sample of young children with behavior disorders and 58% of the total sample of children in the 4.5-8-year-old age group were characterized as aggressive. (These percentages for aggression for the 4.5-8-year-old age group are higher than the percentages for aggression presented above for this age group because the above statistics are based on the total sample of 96 behavior problem children and the statistics here are based on only the 22 children with behavior problems in this age group.)

In cluster analysis of behavior characteristics across age groups, it was discovered that 6 (18%) of 34 children characterized as aggressive used passive methods of suicidal behavior such as poison while 15 (44%) characterized as aggressive used active methods such as hanging, running into traffic, or shooting.

Males had a higher percent of every behavior problem than females except for disobedience which was shared equally (50% for each sex). The behavior problem which occurred most frequently for both males and females was delinquency (57.1% for all behavior problems for females and 57.4% for all behavior problems for males).

A rejecting mother had suicidal children who were highest in the negative behaviors of aggression, withdrawal, delinquency, truancy, running away, and of enuresis and encopresis. Hyperactive children had ambivalent mothers. Those children who were high in disobedience had mothers most frequently characterized as caring.

Hyperactive children used jumping from a high place as the most common method of suicide attempt. Other behavior problems of disobedience, withdrawal, delinquency, truancy, running away, and enuresis and encopresis were linked with poison as the most often used method of suicide attempt.

## Depression

Depression was reported in 59 (35.3%) of the total of 167 case studies. Children who were diagnosed as depressed were highest in the negative behaviors of withdrawal and enuresis and encopresis. Children who were not diagnosed as depressed were highest in the behaviors of hyperactivity, aggression, disobedience, delinquency, truancy, and running away (see Table 15).

Though results are not significant for behavior problems and depression, there is a trend for depressed children to show more "passive" behavior characteristics, such as withdrawal, while children not characterized as depressed show more "active" behavior characteristics such as hyperactivity, aggression, and behaviors characterized as delinquent.

Table 15  Behavior Problems and Depression Categorization of Suicidal Children and Adolescents

| | Behavior problems | | | | | | | | | | | | | | | |
| | Hyperactive | | Aggressive | | Disobedient | | Withdrawn | | Delinquent | | Truant | | Run Away | | Enuretic | |
| | N | Percent | N | Percent | N | Percent | N | Percent | N | Percent | N | Percent | N | Percent | N | Percent |
|---|---|---|---|---|---|---|---|---|---|---|---|---|---|---|---|---|
| Depressed | 0 | 0 | 10 | 29.4 | 2 | 25.0 | 10 | 55.6 | 20 | 36.4 | 10 | 40.0 | 4 | 22.2 | 6 | 60.0 |
| Not depressed | 6 | 100.0 | 24 | 70.6 | 6 | 75.0 | 8 | 44.4 | 35 | 63.6 | 15 | 60.0 | 14 | 77.8 | 4 | 40.0 |
| Totals[a] | 6 | | 34 | | 8 | | 18 | | 55 | | 25 | | 18 | | 10 | |

N = 174.

[a]These totals are based on instances of behavior problems and not subjects (because a single subject could have more than a single behavior problem) and thus the total is more than the 167 subjects.

## Delinquent Behavior

There were eight behaviors described as delinquent, which represent a further breakdown of behaviors classed as delinquent by the authors whose case studies are analyzed here. These delinquent behaviors are running away and truancy (which also appear under behavior characteristics) and stealing, fire-setting, violent acts, rebelliousness, sexual acting out, and other (which are classed as delinquent behaviors only). These delinquent behaviors appear in the following numbers and relative percentages: running away, 18 children (10.8%); truancy, 25 children (15%); stealing, 18 children (10.8%); fire-setting, 7 children (4.2%); violent behavior, 14 children (8.4%); rebelliousness, 6 children (3.6%); sexual acting out, 2 children (1.2%); and other, 9 children (5.4%).

These cases of delinquent behavior come from 55 children from the total sample of 167 case studies of children (33%). There are 26 cases (15.6%) of children displaying a single delinquent behavior and 29 cases (17.4%) of children displaying multiple delinquent behaviors. Running away always clustered with stealing and also frequently clustered with truancy. This indicates that a variety of delinquent behaviors often occur together in suicidal children.

## IQ

There were 62 cases in which IQ was reported. Of these, 9 cases (14.5%) were below average intelligence, 25 cases (40.3%) were of average intelligence, 20 cases (32.3%) were judged to be above average intelligence, and 8 cases (12.9%) were judged to be of superior intelligence.

## Precipitating Factors in Suicidal Behavior

Precipitating factor as discussed here means the specific event mentioned by the child for the suicide attempt. This may be different than the underlying reason (which may be termed the "actual reason" for the behavior and which is often determined later), or it may be the same as the underlying reason. The precipitating factor is usually mentioned right away by the child, while the underlying reason, if it is different than the immediately-given precipitating factor, is usually pieced together by the psychiatrist based on conversations with the child and often with friends and relatives of the child. The precipitating factor for the suicidal behavior was reported in 67 cases.

The following precipitating factors for the suicide attempt were given: everyone would be better off, 2 children (3%); as a reaction to a quarrel, 11 children (16.4%); romance difficulties, 9 children (13.4%); feelings of being rejected, 11 children (16.4%); school problems, 8 children (12%); an effort to join a dead relative, 2 children (3%); feelings of hopelessness, 7 children (10.2%); and other miscellaneous reasons, 17 children (25.4%).

## Underlying Reasons

There were eight possible underlying reasons: rejection, loss, separation, depression, illness (physical or mental), hostility directed at the child from significant others, school difficulties, and other. The children in the case studies could be counted as having more than one underlying reason if that was appropriate. The statistics are based on the number of responses, therefore, instead of the number of respondents, and relative frequencies are reported. Underlying reasons included: rejection, 46 children (27.5%); loss, 14 children (8.4%); separation, 29 children (17.4%); depression,* 30 children (18%); illness, 16 children (9.6%); hostility directed at the child, 41 children (24.6%); school problems, 14 children (8.4%); and other, 26 children (15.6%).

For the age group 4.5-8 years, rejection was the most prevalent underlying reason (47.6%). For age group 9-11 years, hostility directed at the child was reported most frequently as the underlying reason (38.7%). The 12-15-year-old group also had rejection reported as the most frequent underlying reason (34.6%), but not as often as the 4.5-8-year-old age group. The oldest age group (16-20 years) had depression as the most frequently reported underlying reason (38.1%).

---

*Depression was reported in a total of 59 cases, but as an underlying reason in only 30 cases. In the other 29 cases, depression was not found to be the main reason for the suicidal act.

Males experienced loss, separation, and illness (either physical or mental) as more frequent underlying reasons than did females; females experienced depression and hostility directed at the child as more frequent underlying reasons than did males. Males and females split evenly on rejection and school difficulties as underlying reasons (see Table 16).

For all underlying reasons, poison was the most common method of suicide attempt used except for those children for whom illness (physical or mental) was reported as the underlying reason; for those who were reported as ill, running into traffic was the most common suicide attempt method.

The underlying reason was listed as depression at a much higher rate for the completed suicide group (30%) than for the attempted plus threatened suicide group (16.3%). Other underlying reasons for the completed suicide group were: rejection, 15%; loss, 5%; separation from significant others, 5%; and illness, 5%. For the attempt plus threatened group, precipitating causes were rejection, 29.3%; loss, 8.8%; separation, 19%; illness, 10.2%; hostility directed at the child from the environment, 27.9%; and school problems, 9.5%. Subjects may have more than one underlying reason so percentages for suicide attempters plus threateners equal more than 100%. Missing data account for the lower total percent of underlying reasons for suicide completers.

## Preceding Threats, Previous Attempts

There were reports in 22 cases (13.2%) that threats of suicide had preceded the attempt, and reports in 3 cases (1.8%) that threats followed the suicide attempt. Previous suicide attempts were made in 44 cases (26.3%). In 21 cases (12.6%), the child had made one previous suicide attempt; in 11 cases (6.6%), the child had made two previous attempts; and in 12 cases (7.2%), the child had made more than two previous attempts. In 2 cases (1.2%), the child made a subsequent attempt to the one reported in the case study. These are reported in relative frequencies.

More of the completed suicide group members had made previous suicide attempts than had the attempt plus threatened group.

**Table 16  Underlying Reasons and Sex of Suicidal Children and Adolescents**

| | | | | | | | Underlying reasons | | | | | | | | | |
|---|---|---|---|---|---|---|---|---|---|---|---|---|---|---|---|---|
| | Rejection | | Loss | | Separation | | Depression | | Illness | | Hostility | | School | | Other | |
| Sex | N | Percent | N | Percent | N | Percent | N | Percent | N | Percent | N | Percent | N | Percent | N | Percent |
| Female | 23 | 50.0 | 4 | 28.6 | 12 | 41.4 | 16 | 53.3 | 5 | 31.2 | 23 | 56.1 | 7 | 50.0 | 11 | 42.3 |
| Male | 23 | 50.0 | 10 | 71.4 | 17 | 58.6 | 14 | 46.7 | 11 | 68.8 | 18 | 43.9 | 7 | 50.0 | 15 | 57.7 |
| Totals | 46 | | 14 | | 29 | | 30 | | 16 | | 43 | | 14 | | 26 | |

N = 218. (Note: Number reported here is based on instances of underlying reasons and not number of subjects (because a single subject could have more than a single underlying reason) and thus the total is more than the 167 subjects included in this book.

For the 20-member completed group for whom a previous attempt was reported, 35% made one attempt, 5% made two attempts, and 15% made more than two attempts. For the attempt plus threatened suicide group, 9.5% made one previous attempt, 6.8% made two attempts, 6.1% made over two attempts, and 1.4% made a subsequent attempt after the one reported for this study.

## Affective Characteristics

There were five negative affect characteristics included in the case studies: anger, fearfulness, unhappiness, resentfulness, despair, and other, composed of miscellaneous negative affective characteristics. Children could fall into one or more categories of affective characteristics; therefore, frequencies are reported as relative. The numbers and percentages are as follows: anger, 34 children (20.4%); fearfulness, 7 children (4.2%); unhappiness, 13 children (7.8%); resentfulness, 4 children (2.4%); despair, 31 children (18.6%); and other, 7 children (4.2%).

Out of the total sample of 167 children, there were 46 children with a single negative affective characteristic (27.5%) and 19 children with multiple negative affective characteristics (11.4%), for a total group of 65 children (38.9%) who were noted in the case studies to have negative affect.

The affective characteristics most often found in the 4.5-8-year-old age group are anger (40%) and despair (33.3%). For the 9- to 11-year-old group, anger (25%) and fearfulness (25%) are the most common affective characteristics. The most common affects for the 12- to 15-year-old age group are despair (58.3%) and anger (45.8%). For the 16- to 20-year-old group, anger (66.7%) and despair (47.6%) were the most common affects. Suicide attempters may be considered to have more than one negative affect characteristic (and these characteristics were each coded individually) so an age group's total affective characteristics might add up to more than 100% and, because the percentages are based on an affect characteristic for each age group taken independently of other age groups, a particular affect may also total more than 100%.

Males showed the affects of anger (61.8%), fearfulness (71.4%), unhappiness (61.5%), resentfulness (75%), and despair (54.8%)

more frequently than did females. Female affect was concentrated around the affects of anger and despair, while males had a tendency to have a higher negative affect with regard to fearfulness and unhappiness.

## Personality Characteristics

Personality characteristics reported in the case studies all tended to be negative. Those included in the analysis were anxiousness, impulsiveness, instability, hysterical, restlessness, passiveness, feeling unwanted, immaturity, cruelty, and other. Children could have been included in more than one of these categories. Numbers and relative percentages are as follows: anxiousness, 10 children (6%); impulsiveness, 7 children (4.2%); instability, 8 children (4.8%); hysterical, 6 children (3.6%); restlessness,* 2 children (1.2%); passiveness, 11 children (6.6%); feeling unwanted,† 1 child (.6%); immaturity, 12 children (7.2%); cruelty, 5 children (3%); and other, 23 children (13.8%). There were 73 children (43.7%) reported to have negative personality characteristics. Of these 58 children (34.7%) had a single negative personality characteristic and 15 children (9%) had multiple negative personality characteristics.

Based on the 73 children for whom personality characteristics were reported, the personality characteristic most common to the 4.5- to 8-year-old age group is cruelty (33.3%) For the 9- to 11-year-old age group, passivity (25%) is the most common personality characteristic. For the age group 12- to 15 years old, instability (17.4%), hysterical behavior (17.4%), and passivity (17.4%) are the most common personality characteristics, and this age group also ranks higher on these traits than any of the other age groups, as well as being higher on impulsiveness than any other age group. The oldest age group (16- to 20-years) ranks highest on immaturity (25%) than on any other personality trait, and also ranks higher on immaturity and anxiousness than any other age group.

---

*This includes children not necessarily diagnosed as hyperactive but whose personality was predominated by being uneasy or in perpetual motion.
†These are children whose personality is dominated by feelings of being unwanted or rejected.

Males were higher than females on the personality traits of anxiousness (90%), impulsiveness (71.4%), instability (62.5%), restlessness (100%), and immaturity (58.3%). Females ranked higher than males on the personality traits of hysterical behavior (66.7%) and passiveness (54.5%).

## Loss

There were a total of 54 cases in which separations and/or losses occurred before the child's suicide attempt. Of these 54, 36 children (66.7%) incurred one separation and/or loss; 11 children (20.4%) incurred two separations and/or losses; 3 children (5.6%) incurred three separations and/or losses; and 4 children (7.4%) incurred over three separations and/or losses. These separations included instances when the parents separated or divorced, and also instances when a significant other besides the parents, such as a sibling or grandparent, left the home.

As for bereavements, there were 27 cases in which the death of a significant other was reported as occurring before the child's suicide attempt. These numbers and percentages are as follows: one bereavement, 22 cases (81.5%); two bereavements, 4 cases (14.8%); and three or more bereavements, 1 case (3.7%).

The ages and frequencies with which the children experienced the separations and/or losses were as follows: age 0-8 years*, 23 children (74.2%); ages 9-11 years, 3 children (9.7%); ages 12-15 years, 1 child (3.2%); and ages 16-20 years, 4 children (12.9%). Age of separation and/or loss was not reported for 23 children.

The ages and frequencies with which the children experienced bereavements are as follows: ages 0-8 years, 10 children (47.6%); ages 9-11, 7 children (33.3%); and ages 12-15, 4 children (19%). No bereavements occurred in the oldest age category, 16-20 years of age. Age of bereavement was not reported for 6 of the 27 children for whom bereavements were reported.

The number of children who lost a significant other through

---

*Though ages for children engaged in suicidal behavior begin with the category 4.5-8 years of age, separations, losses and bereavements were recorded as occurring several years before the suicidal incident in some cases.

death and the person lost are as follows: father, 8 children (4.8%); mother, 7 children (4.2%); sibling, 5 children (3%); other relative, 8 children (4.8%); pet, 2 children (1.2%); and other, 3 children (1.8%). Children could fall into more than one of these categories if more than one bereavement was experienced, therefore frequencies are relative.

The form the separation and/or loss took could have been divorce of the parents, abandonment by the father, abandonment by the mother, abandonment by both parents, placement in an institution or foster home, several such placements, or other. A child could fall into one or more of these categories, therefore frequencies are reported as relative. These separations and/or losses occurred in the following frequencies and percentages: divorce, 12 children (7.2%); father abandoned, 16 children (9.6%); mother abandoned, 8 children (4.8%); both parents abandoned, 6 children (3.6%); placed in an institution or foster home, 2 children (1.2%); several such placements, 4 children (2.4%); and other, 7 children (4.2%).

A few of the children in the study were reported as having experienced several deaths and separations. Though the total number of children in this category is small (24), the pattern of these events may be of interest. They were as follows: several deaths in succession, 2 children (8.3%); several separations in succession, 10 children (41.7%); deaths followed by separations, 3 children (12.5%); separations followed by deaths, 7 children (29.2%); and interspersed deaths and separations, 2 children (8.3%).

There were 15% of the completed suicide group who experienced the suicide of their mother before their own suicide, as compared to 4.8% of the attempt group.

## Birth Order, Number of Siblings

The child's birth order was reported in 66 cases. Birth order data was as follows: youngest child, 13 (19.7%); oldest child, 26 (39.4%); only child, 12 (18.2%); and any other position, 15 (22.7%).

The number of siblings was reported in 76 cases. It was as follows: one sibling, 24 (31.6%); two siblings, 18 (23.7%); three siblings, 10 (13.1%); four siblings, 6 (7.9%); more than four siblings, 6 (7.9%); and no siblings, 12 (15.8%).

### Illnesses

The relative frequency of times the suicide attempter was reported as being physically ill was 24 (14.4%) and as being mentally ill was 30 (18%) at the time of the case report. The child was reported as being both physically and mentally ill in 4 cases (2.4%).

### Physical and Sexual Abuse

Children were reported as being physically abused in 25 cases and as being sexually abused in 4 cases. In the case of physical abuse, the abuse was perpetrated by the father in 11 cases (44%), by the mother in 6 cases (24%), by both parents in 3 cases (12%), by a sibling in 1 case (4%), and by someone else in 4 cases (16%). In the sexual abuse cases, the abuse was always carried out by the father.

### Illegitimacy

The child was reported as illegitimate in 7 of the 167 cases (4.2%). While some children were not reported as illegitimate, they were reported as not wanted by the parents. This occurred in 10 cases (6%). Some of the illegitimate children were probably wanted children. However, illegitimate children were reported to be unwanted children in 3 of the cases (1.8%), separately from the 7 cases in which illegitimacy was reported, but the mother did not report if the child was a wanted child or an unwanted child. These frequencies are relative.

### Family Characteristics

*Divorce, Separations.* There were divorces in 22 of the 167 cases (13.2%), parents were separated from each other in 13 cases (7.8%), and frequent quarrels occurred in 3 cases (1.8%). These are relative frequencies.

*Parents' Personalities.* Personality characteristics reported as relative frequencies for the mother included depression, 12 cases (7.2%); passivity, 6 cases (3.6%); hostility, 9 cases (5.4%); feelings of inadequacy, 6 cases (3.6%); being strict, 8 cases (4.8%); being mentally ill, 3 cases (1.8%); anxiousness, 9 cases (5.4%); immaturity, 2 cases (1.2%); and other, 8 cases (4.8%).

Personality characteristics reported as relative frequencies for the father included depression, 1 case (.6%); passivity, 7 cases (4.2%); hostility, 16 cases (9.6%); feelings of inadequacy, 3 cases (1.8%); strict, 7 cases (4.2%); being mentally ill, 3 cases (1.8%); anxiousness, 1 case (.6%); immaturity, 1 case (.6%); indifference, 5 cases (3%); and other, 5 cases (3%).

Parents could fall into more than one of the above personality characteristics, so relative frequencies are reported. These figures are derived from the 53 cases in which the mother's personality was reported (31.7%) and 40 cases in which the father's personality was reported (24%). All categories are identical for mother and father, except for indifferent, which was reported for fathers but not for mothers.

*Family Suicides.* Suicides by family and other close associates of the child were reported in the following numbers and percentages: father, 6 (3.6%); mother, 10 (6%); sibling, 4 (2.4%); other relative, 3 (1.8%); friend, 1 (.6%); and other, 2 (1.2%). These are relative frequencies.

*Illness of Parent.* The parent was reported as mentally ill in 14 cases (8.4%), as physically ill in 14 cases (8.4%), and as both physically and mentally ill in 3 cases (1.8%). Though there were only 6 reports of mentally ill parents under personality characteristics (3 mothers and 3 fathers) above, in that instance the report was of a dominant personality characteristic. This report of mental illness signifies any report of mental illness in the parent, even when that illness is not a dominant characteristic. Illness percentages are relative frequencies.

*Characterization of Parental Role.* The mother's parental behavior was reported in 46 cases and the father's parental behavior was reported in 32 cases. For mothers, parental behavior numbers and percentages were: rejecting, 32 (69.6%); caring 6 (13%); ambivalent, 2 (4.4%); and inadequate, 6 (13%). For fathers, parental behavior numbers and percentages were: rejecting, 20 (62.5%); caring, 7 (21.9%); ambivalent, 1 (3.1%); and inadequate, 4 (12.5%).

While no more of the mothers held a rejecting attitude toward their child in the completed suicide group than in the attempted and threatened suicide groups, the fathers were more rejecting in their attitudes in the completed suicide group (20%) than in the attempt plus threatened groups (10.9%).

*Parental Abuse, Arrests, Alcohol, and Drugs.* One parent was abused by the other in 11 cases. In 2 cases, one parent had been arrested, in one case for a violent crime and in the other case for another type of crime.

Alcohol and/or drug abuse was reported in 25 cases. It occurred in the following relative percentages: father abused alcohol, 17 (10.2%); father abused drugs, 1 (.6%); father abused both alcohol and drugs, 2 (1.2%); mother abused alcohol, 1 (.6%); mother abused drugs, 1 (.6%); and mother abused both alcohol and drugs, 3 (1.8%).

There was more parental alcohol abuse and drug abuse in the completed suicide group chiefly by the father. In the completed suicide group, 20% of the fathers abused alcohol, 5% abused drugs, and 5% of both mothers and fathers of an individual child abused alcohol. In the attempted and threatened suicide group, 8.8% of the fathers abused alcohol, .7% abused drugs, and .7% abused both. Also in the attempted and threatened suicide group, .7% of mothers abused alcohol, .7% of mothers abused drugs, and 1.4% of both fathers and mothers in the same case abused alcohol. These are relative frequencies based on 20 subjects in the completed suicide group and 147 subjects in the attempted plus threatened suicide groups.

### Environmental Characteristics

The child's environment was categorized in the following ways: repressive, 16 cases (11%); punitive, 15 cases (10.3%); rejecting, 60 cases (41.4%); burdening (as in causing the child to assume an adult role), 15 cases (10.3%); deprived (either physically or emotionally), 25 cases (17.2%); overindulgent, 2 (1.4%); nurturing, 3 (2.1%); and other, 9 (6.3%).

## Parent Substitutes

There were 24 cases in which a parent substitute was reported. In 10 cases (41.7%) the substitute was for the father; in 6 cases (25%) the substitute was for the mother; and in 8 cases (33.3%) the substitute was for both parents.

The relationship of the substitute to the suicide attempter was reported in 23 of the 24 cases. In 11 cases (47.8%) the substitute was related to the child and in 12 cases (52.2%) the substitute was not related to the child. The age of the suicide attempter when the substitute entered the home was reported in 16 cases. The child was 0-8 years old in 12 cases (75%); 9 to 11 years old in 2 cases (12.5%); and 12 to 15 years old in 2 cases (12.5%).

The way the child felt about the substitute was reported in 11 of the 24 cases. The child hated the substitute in 4 cases (36.4%); resented the substitute in 3 cases (27.3%); loved the substitute in 2 cases (18.2%); and felt ambivalent toward the substitute in 2 cases (18.2%).

## School Difficulties

There were 71 cases that reported the child's school perform-ance. In 12 cases (16.9%) the child performed well and in the other 59 cases (83.1%) the child had difficulties. Those difficulties were reported as truancy, 18* cases (25.4%); difficulties with school lessons, 25 cases (35.2%); disinterested in school, 2 cases (2.8%); more than one difficulty, 9 cases (12.7%); and other, 5 cases (7%).

## Friends and Romance

The child's relationship with friends was discussed in 28 case studies. Of these cases, in 17 (60.7%), the child had no friends; in 3 (10.7%), the child had no close friends in which to confide; in 4

---

*This information is for difficulties specifically reported under school problems. Truancy reported under behavior characteristics occurred 25 times.

(14.3%), the child had good friends in which she or he could confide; and in 4 (14.3%), the child had friends, but the parents disapproved of them. In 14 of the 167 reported cases (8.4%), it was observed that a break-up with a romantic partner immediately preceded the suicide attempt.

More of those who completed suicide felt they had no friends (15% as compared to 9.5% of the attempted and threatened suicide group). Of the suicide attempters who completed suicide, 20% had experienced the breakup with a romantic partner shortly before their suicide as compared with 6.8% of the attempted and threatened groups. These results are based on relative frequencies for completed and attempted and threatened suicidal behaviors.

## Special Circumstances

The following special circumstances accompanied the suicide attempt: pregnancy, 5 cases (15.6%); in the army, 4 cases (12.5%); recently in or presently in foster care or institutional care, 19 cases (59.3%); homosexual or lesbian, 2 cases (6.3%); and in college, 2 cases (6.3%).

## Statistical Comparison of Completed Versus Noncompleted Suicidal Behavior

While data for completed suicide in comparison with attempted and threatened suicide is reported under the relevant subheadings above, a summary of this information is presented here. There were 20 subjects who completed suicide and 147 subjects who threatened or attempted suicide.

All but one of the subjects who completed suicide were in the oldest age group (16- to 20-years of age); the other was in the 12- to 15-year-old group. Of the suicide completers, 65% were males and 35% were females while in the noncompleted group, 52.4% were male and 47.6% were female.

Suicide completers used poison as the most frequent method of suicide (45%). They also used hanging (20%), shooting (5%); gas (5%); and running into traffic (15%). Noncompleters also used poison most frequently (40.8%) and also the following methods: running into traffic, 7.5%; hanging, 7.5%; jumping from a high place, 6.8%; various methods used in combination, 8.8%; gas, 7%; wrist-slashing, 6.8%; and other, 2%.

Depression was reported as a more common precipitating cause for completed suicide (30%) than for the noncompleted suicide group (16.3%).

More of the completed suicide group had made previous suicide attempts (55%) than had the noncompleted group (22.4%).

A higher percentage of the completed suicide group abused drugs and alcohol (25%) than had the noncompleted group (4.2%).

Among the completed suicide group, 15% had experienced the suicide of their mother before their own suicide, as compared to 4.8% of the noncompleted group.

While no more of the mothers had a rejecting attitude toward their child in the completed suicide group than in the noncompleted suicide group, the fathers of suicide completers were more rejecting in their attitudes (20%) than were the fathers of the noncompleted suicide group (10.9%).

# 19

# Conclusions

Children in this study are analyzed here as if they were a representative group of the entire population of suicidal children. It must be remembered, however, that the data reported here are not extensive enough to make generalizations to the entire population of suicidal children and adolescents with any degree of conclusiveness.

The data from this group of 167 children show that boys are involved in a suicidal incident slightly more frequently than girls and, when analyzed by sex and age, it is clear that there is a much larger number of young boys (4.5-8 years and 9-11 years) who are involved in a suicidal incident than are young girls in the same age categories. Female suicide attempts increase significantly around puberty and drop slightly in the oldest age group (16-20 years). Male suicide rates increase slightly at age 9-11 years and again at 16-20 years, with a slight drop at age 12-15 years. The children who attempt suicide are usually bright (average or above average intelligence with several of superior intelligence), but their environment and personal lives are in turmoil. Many feel a great deal of hostility directed at them and many others experience overt or covert rejection. They often react with behavior problems (most frequently delinquency) which may take the form of running away, truancy, stealing, and/or aggressive behavior. Others are depressed and often withdrawn. They possess a great deal of anger and also despair. Some have experienced separations and deaths, primarily in their younger years, and for some this has formed a pattern of separations and deaths occurring throughout their childhood. They are usually in a special sibling position of firstborn, youngest, or only child. They may be special in other ways, such as being tall for their age, and are often characterized as having negative personality characteristics such as immaturity, passiveness, instability, and cruelty. The mother, the father, and the environment of this child are all overwhelmingly rejecting. School is difficult and is often escaped through truancy. The child attempts suicide, most often as a gesture to draw attention to the situation, and usually tries it either at home with the parents present or with other people nearby. Attempts that will end in death usually occur in isolation.

Those who complete suicide are characterized as being more depressed, they more often abuse drugs and alcohol, have more rejecting fathers, and have more frequently experienced the suicide of their mothers before their own suicide than have noncompleting attempters. Suicide completers are more often male and more often members of older age groups than are suicide attempters who do not complete suicide.

It is clear that the child's family, the child's environment, and the child himself or herself play a role in the suicidal situation. It is probably that none of these factors alone would produce the suicidal incident, but that these factors in combination set the stage for suicidal behavior to occur.

Statistical differences between the children included in the case studies analyzed here may be clarified by the following age and sex profiles.

## PROFILE: 4.5- TO 8-YEAR-OLD BOY

Males with suicidal behavior occur with almost four times the frequency at this age levels as do females. The child in this youngest age group is highly unlikely to complete suicide and is more frequently a suicide threatener than a suicide attempter. This age group uses running into traffic as a method of attempt more frequently than any other age group, and that is usually considered a nonlethal gesture. However, running into traffic was used successfully with 15% of the completed suicide group, so there is a danger that children in this age group will "accidentally" complete suicide while gesturing. This group also used jumping from a high place and hanging as frequent suicidal attempt methods. Also, only in this youngest age group did males outnumber females in the use of poison for suicide attempt, though overall the use of poison as a method increased with age.

Younger ages of suicidal children display more behavior characteristics of hyperactivity, aggression, and disobedience. The youngest age group had the highest proportion of aggressive behavior and disobedience of any of the age groups studied here. Males were more likely to be aggressive than females. These behaviors of aggression, hyperactivity, and disobedience tend to correlate with those children not reported as being depressed.

These young children were more likely to report rejection as the precipitating circumstance than any other cause, and males overall experienced loss, separation, and illness as more frequent precipitating circumstances than did females. These males who reported illness as a precipitating circumstance were more likely to use running into traffic as a method than those with other precipitating circumstances, who were more likely to use poison as a method.

The affective characteristics of this age group are predominated by anger and despair. Also, males are more likely to show the affects of fearfulness, unhappiness, and resentfulness than are females.

Cruelty was the most common personality characterization of this age group.

Because losses, separations, and bereavements occur in the highest numbers for young children, this group is particularly susceptible to loss experience. They are most likely to have experienced some type of loss near the time of their suicide behavior. Also, because males appear more vulnerable to loss (in that they more frequently list it as a precipitating factor), this group of young males would be expected to be more at risk in the area of loss than any other group.

This age group might also expect to be more frequently placed in a foster home in the event of significant family disruption (because of the difficulty in caring for young children) and might be expected to remain in such placement longer before independence.

## PROFILE: 4.5- TO 8-YEAR-OLD GIRL

Much the same profile may be drawn for the youngest female suicide group as for her young male counterpart.

Females are lower in proportion in this age group than in any other group. While poisoning was the most frequent method of suicide attempt for females overall, females in this youngest age group used poison less frequently than males in this group and, presumably, used other methods common to young children such as running into traffic, hanging, and jumping from a high place.

Females were less aggressive and hyperactive than males, but were equally disobedient. Those children who were disobedient were often reported to have mothers who were characterized as caring. Rejection, however, was the most commonly mentioned precipitating circumstance for this age group.

These young females commonly show an affect of anger and despair.

## PROFILE: 9- TO 11-YEAR-OLD BOY

This age produced the highest number of suicide threateners. However, when this age group attempted suicide, jumping from a high place and using various methods in combination were the most frequent methods chosen.

This age group also frequently demonstrated the negative behavior characteristics of hyperactivity, aggression, and disobedience.

Hostility directed at the child was the most common precipitating factor. This age group showed the affective characteristics of anger and fearfulness, and males showed a much higher proportion of these affects than did females. School problems begin to appear with this age group.

Passivity was the most commonly observed personality characteristic.

## PROFILE: 9- TO 11-YEAR-OLD GIRL

When females in this age group attempt suicide, poison is a commonly used method, and running into traffic is not used as a method at all. Females who are involved in a suicidal incident have almost doubled in number from the youngest age category, but this group still includes a large number of suicide threateners and still is only about 1/3 as large in number as males in this same age category.

Hostility directed at the child was the most common precipitating factor both for this age group and for females in this age category.

These females had a higher proportion of anger as an affect. For all this anger, their personalities tended to be passive.

## PROFILE: 12- TO 15-YEAR-OLD BOY

This age group shows a slight drop in male suicide behavior from the previous age group. However, one male in this age category completed suicide, so suicide intent may have gotten more serious.

Poison was the most often used method of this age group. Hanging was used least often by this age group; jumping from a high place showed a dramatic drop from the 9- to 11-year-old group; various methods in combination was still chosen quite frequently; this was one of only two groups who used gas as a method (the other being the oldest age group); and wrist-slashing increased as a method for this group. Only males used gas as a method of suicide attempt.

The behavior characteristics of withdrawal, delinquency, truancy, and running away are more common at this age level, and all of these negative behaviors are more common for this age group than for any other age group studied here. Males showed a higher rate of all these negative behaviors, though females showed an almost equal proportion of delinquency.

Depression tended to correlate with the negative behavior of withdrawal. Because males tended to show more withdrawal than females, it may be that they also showed more depression.

Rejection was the most common precipitating circumstance for this age group, and rejection tended to be experienced in equal proportions by males and females.

Despair and anger were the most common affects for this age group. Males in this group were characterized as having unstable personalities.

## PROFILE: 12- TO 15-YEAR-OLD GIRL

The most dramatic increase in suicidal behavior and the highest percentage of suicidal behavior across age groups occurs among 12- to 15-year-old girls. While none of these females completed suicide, almost twice as many proportionally threatened or attempted suicide at this age level than did males.

Of the most commonly used methods for this age group (poison, various methods in combination, and wrist-slashing), females more frequently use poison and wrist-slashing than do males, and use both of these methods about twice as frequently as males.

Females are about equally classed as delinquent with males, a negative behavior characteristic that emerges with this age group.

Females at this age level experienced rejection as a potent precipitating factor. They also experienced despair and anger as affects. Their personality characteristics were commonly hysterical or passive.

## PROFILE: 16- TO 20-YEAR-OLD BOY

In this age group, the possibility of completed suicide rises dramatically and over twice as many males completed suicide as females. These suicide completers also tend to show more special characteristics, such as being tall for their age or overweight.

Only this age group used shooting as a suicidal method (a very effective means of completing suicide) and it was used only by males. This age group used the highest percentage of poisoning, but also used hanging, wrist-slashing (these latter two methods are used in equal numbers at this age level), and gas as methods. Males tended to be more varied in their method choices than females at this age.

This age group presented the lowest number of behavior problems across age groups.

Depression was the most frequent precipitating factor for this age group, and those who ultimately completed suicide were more depressed than those whose suicide attempts did not end in completed suicide.

Anger and despair were common affective characteristics. Personalities were characterized as immature and anxious, with males showing these characteristics more frequently than females.

At this age level, problems with alcohol and drug abuse could be expected to be most common, and breakups with romantic partners would probably be most traumatic. Also the special problems a male might face of being in college, in the army, or discovering he were a homosexual would probably show up here. And, as has been shown in some cases, if the suicidal individual's life is characterized by a series of separations, losses, and bereavements, this age group would have had an opportunity to experience any number of these, producing a pattern of losses that makes this adolescent more vulnerable to suicide.

## PROFILE: 16- TO 20-YEAR-OLD GIRL

While males of this age group show a small increase in suicidal incidents over the 12- to 15-year-old age group, females show a slight drop in incidences of suicidal behavior over the previous age group. They also show a trend toward stabilizing with poison as a method of suicide behavior, though they still use wrist-slashing more than males. Females don't use gas or shooting as a method of suicidal behavior, and females at this age level don't use running into traffic as a method. They also use hanging and jumping from a high place much less frequently than males. Taken together with the much lower number of completed suicides among females with what may be considered less-lethal methods of poison and wrist-slashing, it might be considered that female attempts at this age level are more often gestures than serious suicide attempts.

Depression was the most common precipitating factor for this age group, and females experienced it more frequently than did males.

Anger and despair, common affective characteristics for this age group, might be demonstrated by females with sexual acting out, though delinquency behaviors were lower for this age group than for 12- to 15-year-olds. At this age group females, in addition to experiencing romance breakups, problems with drugs and alcohol, college, and dealing with possible lesbianism, also might be faced with the dilemma of pregnancy.

# Appendix A
# Annotated Bibliography

Information provided in the books and articles included here are categorized under the following labels: (1) family factors; (2) characteristics and presenting symptoms of the child or adolescent; (3) treatment, and (4) case studies. The number in parentheses after each bibliographic entry indicates the category or categories into which that reference falls. Those titles beginning with a single asterisk (*) contain information pertaining only to child suicide; those titles beginning with a double asterisk (**) contain information pertaining only to adolescent suicide. Those titles unmarked with an asterisk contain information pertaining to both child and adolescent suicide.

*Ackerly, W. C. Latency-age children who threaten or attempt to kill themselves. *Journal of the American Academy of Child Psychiatry*, 1967, *6*, 242-261.

Study of 31 latency-age children who threatened (24) or attempted (7) suicide. There were 22 boys and 9 girls in the sample, ranging in age from 4 to 12. Precipitating circumstances may be seemingly minor, or severe (as in the death of a parent). The boys who attempted suicide seemed more disturbed than the girls. A complex of multiple psychic forces are operating when a latency-age child threatens or attempts suicide. A summary of treatment considerations is offered. (1, 2, 3, 4)

*Aleksandrowicz, M. K. The biological strangers: An attempted suicide of a seven-and-a-half-year-old girl. *Bulletin of the Menninger Clinic*, 1975, *39*, 163-176.

Case study of a 7½-year-old girl who made a serious suicide attempt by jumping from a window. The active-aggressive mode of her suicide attempt is considered by the author as typical of a latency-age child. Her family picture is one of intense guilt over an ambivalent relationship with her mother, envy of her siblings, and rage at what she considers to be loss of parental love. From the beginning of her life, this child did not manage to evoke good mothering and supplied little gratification to her mother. The "mismatch" of personalities of mother and daughter made them, in the author's words, "biological strangers." (1, 2, 3, 4)

**American Academy of Pediatrics. Teenage suicide. *Pediatrics*, 1980, *66*, (1), 144-146.

Reviews statistics concerning child and adolescent suicides. Briefly discusses presenting symptoms including depression, feeling unwanted, adolescents with poor impulse control, psychotic adolescents, family history, and adolescents who have experienced a serious trauma. Information important for the management of adolescents who have attempted suicide and survived the attempt is also discussed. These include reasons for the attempt, lethality of the suicide attempt, and the adolescent's support system. (2)

Bakwin, H. Suicide in children and adolescents. *The Journal of Pediatrics*, 1957, *50* (6), 749-769.

This article presents statistical information about childhood and adolescent suicide by age, sex, and country, and reviews the literature related to these statistics. A case history of a 5½-year-old boy who attempts suicide, and case studies drawn from the literature are presented. Literature-based discussions on factors leading to suicide, including social factors and individual factors, as well as age differences, are also presented. Some treatment approaches are discussed. (1, 2, 3, 4)

**Bakwin, H. Teen-age suicide. *Archives of Environmental Health*, 1966, *12*, 276-278.

Literature review and discussion of factors in adolescent suicide. Statistical information, including rates by race, religion, and geographic location (United States cities and various countries), is examined. Suggestions for treatment, based on the discussion, are outlined. (2, 3)

**Barter, J. T., Swaback, D. O., and Todd, D. Adolescent suicide attempts: A follow-up study of hospitalized patients. *Archives of General Psychiatry*, 1968, *19*, 523-527.

Report of prehospital and posthospital adjustment of 45 adolescent suicide-attempters, as determined by review of hospital charts. Three areas were discussed in relation to information found in the charts: family relationships, school adjustment, and the circumstances of the suicide attempt. A follow-up interview was conducted by telephone. It was found the adolescents who are hospitalized for a suicide attempt have often made previous attempts that were either not recognized or ignored by those around the adolescents; that many adolescents continue suicide behavior after hospitalization; and that those who continue suicidal behavior have a living situation that includes inadequate family relationships for the adolescent, parental loss, a minimum social life for the adolescent, and a requirement on the part of the adolescent of continued aid from a social agency. (1, 2)

*Bender, L. *Aggression, hostility and anxiety in children*. Springfield, IL: Charles C Thomas, 1953.

Discusses aggression in children in general. Information is presented on the specific topics of children's attitude toward death, children preoccupied with suicide, children with homicidal aggression, fire-setting in children, the genesis of hostility in children, and anxiety in disturbed children. Extensive case studies of children are presented to describe each specific category, and these case studies are reported from observations of children with behavior problems in the children's service of the Psychiatric Division of Bellevue Hospital in 1934 and 1935. Children ranged in age from 3 to 15 years. (2, 4)

*Bender, L., and Schilder, P. Suicidal preoccupations and attempts in children. *The American Journal of Orthopsychiatry*, 1937, 7, 225-234.

Case studies of children 6 through 15 are presented and discussed regarding underlying characteristics of children and factors that appeared to provoke preoccupations with and threats of suicide. Some preliminary formulations about suicidal tendencies in childhood are drawn based on the cases presented here. (1, 2, 4)

Bergstrand, G. G., and Otto, U. Suicidal attempts in adolescence and childhood. *Acta Paediatrica Scandinavica*, 1962, 51, 17-26.

Data collected for 1955-1959 from hospitals in Sweden on 1727 children and adolescents who have attempted suicide (351 boys and 1376 girls). Age distribution, seasonal variations, annual rate, social background, school conditions, and family situation, the reason for the attempt, and the method employed are recorded and discussed. (1, 2)

**Bigras, J., Gauthier, Y., Bouchard, C., and Tassé, Y. On the depressive illnesses in childhood: Suicidal attempts in adolescent girls: A preliminary study. *Canadian Psychiatric Association Journal*, 1966, *11* (Supplement), 275-282.

A detailed study of 21 adolescent girls between the ages of 14 and 17 who attempted suicide. The method of attempt, the structure of the family and parents' personalities, the precipitating event, and the girl's image of herself, her father, and her mother are discussed. Case studies are presented in segments in comparison with each other. Psychotherapy with these suicidal girls is described. (1, 2, 3, 4)

**Blanchard, J. D., Blanchard, E. L., and Roll, S. A psychological autopsy of an Indian adolescent suicide with implications for community services. *Suicide and Life-Threatening Behavior*, 1976, *6* (1), 3-10.

Case report of an adolescent Pueblo Indian boy, Juan, who committed suicide with drugs and alcohol. The article includes a family history, a history of Juan's difficulties, and a report of his psychological evaluation. The authors make an attempt to understand the societal and family factors that may have predisposed Juan to commit suicide. A recommendation for community resources that might prevent suicide in this setting is delineated. (1, 2, 3, 4)

**Cantor, P. The adolescent attempter: Sex, sibling position, and family constellation. *Life-Threatening Behavior*, 1972, *2* (4), 252-261.

Data from 17 adolescents who attempted suicide were collected at Payne Whitney Psychiatric Hospital in New York City to determine information related to sex, birth order, sex of siblings, and family constellation. There was an overrepresentation of females with younger brothers in the sample, and only or firstborn children were overrepresented in the sample regardless of sex. There was also an extremely high degree of family disorganization within the sample, notably with the father absent from the home. Elements of a suicide attempt among adolescents include: (1) the wish to seek contact; (2) the wish to move toward and be with other people; (3) the desire to make an appeal for help, love, and protection; and (4) the wish to express anger and aggressions that have otherwise not been expressed. (1, 2)

Carlson, G. A., and Cantwell, D. P. A survey of depressive symptoms in a child and adolescent psychiatric population. *Journal of the American Academy of Child Psychiatry*, 1979, *18* (4), 587-599.

Of 28 children ages 7 to 17 judged to have an affective disorder, 88.9% exhibited suicidal ideation as a symptom. Other symptoms common to this group included dysphoric mood (70.4%), low self-esteem (74.1%), poor school performance (48.1%), anhedonia (66.7%), changed appetite (40.7%), tired (66.7%), insomnia (70.4%), somatic complaints (70.4%), and hopelessness (70.4%). (2)

Carlson, G. A., and Cantwell, D. P. Suicidal behavior and depression in children and adolescents. *Journal of the American Academy of Child Psychiatry*, 1982, *21* (4), 361-368.

The authors, in an effort to understand why some psychiatrically referred children attempt suicide and others do not, examined a group of 102 children and adolescents in a psychiatric setting on the factors of: (1) feelings of hopelessness, (2) duration of psychiatric illness, (3) feelings of depression, (4) psychiatric diagnoses, (5) family history of psychopathology, and (6) the relationship of age to the foregoing variables. They used the Children's Depression Inventory and semistructured interviews to study the suicidal ideas of these children. The authors found that 63% of subjects with depressed Children's Depression Inventory scores were suicidal, but that 34% of the suicidal children did not have high scores for depression. They also found that 71% of the children and adolescents with suicidal ideation and high depression scores met criteria for depressive disorders. They did not find, however, that the frequency and intensity of suicidal ideation increased with chronological age. (2)

*Connell, H. M. Attempted suicide in schoolchildren. *Medical Journal of Australia*, 1972, *1*, 686-690.

Fifteen children under the age of 15 were seen after being admitted to the hospital after taking an overdose of barbiturates or other drugs. All children lacked normal supportive adult relationships, either because a parent was absent from the home or because of marital discord or alcoholism in one or both parents. In most, a seemingly trivial event tipped the scale and aggressive feelings meant for the disappointing love object were directed toward the self. This study highlights both the stress to which many children may be subjected without parents being aware of their plight and the ease with which drugs may be obtained by children in many households. A detailed case study and treatment suggestions are included. (1, 2, 3, 4)

**Corder, B. F., Shorr, W., and Corder, R. F. A study of social and psychological characteristics of adolescent suicide attempters in an urban, disadvantaged area. *Adolescence*, 1974, *9* (33), 1-6.

Study of 11 adolescents admitted to a mental health adolescent unit with a history of suicide attempts matched for age, sex, I.Q., and socioeconomic level with a control group of 11 adolescents admitted to the unit but without a history of suicide attempts. The two groups were compared on 12 factors, and the suicidal group was found to significantly differ from controls on seven of the factors: absence of any warm adult parental figure with whom to identify; lack of investment in the future and absence of future goal orientation; lack of control over the environment; high activity level; low level of school involvement; low impulse control; and active parental conflict and negative attitude expressed toward child by parent. (1, 2)

*Crook, T., and Raskin, A. Association of childhood parental loss with attempted suicide and depression. *Journal of Consulting and Clinical Psychology*, 1975, *43* (2), 277.

This was a report of a study of 115 depressed inpatients with a history of attempted suicide, 115 nonsuicidal depressed patients, and 285 normal subjects, matched for age and sex. Results indicate the major difference between suicide attempters and the other two groups is the amount of parental discord and intentional separation of parents from the patients in their childhood, with the suicide-attempters experiencing a significant excess of parental loss from divorce, desertion, or separation in their childhood. The results did not indicate an association between attempted suicide and the loss of a parent from natural causes. (1, 2)

**Daniel, W. A., Jr. Suicide in adolescence. *Acta Paediatrica Scandinavica*, 1975, No. 256 (Supplement), 36.

Short article, from the Adolescent Unit of the University of Alabama Medical Center, on suicide in adolescence with information about the general causes of suicides and major points of therapy for the adolescent who has unsuccessfully attempted suicide. (2, 3)

**Dizmang, L. H., Watson, J., May, P. A., and Bopp, J. Adolescent suicide at an Indian reservation. *American Journal of Orthopsychiatry*, 1974, *44* (1), 43-49.

Comparison of 10 Shoshonean Indians age 15-24 who completed suicide with 40 controls matched for age, sex, and degree of Indian blood. Seventy percent of completed suicides had more than one significant caretaker before age 15, as compared with 15% of controls, and 40% of the suicides' caretakers had five or more arrests compared with 7.5% of controls. The Indian adolescents who completed suicide also had significantly more homes broken by divorce or desertion, more personal arrests, and a larger number of attendances at boarding school by or before ninth grade. Prevention and treatment suggestions are offered. (1, 2, 3)

Dorpat, T. L., Jackson, J. K., and Ripley, H. S. Broken homes and attempted and completed suicide. *Archives of General Psychiatry*, 1965, *12*, 213-216.

A study of 114 subjects who completed suicide and 121 subjects who attempted suicide; 50% of those who completed suicide and 64% of those who attempted suicide had broken homes in childhood. In the completed suicide group, a home broken by death was most common, while in the attempted suicide group, homes broken by divorce were significantly higher. (1)

**Eisenberg, L. Adolescent suicide: On taking arms against a sea of troubles. *Pediatrics*, 1980, 315-320.

Discussion of violence in general among adolescents, suicide rates, and completed suicides as compared with attempted suicides. Suicides at college among American and British youth are discussed. Barbiturate control and gun control as it relates to adolescent suicide is analyzed. Clinical decision-making regarding treatment of suicidal adolescents is outlined. (2, 3)

Erikson, E. H. *Childhood and society*. New York: W. W. Norton and Company, Inc., 1950.

Extension of psychoanalytic concepts to include the entire life cycle (defined as the Eight Stages of Man). A discussion of the relevance of using case histories, and use of case histories to illustrate basic concepts are included. Uses a combination of historical narrative and psychoanalytic case studies to discuss Adolf Hitler's childhood as described in *Mein Kampf* and Maxim Gorky's childhood and youth from a film; discusses the childhood training of two Indian tribes, the Sioux and the Yorok. (2)

**Erlich, H. S. Adolescent suicide: Maternal longing and cognitive development. *The Psychoanalytic Study of the Child*, 1978, *33*, 261-277.

Reviews literature regarding suicidal behavior in adolescence. Discusses the contribution of the developmental period of adolescence to suicidal behavior. The longings for the preoedipal mother are described as reawakening in adolescence and the adolescent propensity to a rise in egocentrism is discussed. These two factors, the author suggests, may give rise to suicidal preoccupation and actions in adolescents. These factors are supported with clinical illustrations. (1, 2, 4)

**Finch, S. M., and Poznanski, E. O. *Adolescent suicide*. Springfield, IL: Charles C Thomas, 1971.

Statistics, precipitating factors, and methods of suicide are discussed. Types of suicidal adolescents are described as impulsive character disordered, depressed adolescents, and psychotic adolescents. Wrist-cutting syndrome is described as a variant of the psychotic pattern. Family background and environmental factors are described. Such factors as inheritance, menstruation, and pregnancy are discussed briefly in relation to suicide. Suicide and aggressive behavior are compared. There is a chapter on suicide among college students. Assessment and management of suicidal behaviors are outlined, and case studies are used to illustrate some aspects of adolescent suicidal behavior. (1, 2, 3, 4)

Freud, A. *Normality and pathology in childhood: Assessments of development.* New York: International Universities Press, Inc., 1965.

Reviews the history of child psychoanalysis and techniques employed, and compares child analysis and adult analysis. Discusses development in childhood in terms of dependency to emotional self-reliance from sucking to rational eating, from wetting and soiling to bladder and bowel control, from irresponsibility to responsibility in body management, from egocentricity to companionship, from body to the toy, and from play to work in terms of psychological implications. Regression in normal development is outlined. Pathology is described at some length, and therapeutic possibilities are also described. (1, 2)

**Gabrielson, I. W., Klerman, L. V., Currie, J. B., Tyler, N. C., and Jekel, J. F. Suicide attempts in a population pregnant as teenagers. *American Journal of Public Health*, 1970, *60*, 2289-2301.

Of 105 New Haven residents who were 17 and under when they had a baby, 14 subsequently attempted or threatened suicide. The risk of suicide in this population was higher for single women, Catholics, those not from poverty areas, and those with pregnancy complications and venereal disease. Preventive measures are suggested. (2, 3)

Garfinkel, B. D., and Golombek, H. Suicide and depression in childhood and adolescence. *Canadian Medical Association Journal*, 1974, *110*, 1278-1281.

Review of the literature on depression and suicide in children and adolescents. Information on epidemiology, psychopathology, and clinical picture is presented, and suggestions for examination and treatment of depressed children and for prevention of suicide are included. (1, 2, 3)

Glaser, K. Attempted suicide in children and adolescents: Psychodynamic observations. *American Journal of Psychotherapy*, 1965, *19*, 220-227.

Suicidal behavior in children and adolescents from a middle-class urban population is discussed. Assessment of the behavior is categorized as "just talk," "gesture," "threat," and "attempt," with case study examples for each category. Interfamily tensions and conflicts within the child are described, with prevention and treatment suggestions offered. (1, 2, 3, 4)

**Glaser, K. The treatment of depressed and suicidal adolescents. *The American Journal of Psychotherapy*, 1978, *32*, 252-264.

Discussion, based on the author's experience as director of a residential adolescent unit, on depression and suicidal behavior in adolescence. Includes information on adolescent reaction to loss and low self-esteem, and on the manipulative suicidal patient. Suggestions for management and treatment of depressed and suicidal adolescents are brought in throughout the discussion, and there is a section on psychological aspects of psychopharmacological treatment. (1, 2, 3, 4)

*Glaser, K. Suicidal children—management. *American Journal of Psychotherapy*, 1971, *25* (1), 27-36.

Discussion of child suicide focusing on crisis-intervention and management. In the child, where completed suicides are rare, the first goal is to assess the suicidal behavior as a sign of emotional disturbance, and then to initiate appropriate intervention when emotional disturbance is present. Factors leading to suicidal behavior are discussed. The role of the psychiatrist as an educator or others (professionals and parents) who will be the first to observe suicidal behavior in children is outlined. (1, 2, 3, 4)

Gould, R. E. Suicide problems in children and adolescents. *American Journal of Psychotherapy*, 1965, *19*, 228-246.

Suicide in children and adolescents is discussed in terms of psychodynamic factors, sociocultural influences, and therapeutic management in a hospital setting. Children are differentiated from adolescents and both these groups are differentiated from adults. Sex, race and religion are discussed in terms of suicidal behavior. (1, 2, 3).

*Green, A. H. Self-destructive behavior in battered children. *American Journal of Psychiatry*, 1968, *135* (5), 579-582.

A study of 60 children, confirmed as being physically abused, and 30 neglected and 30 normal children. The physically abused children had a significantly higher incidence of suicide attempts, self-mutilation, and suicidal ideation. The suicidal behavior might serve as an escape from a traumatic situation; act as a "cry for help"; as an imitation of an aggressive, impulsive parent; as a reaction to loss; or include other psychodynamic significance. Global ego function defects appear to be a characteristic of abused children. (1, 2)

Greer, S. Parental loss and attempted suicide: A further report. *British Journal of Psychiatry*, 1966, *112*, 465-470.

A study of 81 suicidal and 385 nonsuicidal patients with neurotic and sociopathic disorders compared in terms of parental loss in childhood, age at the loss, whether loss was of one or both parents, sex of the absent parent, the cause of the loss, and the child's subsequent environment. Most of the patients who attempted suicide were young adults (under 30). Suicidal neurotics had significantly more parental loss, more often experienced the loss before age 5, and more often lost both parents than nonsuicidal neurotics. However, no difference was noted between suicidal and nonsuicidal neurotics regarding the sex of the absent parent, the cause of the parental loss, and the subsequent environment of the patients. Differences between suicidal and nonsuicidal sociopaths failed to reach levels of significance as determined by the authors through psychic interview data. (2)

**Greuling, J. W., and DeBlassie, R. R. Adolescent suicide. *Adolescence*, 1980, *15* (59), 589-601.

Reviews the literature regarding characteristics and presenting symptoms and treatment aspects of suicidal adolescents. In addition to reviewing causal factors described by a variety of authors of adolescent suicidal behavior, literature discussions of prevention, management, and treatment of the suicidal adolescent are described in some detail. (2,3)

Haider, I. Suicidal attempts in children and adolescents. *British Journal of Psychiatry*, 1968, *114*, 1133-1134.

A report of a study of 64 children and adolescents (22 males and 42 females, 43 between the ages of 14 and 17) who attempted suicide. Of this group, 20 were eldest children. Only 32 lived with both parents, but all but 8 of the remaining families were plagued by disorganization and discord. In 50 of these children and adolescents, suicide was attempted by ingesting drugs, with violent attempts more common among males. (1, 2)

Haldane, J. D., and Haider, I. Attempted suicide in children and adolescents. *The British Journal of Clinical Practice*, 1967, *21* (12), 587-591.

A study of 30 children and adolescents who attempted suicide revealed an association between suicide attempts and family disorganization and also between suicide attempts and antisocial behavior. In this study, 43% were eldest siblings, and the majority were female adolescents diagnosed as having character disorders or reactive behavior disorders, and who were reacting to stressful situations. In the majority (66%) the suicide attempt method used was injection of drugs, and 10% of the 30 in the study made subsequent attempts. Case summaries are included in an appendix. (1, 2, 3, 4)

**Hankoff, L. D. Adolescence and the crisis of dying. In Hankoff, L. D. and Einsidler, B. (eds.), *Suicide: Theory and clinical aspects*. Littleton, MA: PSG Publishing Company, 1979.

Discusses physiological and cognitive development and sociocultural aspects of adolescence. Speaks of Western culture's lack of initiation rituals and of high school graduation as the nearest approximation. Discusses death encounters among adolescent males in terms of thrill-seeking behaviors such as driving fast or recklessly and perhaps being a soldier who performs daring acts in warfare. Describes the higher suicide attempt rate for females as the only acceptable encounter with death open to females. Discusses suicide in terms of broken homes and initiation ritual. The crisis reactivity common to adolescents is discussed relative to maturation. (2)

**Hendin, H. Growing up dead: Student suicide. *American Journal of Psychotherapy*, 1975, *29*, 327-338.

Family constellations that require an emotional deadness to be observed in parents and children are described. Seriously suicidal college students, unable to deal with college and becoming involved with friends or in intimate relationships, choose suicide rather than unravel the death knot with their parents. Case studies and therapeutic interventions are presented. (1, 2, 3, 4)

**Holinger, P. C. Adolescent suicide: An epidemiological study of recent trends. *American Journal of Psychiatry*, 1978, *135*, (6), 754-756.

Review of the literature and discussion of statistics and methods of suicide among adolescents. The authors feel it is unclear whether increased suicide rates among the young represent a real change or if this increase indicates such factors as greater acceptance of the existence of suicide among adolescents and better diagnosis, or if it is a combination of these factors. (2)

**Holinger, P. C. Violent deaths among the young: Recent trends in suicide, homicide, and accidents. *American Journal of Psychiatry*, 1979, *136* (9), 1144-1147.

Review of the literature comparing adolescent death by suicide, homicide, and accidents including methodological problems, general perspectives, and current trends. Statistics are for the period from 1961-1975, during which suicide and homicide rates have doubled for the age group 10-24, but accident rates have changed very little. The author feels the statistics call into question the view that suicide and homicide rates are inversely related and that suicide rates are higher among the nonwhite population. This author found that rates among white adolescents increased more and are still higher than among nonwhites for the period studied (1961-1975). (2)

*Hug-Hellmuth, H. von. The child's concept of death. *Psychoanalytic Quarterly*, 1965, *34*, 499-516.

Author's report from and discussion of a parents' diary of a boy, Ernie, and his encounters with death concepts, beginning at age 3½. The diary records the child's changing death concept over a period of almost two years. The author reports many excerpts in detail and discusses them in light of literature available on children's death concepts. (2)

*Husband, P., and Hinton, P. E. Families of children with repeated accidents. *Archives of Diseases in Childhood*, 1972, *47*, 396-400.

Twenty-four children who have appeared at accident clinics with repeated injuries are profiled as are their families. The children in this group frequently had extroverted personalities. There were serious physical or psychiatric illnesses in other family members in 50% of the families, and the accident-prone children reacted to a difficult family situation by hurting themselves. (1, 2, 4)

Inhelder, B., and Piaget, J. *The growth of logical thinking from childhood to adolescence*. New York: Basic Books, 1958.

Examines the child's emergence from the stage of Concrete Operations (7-11 years) into Formal Operations (beginning at 11-12 years). At this stage, the young adolescent begins to structure certain methods of experimental induction, and is able to systematically verify events. These methods are not available to the younger child. This change in thinking is illustrated by the use of descriptions of children and adolescents 5-16 years old attempting to solve a variety of problems requiring logical thinking. The concluding chapter is a summary of adolescent thinking. (2)

**Jacobs, J. *Adolescent suicide.* New York: Wiley-Interscience, 1971.

Discusses theories of suicide and proposes a theoretical-methodological orientation to the study of adolescent suicide. Describes suicidal attempts in adolescence as occurring after a long-standing history of problems, a period of escalation of problems, a failure of adaptive techniques, that leads to a progressive social isolation from meaningful social relations, and a final phase of dissolution of any remaining meaningful relationships in the weeks and days prior to the attempt. Case study information drawn from interviews and suicide letters illustrate these events mentioned above. (1, 2, 4)

**Jacobs, J., and Teicher, J. D. Broken homes and social isolation in attempted suicides of adolescents. *The International Journal of Social Psychiatry*, 1967, *13* (2), 139-149.

The authors studied 50 adolescents ages 14-18 admitted to Los Angeles County General Hospital from September 1964 to May 1965. Adolescents were interviewed 24-48 hours after the attempt, and both adolescents and their parents completed identical questionnaires. It was found that there was a long-standing history of problems from childhood to adolescence, a period of escalation of problems following adolescence, and a dissolution of meaningful social relationships in the days and weeks preceding the attempt. (1, 2)

Jacobziner, H. Attempted suicide in children. *The Journal of Pediatrics*, 1960, *56* (4), 519-525.

A study of children and adolescents aged 8-19 reported for poisoning by physicians and hospitals in New York City. There was a higher incidence of poisoning among Puerto Ricans than among other groups, and there was a higher incidence among children from broken and disorganized homes. Incidence was lowest in autumn and highest in spring. There was a ratio of 50:1 of attempts to completed suicides among adolescents, and these attempts occurred more frequently among medium- and low-income groups. There are suggestions for prevention, follow-up and aftercare. (2, 3)

**Jacobziner, H. Attempted suicides in adolescence. *Journal of the American Medical Association*, 1965, 191 (1), 101-105 (a).

Reviews statistics of suicides in general and adolescent suicides and suicide attempts in the United States. Factors surrounding 597 suicide attempts in the age group 12-20 reported to the New York City Poison Control Center from 1960 to 1961 are discussed. Case studies are presented briefly. Some preventive measures are outlined. (1, 2, 3, 4)

**Jacobziner, H. Attempted suicides in adolescents by poisoning. *American Journal of Psychotherapy*, 1965, *19*, 247-252 (b).

Provides general statistical information about suicides, including suicide rate by countries and by race. Statistical information about adolescent suicides includes information by sex and ethnic distribution and information about previous attempts. Case studies illustrate the statistics. (2)

**Johnson, R. J. Youth in crisis: Dimensions of self-destructive conduct among adolescent prisoners. *Adolescence*, 1978, *13* (51), 461-482.

Study of adolescent prisoners' self-mutilation and attempted suicide in New York penal institutions from 1971 to 1974. The data were collected with a semi-structured descriptive interview. The imprisoned adolescents' reactions are presented as interview excerpts and cover such topics as segregation from other prisoners, which means social isolation for some, breakdown of social supports, and the marginal existence common to many adolescent prisoners. (2)

**Kenny, T. J., Rohn, R., Sarles, R. M., Reynolds, B. J., and Heald, F. P. Visual-motor problems of adolescents who attempt suicide. *Perceptual and Motor Skills*, 1979, *48*, 599-602.

In a study of 18 adolescents age 11 to 18 years who attempted suicide, the authors concluded that learning disabilities may be a significant unrecognized factor in such attempts. The adolescents were administered the Bender Visual Motor Gestalt Test and the

Canter Background Interference Procedure after their attempt, and the scores were compared with a control group of adolescents of similar age, race, and socioeconomic background. The suicide attempters had significantly higher scores indicating neurologic dysfunction and learning disabilities. School histories also revealed significantly more problems in adjustment and a higher rate of school failure than among controls. (2)

**Koocher, G. P. Talking with children about death. *American Journal of Orthopsychiatry*, 1974, *44* (3), 404-411.

Four questions about death were asked of 75 children aged 6-15: (1) What makes things die? (2) How do you make dead things come back to life? (3) When will you die? and (4) What will happen when you die? Responses of subjects fell into the expected response categories reflecting Piaget's Preoperational, Concrete Operations, and Formal Operations levels of cognitive development, according to appropriate age levels of the subjects for these categories. (2)

**Kreider, D. G., and Motto, J. A. Parent-child role reversal and suicidal states in adolescence. *Adolescence*, 1974, *9* (35), 365-370.

In this situation the child develops some parental behavior, and the parent becomes more like a child. Unresolved dependency needs in the parent may lead to parent-child role reversal. A child in this situation has been deprived of a position of nurturance, restricted in the range of behaviors available, is required to carry the burden placed upon her/him without asking for it, and may experience severe anxiety because of a sense of inability to fulfill the parental role. This may generate hostility and feelings of rejection. Clinical examples are given to illustrate parent-child role reversal. (1, 2, 3, 4)

**Lawler, R. H., Nakielny, W., and Wright, N. A. Suicidal attempts in children. *Canadian Medical Association Journal*, 1963, *89* (14), 751-754.

Assessment and management techniques with 22 children ages 8 through 15 who attempted suicide are discussed. Most (68%) took medicinal drugs, and intrapsychic and interpersonal conflicts were present in all cases. Many of these children gave previous warnings of their disturbed states, but these had gone unheeded. The child's position in sibling order appeared to be of some significance, and all but one were of superior intelligence. (1, 2, 3)

**Lee, E. E. Suicide and youth. *Personnel and Guidance Journal*, 1978, *57*, (4), 200-204.

Review of the literature discusses statistics, cultural factors, minority status, and sex difference and suicide rates. Possible causes discussed include interaction of sex, sibling position, and family constellation; family disorganization; loss of love object; personality characteristics; depression; and increased stress on women. Case studies illustrate symptoms of suicidal behavior. Treatment suggestions, including the role of teachers and counselors, are offered. (1, 2, 3, 4)

Lourie, R. S. Clinical studies of attempted suicide in childhood. *Clinical Proceedings of the Children's Hospital of the District of Columbia*, 1966, *22* (6), 163-173.

Review of the literature, beginning in the 1800s, of child and adolescent suicides, and an examination of the nature of childhood suicide and suicide attempts. Patterns of thinking and relationships originating in the first years of life are included as components in suicidal efforts. Case studies of children ages 7 through 12 illustrate underlying causes and methods in suicide attempts. (2, 4)

*Lukianowicz, N. Attempted suicide in children. *Acta Psychiatrica Scandinavica*, 1968, *44*, 415-435.

Review of the literature on attempted suicide in children and illustration of this review with 10 detailed case studies of children who threatened, attempted, or contemplated suicide, drawn from a sample of 120 children admitted to one of two child guidance clinics in Northern Ireland, for various reasons. The etiology, symptoms, and psychodynamics of attempted suicide in children are presented, and conclusions are drawn regarding treatment and prevention of suicide in children. (1, 2, 3, 4)

**McAnarney, E. R. Adolescent and young adult suicide in the United States—A reflection of societal unrest? *Adolescence*, 1979, *14* (56), 765-774.

Review of the literature regarding family, religion, transition and mobility, achievement orientation, and aggression and their role in adolescent suicidal behavior. The author comments that the United States is undergoing changes in the family, the role of women, minority status, formal religion, mobility, achievement, and expression of aggression. Societal pressures are present because of potential fuel shortages, population problems, and pollution. Society may seem insecure to the adolescent, who is also experiencing a personal transitional stage of development. (1, 2)

McIntire, M. S., and Angle, C. R. The taxonomy of suicide as seen in poison control centers. *Pediatric Clinics of North America*, 1970, *17* (3), 697-706.

Self-poisoning in 1,103 children, 6 to 18 years of age, was examined. The authors conclude that self-poisoning in children over 6 is rarely accidental, though in older children, intoxication may have been the goal and completed suicide might be the result of a toxicological mishap. Demographic data and the child's concept of death are discussed. (2)

McIntire, M. S., and Angle, C. R. "Suicide" as seen in poison control centers. *Pediatrics*, 1971, *48* (6), 914-921.

Study of 1,103 self-poisoning cases, age 6 to 18, seen at 50 poison control centers. Of these cases, 13% were judged intentional, 13% intoxication, 26% suicide attempts, and 48% suicide gestures. Of the 6- to 10-year-old group, 63% were male and 40% were black. About 50% gave a history of stress or referral for behavior problems. There is an abrupt increase in self-poisoning for girls aged 12-16, and male self-poisonings increase with age. Of the 17- to 18-year-olds, 16% had immature death concepts. (1, 2, 3)

McIntire, M. S., Angle, C. R., and Struempler, L. J. The concept of death in Midwestern children and youth. *American Journal of Diseases of Children*, 1972, *123*, 527-532.

Structured interviews were conducted at church schools and clinics of 598 children and adolescents ages 5-18 to determine their views of causes, images, and finality of death. Death was seen as more violent among the clinic group. By ages 13-16, 20% of the sample still thought the dead were cognizant, 60% expressed belief in spiritual continuation, and 20% denied death as final. The 7-9 age group were more willing to tolerate the realism of death for a pet than for themselves. Children who had lost a parent through death used less fantasy or imagery to describe death, while those children who had lost a parent through divorce used a maximal amount of fantasy. (2)

McIntire, M. S., and Angle, C. R. Psychological "biopsy" in self-poisoning of children and adolescents. *American Journal of Diseases of Children*, 1973, *126*, 42-46.

Using a psychological "biopsy" to assess suicidal intent, public health nurses at two Omaha poison control centers interviewed 50 consecutive patients, ages 6 to 18, treated at the centers. The 50 patients were interviewed at home, and 50 controls of the same age, sex, race, religion and family status as each patient were also interviewed. The hospital diagnosis had been 42% accident and 58% suicide attempt, but after assessment, the diagnoses were 4% accident, 70% suicide gesture, 2% suicide attempt, 22% intoxication, and 2% homicide. There had been prior suicide gestures in 26%, but none of the controls had made such gestures. Extremes of parental control and expectations appeared as a dominant theme among subjects, which were associated with high depression scores for the subjects. In contrast to high parental control and expectations, there was also a pattern of parental rejection manifested as indifference. (1, 2, 3, 4)

**McIntire, M. S., Angle, C. R., Wikoff, R. L., and Schlicht, M. L. Recurrent adolescent suicidal behavior. *Pediatrics*, 1977, *60* (4, Part 2), 605-608.

In Omaha, 26 adolescents from an original group of 50 aged 14 to 18 admitted to psychiatric services after self-destructive behavior were followed up with an evaluation 6 to 24 months later.

Risk for repeated suicide was predicted as low for 6 and high for 20 subjects. Prior attempts occurred in 60% of the 20 high-risk subjects, and subsequent attempts occurred in 31% of this group. There was only one prior attempt in the 6 low-risk attempters, and no subsequent attempts. Only 6 of the 26 adolescents improved with treatment, and this was uniformly associated with an improved environment. (2, 3)

McIntire, M. S., and Angle, C. R. *Suicide attempts in children and youth.* Hagerstown, MD: Harper and Row, 1980.

Discusses statistics reflecting number of suicides to suicide attempts in adolescence and the most common method used. Defines the concept of lethality of intent to commit suicide. Describes death concept among children and adolescents. Explains taxonomy of self-poisoning as seen in poison control centers based on a study conducted by the authors from data on a group of 1,103 children and adolescents ages 6-18 from 50 poison control centers. Recurrent suicidal behavior is discussed, and management and treatment measures are critiqued. The role of the health professional in evaluating the suicidal adolescent is described in terms of goals. Diagnosing and treatment of acute overdoses in adolescents are described. Case studies are provided. (1, 2, 3, 4)

**McKenry, P. C., Tishler, C. L., and Christman, K. L. Adolescent suicide and the classroom teacher. *The Journal of School Health*, 1980, *50* (3), 130-132.

Review of the literature regarding theories of suicide and possible precipitating factors, which may act as warning signs of adolescent suicidal behavior. This information is directed at the classroom teacher, with suggestions related to the teacher's role in identifying potentially suicidal adolescents and in suicide-prevention. (2)

**Margolin, N. L., and Teicher, J. D. Thirteen adolescent male suicide attempts: Dynamic considerations. *Journal of the American Academy of Child Psychiatry*, 1968, 7, 296-315.

Thirteen boys, ages 14-18, were studied following a suicide attempt. Chronic separation trauma, role reversal, and identification with maternal depression were reported in these cases. Detailed case studies are given on 3 of the boys, with a brief case report on all 13 to illustrate loss, and depression of the parents. (1, 2, 4)

**Marks, A. Management of the suicidal adolescent on a non-psychiatric adolescent unit. *The Journal of Pediatrics*, 1979, *95* (2), 305-308.

Retrospective analysis of first 100 suicidal adolescents admitted to a general adolescent inpatient unit of a New York hospital to determine safety, practicality, and efficaciousness of this method. The admission to the unit was allowed for evaluation and disposition of the suicidal adolescents; the adolescents appeared to integrate rapidly and well with the milieu and activities of the unit; and only 12 of the adolescents required transfer to a psychiatric unit, although all needed further professional attention. The authors recommend this method as a model of care for the suicidal adolescent. (3)

Mattsson, A., Seese, L. R., and Hawkins, J. W. Suicidal behavior as a child psychiatric emergency: Clinical characteristics and follow-up results. *Archives of General Psychiatry*, 1969, *20*, 100-109.

A retrospective and follow-up study of 75 children and adolescents who had made suicidal gestures or suicide attempts is discussed and compared with 95 nonsuicidal child psychiatric emergency cases seen at the same time, both in a general hospital emergency room. While there were differences in the two groups as to age and sex, the pattern of family disorganization was similar. The suicidal patients, unlike the comparison group, required a high rate of hospital admissions and extensive aftercare through clinics, agencies, and treatment centers. Such factors for the suicide group as intentions, nature of the suicidal behavior, methods employed, and therapeutic considerations were discussed. Observation of typical signs of depression often weeks before the suicidal behavior offers insight into community-education efforts aimed at early identification of potentially suicidal children and adolescents. (1, 2, 3)

**Miller, J. P. Suicide and adolescence. *Adolescence*, 1975, *10* (37), 11-24.

Reviews the literature of suicide in adolescence as distinct from suicide among other groups. High-school-age young people and college students are included in the discussion. Case studies and autobiographical material are used to explain environmental conditions, psychological states, individual constitution, behavior and "the cry for help" aspects of adolescent suicides. College student suicides in the United States and England are discussed. (2, 3)

Morrison, G. C., and Collier, J. G. Family treatment approaches to suicidal children and adolescents. *Journal of the American Academy of Child Psychiatry*, 1969, *8*, 140-153.

A discussion of 34 of the first 100 families seen by a child psychiatry emergency service because of suicide threat or attempt by a child or adolescent in that family is presented. Case studies of several of the children, which includes family background information, are offered. In 76% of these cases, the suicidal threat or attempt was precipitated by an important loss or separation of a parent or parent surrogate by death, illness, marital separation, hospitalization, or household move, or the anniversary of such a loss. Treatment methods are described, with an emphasis on matching a treatment plan with a family's or individual's ability to work within the problem-solving process. (1, 2, 3, 4)

*Nagy, M. H. The child's theories concerning death. *The Journal of Genetic Psychology*, 1948, *73*, 3-27.

Study of written compositions, drawings, and discussions of 378 children ages 3-10 living in Budapest concerning their attitudes toward and images of death. The author found three stages of development concerning death: denial of death as a regular and final process (ages 3-5); death personified (ages 5-9); and death as a pro-

cess which is universal and the perceptible result is dissolution of
bodily life (ages 9-10). Extensive examples from the interviews are
provided. (2)

*Nagy, M. H. The child's view of death. In Feifel, H. (ed.), *The
meaning of death*. New York: McGraw-Hill, 1959.

Children 3 to 10 years old living in Budapest were interviewed
about their concepts of death. Also, children ages 7-10 were asked
to write about everything that came to their mind about death,
and children aged 6-10 were asked to make drawings about death.
From this sample of 378 children, three developmental stages regarding death concept were discovered. In Stage 1, the child under
5 does not see death as an irreversible fact; death is a departure or
sleep, death is seen as gradual or temporary, or death is denied. In
Stage 2, between ages 5-9, death is personified. Death may be
thought of as a separate person or identified with the dead. In Stage
3, after age 9, death is seen as a process, which happens to people
according to certain laws. It is also recognized as universal. A sam-
pling of interviews with children at each stage is presented. (2)

*Ohara, K. Characteristics of suicides in Japan especially of parent-
child double suicide. *American Journal of Psychiatry*, 1963,
*120*, 382-385.

Report on suicide in Japan, offering some information on child
suicides, but concentrating on mother-child suicides with the
mother killing the child or children then killing herself. Such multiple suicides are frequent in Japan (parent-child suicides account
for 22% of multiple suicides) and reflect the Japanese attitude that
suicide is admirable.

*Orbach, I., and Glaubman, H. Children's perception of death as a
defensive process. *Journal of Abnormal Psychology*, 1979, *88*
(6), 671-674. (a)

Study of 27 children aged 10-12 years old (15 boys and 12 girls)
born of Israeli immigrant parents in Israel, who were suicidal, aggressive, or normal (9 in each group). The authors found that sui-

cidal children distorted the death concept more frequently than the other two groups, but that this seemed to be independent of general cognitive functioning. Wishful thinking about death as a defensive process occurred more frequently among suicidal children. The authors suggest that a discussion of the meaning of death should be an important part of the treatment of suicidal children. (2)

*Orbach, I., and Glaubman, H. The concept of death and suicidal behavior in young children. *Journal of the American Academy of Child Psychiatry*, 1979, *18* (4), 668-678. (b)

Three detailed case studies, including partial interviews, relating child suicide to distorted death concepts. This distorted death concept in the three children interviewed for this study appeared to be limited to personal conceptions of death only, and was seen to reflect the result of a defensive process in the children. The authors speculate that if this distorted death concept is in fact the result of a defensive process, then suicidal children should have a more distorted death concept than would be true of other related, but more neutral concepts. Therapy with suicidal children is discussed. (2, 3, 4)

Otto, U. Changes in the behavior of children and adolescents preceding suicidal attempts. *Acta Psychiatrica Scandinavica*, 1964, *40*, 386-400.

A study of a sample of 1,727 Swedish children and adolescents who attempted suicide in a five-year period found no specific presuicidal syndrome that makes it possible to predict if a person will commit a suicidal act. The most common behavior change discovered was an addition of depressive and neurotic symptoms such as anguish, unrest, sleep difficulties, and psychosomatic symptoms. Character symptoms—aggressiveness, labile affectivity, increased irritability, and social behavior disorders—are more unusual. (2, 4)

Otto, U. Suicidal attempts made by children and adolescents because of school problems. *Acta Paediatrica Scandinavica*, 1965, *54*, 348-356.

Among 1,727 Swedish children and adolescents who have attempted suicide, 62 indicated school problems as the provoking cause. Poor school results was the major cause, followed by adjustment difficulties and a desire to quit school which was prevented. School problems seemed to be a minor factor overall as a reason given for suicidal behavior. (1, 4)

*Otto, U. Suicidal attempts made by children. *Acta Paediatrica Scandinavica*, 1966, *55*, 64-72.

Of 1,727 Swedish children and adolescents who were admitted to the hospital following a suicide attempt, 42 cases who were under age 14 are investigated here. The youngest is a 10-year-old boy. There is a marked preponderance of girls in this group, and home and parental problems, followed by school problems, are the major precipitating factors. Passive methods (i.e., taking drugs) predominate in this sample. (1, 4)

Otto, U. Suicidal attempts made by psychotic children and adolescents. *Acta Paediatrica Scandinavica*, 1967, *56*, 349-356.

Study of psychotic children and adolescents identified in a sample of 1,727 Swedish children and adolescents who attempted suicide. While exogenous events have been more often identified as precipitating factors for the entire sample, the illness itself appears to be the dominant cause in suicide attempts in psychotic patients. Boys constitute a major part of the group. Depressive reactions dominate the mental state of both schizophrenic and manic-depressive suicide-attempters, and behavior change during the three months preceding an attempt is more common in psychotic children and adolescents than in any other diagnosis. (1, 4)

Otto, U. Suicidal acts by children and adolescents: A follow-up study. *Acta Psychiatrica Scandinavica*, 1972 (Supplement), *233*, 5-123.

Report of a prospective study carried out 10-15 years after an initial study conducted from 1955 to 1959 on a sample of 1,727 Swedish children and adolescents. This report includes an extensive review of the original data and a report of the follow-up information. Factors discussed include the child's concept of death; mental illness and personality variables in this suicidal population; pre-suicidal changes in behavior; suicide attempts made by younger children; suicide attempts in connection with school problems, military service, and pregnancy; suicidal acts from a social psychiatric and cultural history point of view, and in comparison with a control group; and completed suicides. Brief case histories illustrate these factors. An extensive review of the literature is included (1, 2, 4)

**Patterson, W. M., Dohn, H. H., Bird, J., and Patterson, G. A. Evaluation of suicidal patients: The SAD PERSONS scale. *Psychosomatics*, 1983, *24* (4), 343-349.

Scale, developed for use with potentially suicidal adults, whose 10 major risk factors spell the acronym SAD PERSONS. Items used to determine suicidal risk include sex, age, depression, previous attempt, ethanol abuse, rational thinking loss, social supports lacking, organized plan, no spouse, and sickness. While some of the items on the scale are not pertinent to adolescent suicide behavior, some item information may be applied to adolescent populations with caution. (3)

*Paulson, M. J., Stone, D., and Sposto, R. Suicide potential and behavior in children ages 4 to 12. *Suicide and Life-Threatening Behavior*, 1978, *8* (4), 225-242.

A study of 34 severely depressed and self-abusive and/or suicidal children, identified from a population of 662 children aged 12 and under seen at the UCLA Neuropsychiatric Institute, was conducted by the authors. Family situations demonstrated acute family breakdown, marital disharmony, and both verbal and physical violence. This was reflected in the behavior of the 34 children studied. A variety of treatment methods, including behavior modification training for parents, psychotherapy, inpatient treatment, foster home placement, and adoption were instituted. Follow-up indicated no child in the group had committed suicide, with a majority of the children showing fair to good recovery and adjustment. (1, 2, 3)

**Perlstein, A. P. Suicide in adolescence. *New York State Journal of Medicine*, 1966, *66* (23), 3017-3020.

This article reviews the literature and compares completed and attempted suicides and suicide threats in adolescence. General statistics, clinical studies, theories of suicide, and the threatment and preventive approach are included in the review. The article suggests there is a psychological continuum from the suicide-threatener to the suicide-completer. (2, 3)

*Pfeffer, C. R. Psychiatric hospital treatment of suicidal children. *Suicide and Life-Threatening Behavior*, 1977, *8* (3), 150-160.

Hospital admission is indicated for suicidal children if: (1) the child is unable to withstand stress; (2) the child is unable to utilize diagnostic interviews as an incentive to delay further self-destructive actions; and (3) the family is unable to provide sufficient environmental stability for the child. Three phases of hospital treatment are discussed: initial phase, working-through phase, and termination phase. Three cases are presented: that of a depressive and hysterical girl, that of a severely behavior-disordered boy with borderline personality organization, and that of a psychotic boy. (1, 2, 3, 4)

*Pfeffer, C. R. Suicidal behavior of children: A review with implications for research and practice. *American Journal of Psychiatry*, 1981, *138* (2), 154-159.

Review of the literature concerning suicide among latency-age children. Topics include incidence, demographic variables, family influences, depression, the child's concept of death, ego functioning, and suicidal motivations in children. Clinical practice considerations for future investigations are outlined. (1, 2, 3)

*Pfeffer, C. R., Conte, H. R., Plutchik, R., and Jerrett, I. Suicidal behavior in latency-age children: An empirical study. *Journal of the American Academy of Child Psychiatry*, 1979, *18* (4), 679-692.

Empirical study of 58 children, ages 6-12, evaluated for suicidal potential after admittance to psychiatric hospitals. A battery of scales used to assess suicidal potential was used, and 72% of the children were found to have some degree of risk. Behaviors significantly correlated with suicide potential included depression, feelings of hopelessness and worthlessness, the wish to die, preoccupations with death, and family factors of severe depression and suicidal behavior. The child's concept of death is of a temporary and pleasant state. (1, 2, 3)

*Pfeffer, C. R., Conte, H. R., Plutchik, R., and Jerrett, I. Suicidal behavior in latency-age children: An outpatient population. *Journal of the American Academy of Child Psychiatry*, 1980, *19*, 703-710.

Comparison study of 13 suicidal children (11 males, 2 females) admitted to a municipal hospital psychiatric outpatient clinic and an inpatient population of the same hospital. The children in this population displayed suicidal ideas, threats, or attempts, and were characterized by increased psychomotor activity, intense preoccupations with death, and had parents who made suicidal gestures or attempts. The inpatient comparison group had a higher incidence of ego deficits and more serious suicidal behavior. The study reports a higher incidence of childhood suicidal behavior in psychiatric outpatients than has been previously reported. (1, 2)

Piaget, J. *The child's conception of the world*. Paterson, NJ: Littlefield, Adams and Company, 1960. (Originally published by Harcourt Brace and Company, 1929.)

Piaget begins the book with a discussion of his method of observing children and his rules for interpreting the results of his observations. He then discusses his concept of thought development in children and then children's concepts and how they evolve through stages of child development. These include names, dreams, realism, consciousness attributed to things, "life," and animism. He also discusses a child's concepts of the origin of natural phenomena such as the sun, the moon, water, trees, mountains, and the earth. (2)

**Powers, D. The teacher and the adolescent suicide threat. *The Journal of School Health*, 1979, *49* (10), 561-563.

Suggestions for teachers in the event of contact with an adolescent who completes suicide, attempts suicide, or threatens suicide. General information for dealing with each of the three possibilities is described in terms of dealing with the suicidal adolescent and dealing with others in the school environment, particularly if an adolescent completes suicide. (3)

**Rabkin, B. *Growing up dead*: *A hard look at why adolescents commit suicide*. Nashville: Abingdon, 1978.

Case studies which describe, from interviews with suicidal adolescents, events that lead to suicidal attempts in these adolescents' lives. Extensive account of year preceding the death of an adolescent who completed suicide taken from his journals, poetry, suicide note, and interviews with his friends and family. (1, 2, 3)

Rosenberg, P. H., and Latimer, R. Suicide attempts by children. *Mental Hygiene*, 1966, *50*, 354-359.

Study of 51 children (37 females, 14 males) based on records collected on all children 18 and under admitted to a children's ward of a hospital from 1950 to 1963. Information on twins and on birth order is presented, and there is summary information separating groups by sex. Treatment recommendations based on the fundamental needs of children are presented. (1, 2, 3)

**Rosenkrantz, A. L. A note on adolescent suicide: Incidence, dynamics and some suggestions for treatment. *Adolescence*, 1978, *13* (50), 209-214.

Review of the literature regarding incidence, psychodynamics, and treatment of adolescent suicidal behavior. There is a suggestion that treatment of the suicidal adolescent should include treatment of the family as a whole. (1, 2, 3)

**Sabbath, J. C. The suicidal adolescent—the expendable child. *Journal of the American Academy of Child Psychiatry*, 1969, *8*, 272-285.

This article presumes a parental wish, which may be conscious or unconscious, that the child be gone, or dead (the expendable child), in some cases of suicidal behavior in adolescence. In the cases presented here, this situation reaches a critical point during the adolescent level of development. Three case studies are presented in some detail and discussed with regard to the existing literature relevant to the phenomenon of the expendable child. (1, 2, 4)

*Safier, G. A study of relationships between the life and death concepts in children. *The Journal of Genetic Psychology*, 1964, *105*, 283-294.

Study focused on children's concepts of death and "animism" (attributing life and lifelike qualities to inanimate objects). Three groups of boys (10 in each group) were tested and included Group 1, aged 4-5; Group 2, aged 7-8; and Group 3, aged 10-11. The scores showed a decrease in animism with age, and a positive correlation between decreasing animism scores and more adult responses concerning death. Life- and death-concept formation appear to be parallel in their development. (2)

**Schechter, M. D., and Sternlof, R. E. Suicide in adolescents. *Postgraduate Medicine*, 1970, *47* (5), 220-223.

Factors associated with suicidal behavior in the 15-24 age group, such as masked depression, excessive use of fantasy, accident proneness, broken homes, attempts to escape punishment, and psychosis are discussed and the literature reviewed. Treatment suggestions are included. (1, 2, 3)

Schrut, A. Suicidal adolescents and children. *Journal of the American Medical Association*, 1964, *188* (13), 1103-1197.

Suicidal adolescents and children are divided into two groups: withdrawn, chronically depressed, and schizophrenic; and hyperactive as infants or children and aggressive and hostile as older children and adolescents. Group 1 children tend to have mothers who are totally rejecting of the parental role. Group 2 children have mothers whose distaste for the maternal role was modified by guilt or remorse. Case studies and discussion elaborate on these mother-child relationships. (1, 2, 4)

Shaffer, D. Suicide in childhood and early adolescence. *Journal of Child Psychology and Psychiatry*, 1974, *15*, 275-291.

Detailed analysis over a 7-year period of personality and other characteristics of a group of children between 12 and 14 who successfully committed suicide. Two personality stereotypes emerged: (1) solitary children, tall for their age and of superior intelligence, often with mental illness in their families, and whose suicide notes hinted at internal conflicts; and (2) impulsive, aggressive, and sometimes violent children who were sometimes in trouble at school. Factors that the authors feel determine a child's death by suicide include a degree of conceptual maturity, a disturbed family background, depression, a precipitating incident that may be humiliating, access to a method of suicide, an opportunity to use the method in isolation, and experience of suicidal behavior because of its occurrence in a family member, a peer, or at fantasy level. (1, 2)

*Shaw, C. R., and Schelkun, R. F. Suicidal behavior in children. *Psychiatry*, 1965, *28* (2), 157-168.

Survey of the literature on suicide in children, with implications for treatment presented from the literature and from the senior author's own experience. The authors indicate that suicide in children may be classed as accident due to the method employed (running into traffic, jumping from a high place), lack of communication (no suicide note), and tradition (underestimation of the strength of a child's emotions and motivations). Constitutional correlations (hypersensitivity, suggestibility, psychological or physical pathology, and developmental disturbances); social and environmental correlations (loss and stress); affective correlations (depression, loneliness, hopelessness, and a sense of being different); and behavioral correlations (aggression, impulsiveness, sadism-masochism, and magical thinking) are discussed. Prognosis, including a checklist for evaluating the risk of suicidal behavior, and treatment information are presented. (1, 2, 3)

**Stanley, E. J., and Barter, J. T. Adolescent suicidal behavior. *American Journal of Orthopsychiatry*, 1970, *40* (1), 87-96.

Follow-up study of 44 suicidal adolescents and 25 controls (psychiatric patients, but not suicidal) approximately 22 months after the initial contact was made with these patients. Initial contact had been made before the subjects self-admitted themselves to the hospital. There were no differences between suicidal adolescents and controls regarding incidence of parental loss, frequency of family conflicts, social adjustment, and precipitating events at the pre-hospital-admission contact, as determined by the authors. Suicidal adolescents who did not repeat their attempt in the 22-month follow-up and after release from the hospital did not differ from controls on those factors included in the study and mentioned above. However, suicidal adolescents who repeated the suicide attempt during the 22-month follow-up had significantly fewer peer relationships, a poorer academic record, and were less likely to be living with a parent than were controls. (1, 2)

Suicide and suicidal attempts in children and adolescents. *The Lancet*, 1964, *2*, 847-848.

Examines statistics related to suicide and suicide attempts in children and adolescents and reports that suicide attempts for young people are on the increase. Psychodynamics of suicidal behavior and family factors are considered. It is recommended that the children and adolescent populations should be broken down into age groups of five or even three years each in order to relate behavior to developmental phases and to changing social roles. (1, 2)

**Teicher, J. D. Children and adolescents who attempt suicide. *Pediatric Clinics of North America*, 1970, *17* (3), 687-696.

Adolescent suicides are viewed in three stages: a long previous history of problems; an escalation of these problems in adolescence; and a final stage of dissolving relationships, isolation, and alienation. Physical or mental illness in the family is common, and often a relative has made a suicide attempt. Family disruption with deprivation of love is frequently a component. The physician's role in the situation may be literally as the "lifeline" for the adolescent. (1, 2, 3)

**Teicher, J. D., and Jacobs, J. The physician and the adolescent suicide attempter. *The Journal of School Health*, 1966, *36* (9), 406-415.

Three stages to suicidal behavior in the adolescent are described. These are: (1) a long-standing history of problems; (2) an escalation period, which is marked by a feeling by the adolescent that the number and intensity of problems have been mounting since puberty; and (3) a final stage, marked by a chain reaction dissolution of what remains of the adolescent's meaningful social relationships. This discussion includes information about discipline in the family, school, and peers. The physician's involvement with the suicidal family (in 48% of cases of suicidal adolescents, the adolescent, parent, or sibling have been treated for a serious physical or mental ailment in the five years preceding the attempt) and the physician's role in aiding the suicidal adolescent are discussed. (1, 2, 3)

*Tishler, C. L. Intentional self-destructive behavior in children under age ten. *Clinical Pediatrics*, 1980, *19* (7), 451-453.

This article discusses 4 case studies of children under age 10 relating the family conditions that often are present in suicidal children and the child's reactions. A short summary of the treatment methods used with each child has been added to the end of each case study. (1, 3, 4)

*Toolan, J. M. Suicide and suicidal attempts in children and adolescents. *The American Journal of Psychiatry*, 1962, *118* (8), 719-724.

Reviews statistics of 102 children and adolescents with suicidal behavior (in age groups of 5-9, 10-14, and 15-19) and the religion, race, I.Q., ordinal position, current living arrangements, and psychological diagnosis of these children and adolescents. Reasons for the suicidal behavior are discussed, and some brief case studies are presented. (1, 2, 4)

Toolan, J. M. Suicide in children and adolescents. *American Journal of Psychotherapy*, 1975, *29*, 339-344.

Statistics generally are an underestimation of the number of children and adolescents who attempt or complete suicide. The family situations of suicidal children and adolescents are discussed. Suicide theory for this age group, symptoms of suicidal children and adolescents (primarily information on depression), and treatment approaches are considered. (1, 2, 3)

Toolan, J. M. Therapy of depressed and suicidal children. *American Journal of Psychotherapy*, 1978, *32*, 243-251.

This article is based on the premise that depression can be diagnosed in children, provided that different criteria are used than for adults. Such factors as the child's age, intelligence, level of ego development, defenses utilized, attitude of the parents, and community facilities must be taken into consideration. The author theorizes that depression is a reaction to loss and recommends analytically oriented psychotherapy as the effective treatment approach. Depressive symptoms and case studies to illustrate some of the symptoms are presented. (2, 3, 4)

**Tuckman, J., and Connon, H. E. Attempted suicide in adolescents. *The American Journal of Psychiatry*, 1962, *119* (3), 228-232.

The study was conducted over a two-year period of 100 children and adolescents under age 18 who attempted suicide who came to the attention of the Philadelphia Police Department. The authors found an association between attempted suicide and family disorganization, and also an association between attempted suicide and delinquent behavior. Statistics related to adolescent suicide are also discussed. (1, 2, 3)

Tuckman, J., and Youngman, W. F. Attempted suicide and family disorganization. *The Journal of Genetic Psychology*, 1964, *105*, 187-193.

Study focuses on 186 families with an adult member who has attempted suicide. The study clearly shows pervasive family breakdown in those families with a suicidal adult member, demonstrated by contacts with community agencies providing health and welfare services. In 63% of the families with agency contacts, 2 or more family members were involved in independent contacts. In 53% of the sample, 2 or 3 generations were involved. (1)

**Tuckman, J., and Youngman, W. F. A scale for assessing suicide risk of attempted suicides. *Journal of Clinical Psychology*, 1968, *24*, 17-19.

Seventeen-item scale developed to identify individuals who have attempted suicide, who are high-risk for completed suicide. The scale was validated by following up 3,800 attempted suicides and evaluating those who subsequently completed suicide. The scale's 17 factors are considered by the authors to be objective and easily determined. (2)

**Weiner, I. W. The effectiveness of a suicide prevention program. *Mental Hygiene*, 1969, *53* (3), 357-363.

Report on the effectiveness of a community suicide-prevention program initiated by the Los Angeles Suicide Prevention Center in 1961, as determined by comparison of suicide rates in Los Angeles County before and after the introduction of the suicide-prevention service, and comparison with some other California counties without such a service. The findings did not support the hypothesis that there would be a significant reduction in suicide rates in Los Angeles County after the introduction of the suicide-prevention service. In fact, suicide rates went up, while they remained stable in other counties studied. The author speculated that those who call in on a crisis line may not be the same group who complete suicide. (3)

**Weisman, A. D., and Worden, J. W. Risk-rescue rating in suicide assessment. *Archives of General Psychiatry*, 1972, *26*, 553-560.

The article is an explanation of the risk-rescue rating scale, developed to assess the lethality of suicide attempts. Five risk factors and five rescue factors have been operationally defined, weighed, and scored. Risk factors include agent (method) used in the attempt, whether consciousness is impaired, toxicity, reversibility, and treatment required. Rescue factors are location, person initiating rescue, probability of discovery by any rescuer, accessibility to rescue, and delay until rescue. The authors concede that the risk-rescue scale is not a predictive instrument taken alone, but when considered with such factors as intentionality and psychosocial involvement, it can add to the basis of individualized suicide prognosis. (4)

**Weiss, J. M. A. The suicidal syndrome: Relationship to clinical entities. In Achte, K., Aalberg, V. and Lonnqvist, J. (eds.), *Psychopathology of Depression*. Helsinki, Finland: Psychiatria Fennica Supplementum, 1980.

A study of 102 patients for whom the proximate cause of admission to a psychiatric hospital was an actual suicidal attempt indicated significant differences between the patterns of younger and older patients. A large proportion of subjects aged 14-25 years demonstrated relatively low psychological intent but produced relatively severe medical damage. The moderating variables increasing lethality among adolescents and young adults appeared to be more impulsivity, higher "risk-taking" propensity, and the common ingestion of dangerous drugs of unrealized toxicity. Loss of significant others during childhood or recently, psychosocial isolation, and clinical depression were as common among younger as among older attempters. Younger attempters demonstrated a different quality of depression, however, with less psychosis, less self-directed hostility, and motivation more commonly related to breakdown of interpersonal relationships. (1, 2)

**Wenz, F. V. Self-injury behavior, economic status and the family anomie syndrome among adolescents. *Adolescence*, 1979, *14* (54), 387-398. (a)

The article reports on a whole family study of 30 low economic families and 25 high economic families with suicidal adolescent members and a control group of 30 low economic and 25 high economic families with no suicidal member. There was a positive relationship between family normlessness and adolescent suicidal behavior in the low economic families. It was also found that low economic families with a suicidal adolescent were families experiencing the greatest powerlessness. Normlessness and powerlessness were also correlated with adolescents who were high risk for suicide (as determined by a suicide attempt) in the high-economic-status families. These findings indicate a consistent association between normlessness and attempted suicide and powerlessness and attempted suicide among adolescents in the families studied, regardless of the economic status of the families. (1)

**Wenz, F. V. Sociological correlates of alienation among adolescent suicide attempts. *Adolescence*, 1979, *14* (53), 19-30. (b)

The article describes a study of 200 adolescent suicide-attempters chosen from the telephone-caller population to the crisis-intervention center in a northern metropolitan area and from a list of suicide-attempters treated at medical emergency facilities. It was found that the following factors significantly correlated with feelings of alienation among these adolescents: race (white adolescents were significantly more likely to attempt suicide than black adolescents); broken home; broken romance; economic status of parents; geographic mobility; stepparents; both parents working; conflict with parents; (poor or lack of) communication with parents; (poor) school performance; (lack of) social contact with peers; and truancy from school. The author feels that alienation combines with factors mentioned above, which creates a circular process resulting in further alienation. (1, 2)

*Winn, D., and Halla, R. Observations of children who threaten to kill themselves. *Canadian Psychiatric Association Journal*, 1966, *11* (Supplement), 283-294.

General observations of 70 children under 15 years of age of low socioeconomic background who have threatened to kill themselves. Case studies are offered on 12 of these children as representative of the group; most had attempted or threatened suicide by violent means (jumping in front of cars or subways, stabbing themselves, jumping from high places). Detailed information, in percentages, describing the characteristics of these children, is included. (1, 2, 4)

*Winnicott, D. W. A clinical study of the effect of a failure of the average expectable environment on a child's mental functioning. *The International Journal of Psycho-Analysis*, 1965, *46*, 81-87.

Therapeutic consultation described through the case of a 6 year-old boy, diagnosed at 2½ as "simple" but found by the author to be schizophrenic, with the patient making spontaneous recovery. The psychiatrist used drawings to allow the child to express himself more easily. (1, 2, 3, 4)

Zilboorg, G. Considerations on suicide with particular reference to that of the young. *American Journal of Orthopsychiatry*, 1937, *7*, 15-35.

Psychoanalytic discussion of suicide, which is considered a form of instinctual expression, and universal. It is suggested that the clues to the pathogenesis of suicide may best be sought among primitive people and among children. A discussion of suicide among primitive people, and among prepubertal and postpubertal young people is presented. (1, 2, 4)

# Appendix B

# Questionnaire Used to Collect Case Study Analysis Data

### SUICIDE IN CHILDREN AND ADOLESCENTS
*Analysis of Case Studies*

*General Information*

1. Age_____

2. Sex_____

3. Race or nationality_____

4. Physical characteristics (tall, thin, etc.)_____

_____

5. I.Q._____

6. Attempted suicide, threatened suicide or completed suicide_____

7. Location or other circumstances surrounding suicide or suicide attempt

_____

8. Was there a specific reason for the attempt mentioned?_____

   If so, what was it?_____

9. Method of attempt_____

10. Apparent lethality of attempt_____

11. Who reported the incident?_____

12. Was there a suicide note?_____

*Individual Information About the Child or Adolescent*

13. Precipitating factors_____

_____

14. Were there threats or talk of suicide preceding the attempt?_____

15. Were there previous attempts?_____    If so, how many?_____

16. Behavior correlates_____

17. Affective correlates_____

18. Personality characteristics_____

19. Death concept or attitude_____

20. Did the child experience separations before the attempt?_____
    How many?_____

21. Did the child experience losses before the attempt?_____
    How many?_____

22. Did the child experience bereavements before the attempt?_____
    How many?_____

23. At what age were separations experienced?_____

24. At what age were losses experienced?_____

25. At what age were bereavements experienced?_____

26. Relationship of the deceased to the child: Father_____    Mother_____
    Sibling_____    Other_____

27. What form did the separations take?_____

28. What form did the losses take?_____

29. What form did the bereavements take?_____

30. If more than one separation, loss and/or bereavement, in what order did
    they occur?_____

31. Was the child separated from the parent (hospitalization) or did the
    parent separate from the child (death, divorce)?_____

32. Any difficulties in the child's birth and/or infancy?_____

_____

33. Child's birth order_____

34. Mental illnesses_____

35. Physical illnesses_____

36. Alcohol or drug abuse_____

37. Delinquent behavior_____

38. Depression_____

39. Self-esteem_____

40. Was the child abused or punished severely?_____

    If so, by whom?_____

41. Was the child sexually abused?_____    If so, by whom?_____

42. Child's description of herself/himself_____

_____

43. Child's view of the future_____

44. Child's view of parents_____

45. Was the child illegitimate and/or unwanted?_____

46. Did the child feel different from others?_____

47. Was the child hostile?_____    Angry?_____    Aggressive?_____

48. Is the child accident-prone?_____

*Family Information*

49. Age of mother_____          Age of father_____

50. Occupation of parents_____

51. Socioeconomic level of family_____

52. Number of siblings_____

53. Intellectual level of parents and siblings_____

54. Parental reaction to suicide attempt_____

55. Had there been a divorce?_____

56. Had there been a separation?_____

57. Were there frequent quarrels or disagreements?_____

58. Mother's personality_____

59. Father's personality_____

60. Had there been suicides or suicide attempts by other family members?
    If so, who?_____

61. Had there been mental illness in other family members?_____
    Who?_____

62. Had there been physical illness in family members?_____  Who?_____

63. Were parent substitutes present? Substituting for whom?_____

64. Was the substitute any relation to the child?_____

65. At what age of the child did the substitute enter the home?_____

66. What was the child's reaction to the substitute?_____

67. Did the mother feel positively about her role as a parent?_____

    _____

68. Did the father feel positively about his role as a parent?_____

    _____

69. Do the parents see the child as different?_____

70. Was one parent abused by the other?_____

71. Had either parent been arrested for violent acts?_____

72. Had either parent been arrested for other reasons?_____
    If so, what reasons?_____

73. Did either parent abuse alcohol or drugs?_____

74. Did the family accept help from social service agencies?_____

*Environment/Social Situation*

75. General description of environment of child:_____

    _____

    _____

76. Did the family move frequently? Recently?_____

77. How does the child perform in school?_____

78. Does the child have friends?_____

79. Had there been a break with a friend or a romantic partner immediately preceding the attempted or completed suicide?

_____

80. Special circumstances (pregnancy, in the army, in prison, etc.)_____

_____

# Appendix C

# Permissions Annotations

1. *The Psychoanalytic Quarterly*, 1965, 34:499-516. Copyright 1965, *The Psychoanalytic Quarterly*.

2. Copyright 1980, *Clinical Pediatrics*, 19(7):451-453.

3. Reprinted with permission from the *Bulletin of the Menninger Clinic*, 39 (2):163-176. Copyright 1975, The Menninger Foundation.

4. *American Journal of Diseases of Children*, 1973, 126:42-46. Copyright 1973, *American Journal of Diseases of Children*, and the authors, M. S. McIntire and C. R. Angle.

5. Copyright 1965, *American Journal of Psychotherapy*, 19:220-227.

6. Copyright 1966, *Canadian Journal of Psychiatry*, 11(Supplement):283-294.

7. Litman, R. E., Shneidman, E. S., and Farberow, N. L. Los Angeles Suicide Prevention Center. *American Journal of Psychiatry*, 1961, 117:1084-1093.

8. *Psychiatry*, 1965, 28(2):157-168. Copyright 1965, *Psychiatry*.

9. *The Medical Journal of Australia*, 1972, 1:686-690. Copyright 1972, *The Medical Journal of Australia*.

10. *The Journal of the American Medical Association*, 1964, 188:1103-1107. Copyright 1964, The American Medical Association.

11. Copyright 1971, *American Journal of Psychotherapy*, 25(1):27-36.

12. *British Journal of Clinical Practice*, 1967, 21(12):587-591. Copyright 1967, *British Journal of Clinical Practice*.

13. *Archives of General Psychiatry*, 1969, 20:100-109. Copyright 1969, American Medical Association.

14. *Canadian Medical Association Journal*, 89:751-754, 1963. Copyright 1963, Canadian Medical Association.

15. Copyright 1977, Human Sciences Press, printed in *Suicide and Life-Threatening Behavior*, 8(3):150-160.

16. Copyright 1970, *Pediatrics Clinics of North America*, 17(3):687-696.

17. Jacobs, J. *Adolescent Suicide*. Copyright 1971, Wiley-Interscience.

18. Copyright 1978, *Personnel and Guidance Journal*, 57(4):200-204.

19. From Finch, S. M., and Poznanski, E. O. *Adolescent Suicide*. Courtesy of Charles C Thomas, Publisher, Springfield, Illinois, 1971.

20. From *Growing Up Dead*, by B. Rabkin. Copyright 1978 by McClelland and Stewart Ltd., Canada. Published in the United States by Abingdon Press in 1979. Used by permission.

21. *The Psychoanalytic Study of the Child*, 1978, 33:261-277. Copyright 1978, *The Psychoanalytic Study of the Child*.

22. Copyright 1966, *Canadian Journal of Psychiatry*, 11(Supplement):275-282.

23. Copyright 1975, Libra Publishers, printed in *Adolescence*, 10(37):11-24.

24. *Acta Psychiatrica Scandinavica*, 1972, 233(Supplement):5-123. Copyright 1972, *Acta Psychiatrica Scandinavica*.

25. McIntire, M. S., and Angle, C. R. (eds.). *Suicide Attempts in Children and Youth*. Copyright 1980, Lippincott/Harper and Row.

26. From Bender, L. *Aggression, Hostility and Anxiety in Children*. Courtesy of Charles C Thomas, Publisher, Springfield, Illinois, 1953.

27. Copyright 1976, Human Sciences Press, printed in *Suicide and Life-Threatening Behavior*, 6(1):3-10.

28. *The Journal of School Health* 49(10):561-563 (December 1979). Copyright 1979, American School Health Association, Kent, Ohio.

# Index